D1281316

WITHDRAWN

SHAPING MODERN
LIBERALISM

American Political Thought

Edited by

Wilson Carey McWilliams & Lance Banning

SHAPING MODERN LIBERALISM

HERBERT CROLY AND PROGRESSIVE THOUGHT

Edward A. Stettner

 University Press of Kansas

Published by the University Press of Kansas (Lawrence, Kansas 66049), which was
organized by the Kansas Board of Regents and is operated and funded by Emporia
State University, Fort Hays State University, Kansas State University, Pittsburg State
University, the University of Kansas, and Wichita State University

Library of Congress Cataloging-in-Publication Data

Stettner, Edward A., 1940–
    Shaping modern liberalism : Herbert Croly and progressive thought
    / Edward A. Stettner.
        p.   cm. — (American political thought)
    Includes bibliographical references and index.
    ISBN 0-7006-0580-0 (alk. paper)
    1. Croly, Herbert David, 1869–1930—Contributions in political
science.   2. Liberalism—United States—History.   3. Progressivism
(United States politics)—History.   I. Title.   II. Series.
JC251.C76S74   1993
320.5'13'0973—dc20   92-29943

British Library Cataloguing in Publication Data is available.

Printed in the United States of America

10 9 8 7 6 5 4 3 2 1

The paper used in this publication meets the minimum requirements of the
American National Standard for Permanence of Paper for Printed Library Materials
Z39.48–1984.

To C.C.S., F.A.S.

Contents

Preface

This book is a study of the thought and political career of Herbert Croly (1869–1930). My argument is that Croly was an important figure in the theoretical redefinition of American liberalism that took place in the early years of the twentieth century. This intellectual change occurred in the context of the progressive movement, which sought to respond to the abuses that had developed in the American political and economic systems during the "Gilded Age," and progressive politics were central to Croly's theoretical positions and to the wider development of what is now often called "reform liberalism."

Croly's thought has attracted the attention of a number of scholars. Among the more important works, Eric F. Goldman's *Rendezvous with Destiny: A History of Modern American Reform*[1] (1952) focuses in particular on *The Promise of American Life*. In chapter nine ("Mr. Croly Writes a Book"), Goldman emphasizes (and overstates, I think) Croly's influence on Theodore Roosevelt. Goldman also strongly emphasizes (again overstating, I think) the influence on Croly's thought of the Comtean background of his parents.

This strong emphasis on Comtean influences is picked up in Charles Forcey's *The Crossroads of Liberalism: Croly, Weyl, Lippmann and the Progressive Era, 1900–1925*,[2] published in 1961. Forcey portrays the progressive intellectuals as "moths" seeking the flame of political power—and suffering the inevitable disillusionment. However, Forcey's own cynicism about politics sometimes detracts from his ability to present Croly's thought in a full fashion.

The most important book on Croly is David W. Levy's 1985 biography, *Herbert Croly of the New Republic: The Life and Thought of an American Progressive*.[3] I have relied often on Levy's work, but among a number of disagreements I think that he continues to overstate greatly the influence of Croly's father, David Goodman Croly, and his Comtean beliefs. Despite his subtitle, I think Levy also understates the importance for Croly's thought of his political commitment to the progressive movement.

In short, I think that the full logic of Croly's political thought has not been elucidated in any previous treatment. My objective in this work is to treat Croly as he deserves—that is, as a serious political theorist. I have sought to explain the many influences on his thought and to show how his fundamentally liberal theory evolved through his interaction with the political events of his day. I hope that a deeper knowledge of one of the founders of modern American liberalism will be helpful in clarifying some of the dilemmas faced by liberals in the waning years of the twentieth century.

Every scholar accumulates numerous obligations in the course of research, and this work is no exception. A much earlier and very different version was written as a doctoral dissertation at Princeton University under the direction of the late Alpheus T. Mason. I owe much to his wise counsel over the years. Robert K. Faulkner, then of Princeton and now of Boston College, read the dissertation and also very generously gave the current manuscript a very careful reading. His many comments were very useful in helping me clarify my argument. The late John William Ward (who edited *The Promise of American Life* for Bobbs-Merrill) also read the entire manuscript. I'd also like to thank James T. Kloppenberg for his extensive comments on the project. The editors of this series have also made many helpful suggestions, and I would like to thank them for their support.

Various scholars have aided me in uncovering Croly letters and manuscripts. Charles Forcey, formerly of Rutgers University, gave me access to the Eduard C. Lindeman papers, to copies of the Croly–Learned Hand correspondence, and to other notes he made in the course of his own research on Croly. I am also indebted to Fred Ragan and Charles Wrege for other materials. Karolyn Gould, an independent scholar working on a biography of Dorothy Whitney Straight Elmhirst, was extremely helpful with suggestions about material from the 1920s, and I profited greatly from conversations with her. Claire Urion McCully aided me substantially in research on Jane Cunningham Croly, and Karen Huie assisted with the bibliography.

Scholars owe great debts to librarians, and I have been aided by the staff of my own Wellesley College Library and by librarians at Princeton University, Yale University, Harvard University, the Harvard Law School, Columbia University, Rutgers University, Cornell University, Brandeis University, the Library of Congress, the New York Public Library, and by Robin Johnson, the librarian of Dartington Hall, Totnes, England. Mrs. Elsie Douglas, secretary to the late Justice Felix Frankfurter, gave me access to the Frankfurter Papers when they were still in the Supreme Court (they are now at the Library of Congress), and Donald R. Hiss has given permission to quote from these letters. Norris Darrell also gave permission to quote from the Croly–Learned Hand correspondence.

I also gained useful information from talking or corresponding with several of Croly's associates, including Alvin Johnson, Bruce Bliven, Charles Merz, and Leonard Elmhirst. Michael Young and Kenneth Lindsay also helped with information on Croly's work with the Elmhirsts in the 1920s.

The Leopold Schepp Foundation funded part of this research, and Wellesley College's generous provisions for sabbatical leave were instrumental in allowing completion of the work. The Wellesley College Women's Research Center provided support for research on Jane C. Croly.

Finally, I owe a great debt to my family and especially to my wife, Laura, who has lived with Herbert Croly for as long as she has lived with me!

Needless to say, I am responsible for any errors that remain in this work.

Wellesley, Massachusetts
April 1992

1

Introduction

In the year 1900, "liberal" was not a common word in the vocabulary of American political reformers seeking to develop a theoretical or political response to industrialism and its effects. "Liberalism" they recognized as a philosophy that had developed as an assertion of individual rights against the divine right theories of absolute monarchies in the seventeenth and eighteenth centuries.[1] The great theorists of classical European liberalism—such as Locke, Voltaire, Montesquieu, Kant, and Mill—had stressed personal and political rights such as religious freedom, freedom of speech, freedom of the press, and freedom from arbitrary arrest. Most liberal writers had also emphasized constitutionalism and favored legal equality as opposed to the hereditary privileges of the *ancien régime*. These arguments were attractive to Croly and other reformers.

Unfortunately, classical liberal theory also advanced two other positions that were less appealing in the American reform context. First, many classical liberals were at best unenthusiastic democrats. They certainly preferred democracy to autocracy, but they were often unsure that the majority of the population was very concerned about individual freedom; forced to a choice between democracy and freedom, classical liberals didn't hesitate to choose the latter. Second, and even more important, liberalism was closely associated with laissez-faire economic theory. Classical liberals—Locke is the best example—had emphasized private property as a necessary component of individual liberty. At times, the opposition of liberals to arbitrary government seemed to mean opposition to the

regulation of property and of the economy as much as or more than opposition to limitations on personal liberties.

American liberalism had exhibited its own special emphases. In particular, Jefferson, and then even more clearly liberals in the Jacksonian
period as well as Lincoln, had shown themselves open to democracy to a
greater extent than their European cousins. Even so, in the last years of the
nineteenth century, "liberalism" as a political theory was still very closely
identified in the United States with laissez-faire theory and even (in an
exaggerated form) with the radical individualism of the social Darwinist
William Graham Sumner. American reformers were perhaps dimly aware
that English liberalism had begun a transition from the laissez-faire theories of Herbert Spencer to the newer liberalism of T. H. Green and Leonard
Hobhouse,[2] but they did not use the word "liberal" to describe their own
positions.

In the political arena, the reform impulse was disorganized in 1900.
Bryan's Democrats had fought the battle of free silver in 1896 and had been
defeated by William McKinley and Mark Hanna. The populists had begun
exposing the seamier sides of the swiftly developing trusts and had sought
to develop a political opposition to the domination of the political system
by eastern business interests. But populism did not propose a coherent
philosophic alternative to laissez-faire. Labor unions were fighting for
workers' rights, but they also failed to develop a larger political program.
Social reformers of various persuasions were attempting to deal with the
effects of industrialization and urbanization, but again they usually failed
to demonstrate a broader understanding of political change. Of course, a
systematic critique of McKinley's essentially capitalist and imperialist program was to be found in American socialism. However, the socialists'
appeal was limited for many reasons, including the sense that socialism
was "un-American," that its doctrines were foreign and thus not the appropriate basis for a fundamental reformulation of American society.

By 1920, these intellectual and political conditions had all changed
dramatically. Following the political successes of the progressive movement, "liberalism" was now the preferred term for a coherent reformist
political theory. This new liberalism had borrowed extensively from classical liberal theory, but in coming to stress the need for an active role by
government in addressing social problems, progressives had redefined a
number of the central concepts of liberalism, a process continued by their
successors in the New Deal. "Reform liberalism" thus embodied a fundamentally changed view of politics. The new liberalism incorporated some
aspects of socialism, yet it more consistently defined itself against socialism. Indeed, the new liberals very consciously sought to find a "middle
way" between capitalism and socialism.

By 1920, liberals thus viewed themselves as reformers with a comprehensive program that valued the traditional liberal concern for individual rights and what we have come to call "civil liberties." But they also realized that these objectives had to be reconciled with a strong yet democratic government, if they were to be achieved in a regulated yet still fundamentally capitalist economy. In these twenty years, American reformers adopted much of classical liberalism, particularly the emphasis on individual freedoms. But they deemphasized (while not abandoning) property rights and embraced both democracy and a strong government as elements of the new liberal theory. These were important changes, which in many respects set the course for American liberalism for the remainder of the twentieth century.

The political vehicle for these intellectual and political changes was the progressive movement. Progressivism was a broad reform movement that worked through many political groups. It took heart from the presidency of Theodore Roosevelt and was embodied explicitly in his Bull Moose Progressive party of 1912. But progressivism also worked through the Democratic administration of Woodrow Wilson, particularly in the years 1914 to 1918. Progressivism was also advanced by some socialists, by prohibitionists, and by many nonpartisan groups.[3]

Progressives such as Croly sought primarily to use government—particularly the national government and even more particularly the national executive—to control the power of business. They sought to assert the public interest against the trusts and to regulate or to destroy concentrated economic power. They favored such measures as wages and hours legislation, pure food and drug laws, the regulation of the banking system, and the recognition of the rights of organized labor. Progressives also sought to democratize the political system, attacking the political corruption and political bosses that they saw as allied to business interests.

Progressivism in its many forms brought about fundamental changes in the American political, social, and economic systems. In 1920, the Republicans under Harding campaigned for a "return to normalcy" and sought to dismantle some of the new institutions of government that the progressives had constructed. However, they weren't able to return to the *status quo ante*, and when the Great Depression again stirred American reform, the New Deal was able to build on the foundations that the progressives had established. New Deal liberalism also built on the theoretical foundations of the new liberalism of the progressives—adapting the theory, but still holding to the fundamental combination of individual liberties and a reliance on democratic government to solve social problems.

These changes effected by American progressive politics were the work of many men and women. Indeed, the progressive movement was such a broad reform movement that no one historian has fully succeeded in capturing its many parts. Similarly, the changes in American liberalism in the progressive era were wrought by many writers, and no one theorist can claim full credit for developing the new understanding. As R. Jeffrey Lustig has written, the new liberalism has lacked a "synthetic theorist" who could define modern liberalism as Locke or Jefferson had come close to doing for earlier liberal theory.[4] Unfortunately, this lack of a fully systematic statement of modern American liberalism has not been remedied in the New Deal or in liberal reformulations in the later years of the century.

My argument is that Herbert Croly is rightly accorded a place in the front rank among the major writers who were influential in changing liberal theory. A brief review of Croly's career will demonstrate the range and evolution of Croly's thought, an evolution carried on in the context of progressive politics.

Herbert Croly first came to prominence in 1909, when he published *The Promise of American Life*. The book, begun in 1905, was stimulated by the stirrings of political change during Theodore Roosevelt's presidency. Croly agreed that reforms were needed, but very specifically critiqued the developing reform movement, arguing that reformers needed a more coherent political philosophy if they were to have a lasting impact. Croly's purpose was thus to provide an intellectual program for progressivism, and *The Promise* is a strong attack on laissez-faire and a sustained argument for government to act on economic and social ills. Croly refers to "progressives" and "reformers" and calls his own proposals "national democracy" or the "new nationalism." But he does not argue in 1909 that he is developing a new "liberal" political theory. Nonetheless, I shall show that Croly's political theory was fundamentally liberal from the start, that *The Promise* exhibits very significant continuities with classical liberal theory. At the same time, it is a new liberalism, articulated within the context of progressive political reform.

The Promise was complimentary about Theodore Roosevelt's administration, and Roosevelt's *Outlook* returned the compliment with a favorable review.[5] Roosevelt began to adopt more advanced positions in his 1910 campaign to elect progressives to Congress, and particularly as T.R. used Croly's phrase, the "New Nationalism," to describe his position, Croly gained influence in the movement and was (excessively) assumed by political observers to be *the* theorist behind Roosevelt's progressivism. Croly enjoyed this prominence, and while he remained primarily the intellectual critic, he did become involved in the formation of the Progressive party and strongly supported Roosevelt in the 1912 election.

Following Roosevelt's defeat, and his own completion of a biography of Mark Hanna, Croly began work on a sequel to *The Promise*. This book, first delivered as the Godkin Lectures at Harvard, was published in 1914 as *Progressive Democracy*. In this work, Croly refined and even altered a number of his earlier theoretical positions. Again the theory was dependent on classical liberalism in many respects, but Croly used the word only occasionally to describe his own positions, still preferring "progressive." *Progressive Democracy* continued Croly's earlier attack on laissez-faire, and it amplified his argument for government regulation of the economy. But in this work, which was written to guide the reform movement even more explicitly than the earlier book, Croly moved to a much more democratic position, now including a more sustained analysis of society from a pluralist point of view and adopting pragmatist arguments as well. In short, by 1914 Croly had developed a political theory very close in its general outlines to modern reform liberalism.

In that year, Croly was given a vehicle for the further development and dissemination of his ideas when Mr. and Mrs. Willard Straight agreed to provide financial support to establish a weekly "journal of opinion," the *New Republic*. As founding editor, Croly played the dominant role in setting the editorial policy of "the paper" for the next fourteen years, and the *New Republic* gave him an even more prominent position in the reform movement.

Croly's *New Republic* continued his emphasis on political and economic reform spearheaded by a democratic national government, and he now increasingly characterized his theory as "liberal." The reasons for this explicit recognition of his own liberal heritage are several and seem to include the wartime desire to identify his theory with Anglo-American traditions in opposition to German authoritarian theory. Most important, however, was the dismay that Croly and his associates (including Walter Lippmann, Walter Weyl, Felix Frankfurter, Learned Hand, and John Dewey) experienced in response to increased government repression after the United States entered World War I. The recognition that government could oppress individuals politically, as the classical liberals had argued, while at the same time liberating them from economic and social oppression, forced Croly to reemphasize the importance of individual freedoms that had been present but de-emphasized in his earlier books. He came to think explicitly of his theory as a new version of liberalism even as the historic truths of liberalism came alive in his own political life.[6]

By the end of the war, the *New Republic* was clearly the leading liberal journal in the United States. It enabled Croly to speak strongly for liberal principles and guaranteed that his voice would be heard on all major issues of public policy.

In partisan politics, the *New Republic* had been founded to support Theodore Roosevelt's Progressive party. However, the editors soon broke with Roosevelt, supporting Woodrow Wilson in 1916 as he moved toward developing stronger measures for government regulation of the economy. Foreign policy quickly became a dominant concern as the war developed, and Croly and Lippmann attempted to influence Wilson in developing a liberal foreign policy. They used the term "Peace without Victory" in an editorial and advocated a "League to Enforce Peace." When Wilson picked up the former phrase and also supported the idea of a league, the liberal publicists were perceived as being influential with the administration, and the *New Republic*'s circulation soared. However, this political involvement ended abruptly with the publication of the text of the Treaty of Versailles, which Croly thought a betrayal of the stated aims of American entry into the war. He took the *New Republic* into opposition to Wilson and the treaty.

The years 1919 and 1920 were crucial for the testing of Croly's liberalism. After a period of political involvement and some real influence, he was now in opposition. The war and then the treaty and concomitant domestic political events, most notably the "Red Scare" of 1919–1920, forced Croly to try to restate his now explicitly liberal political theory. He wrote yet another book, *The Breach in Civilization*, and then withdrew it, relying instead on a series of long articles in "the paper" to make his thoughts clear. His attempt to state the philosophic supports for liberalism continued for most of the decade of "normalcy."[7] In this period of reaction, Croly supplemented his interest in politics with investigations into a number of other topics that he thought would ground liberalism on a firmer footing, including education, religion, and psychology. His writings in this period illustrate how a liberal political theorist continued to develop in a period of political and cultural adversity.

This introductory review of the development of Croly's political thought should make it clear that he was both a serious thinker, who attempted to develop a liberal political theory, and an important political figure in the progressive movement. I think he came as close as any writer to stating the central assumptions of modern American liberalism: that individual freedoms can be combined with a strong, democratic national government, a government that must assume responsibility to improve social and economic conditions. Even so, it is not clear that Croly succeeded in attaining a full theoretical coherence in his works. By 1919–1920, when the various elements of the theory were in place, Croly was becoming disillusioned with politics. He sought to reformulate his theory in *The Breach in Civilization*, but realized that his analysis was not sufficiently powerful and withdrew the book. Croly's last years exhibit a struggle by a creative thinker to state his views in a final form, a struggle that I believe he ultimately lost. American liberalism lost also, for Croly taught his contemporaries much; his views would have been even more influential if they could have been stated in a final systematic form.

2

Years of Preparation

Herbert Croly was born on January 23, 1869. He first achieved public prominence in 1909, at age forty. What happened in those forty years to prepare Croly to write *The Promise of American Life*? What training had he received? What thinking had he done in those years to prepare himself to write such an influential book on his first excursion into politics? The answers to these questions cannot be certain; Croly indicated only a few of the influences on his thought. However, we have information about many aspects of his life in these years, including the influence of his parents, his education at Harvard, and his work in architectural criticism. We also know something about what Croly read, and most important, we know about the society within which he grew to intellectual maturity.

HERBERT WAS THE third of five children born to Jane Cunningham Croly and David Goodman Croly.[1] His mother was the more prominent of his parents—indeed, she had a national reputation as a journalist and feminist.

Jane Cunningham Croly was born on December 19, 1829, in England and came to the United States in 1841, settling in Poughkeepsie and later in New York City. In 1855, she began a lifelong career in journalism on the staff of the *Sunday Times and Noah's Messenger* (writing under the pseudonym "Jennie June," which she used for many of her writings for the rest of her life).[2] In 1856, she married David Croly, a reporter for the *Herald*.

After a brief period on a Rockford, Illinois, paper, which David edited, the Crolys returned to New York and Jane resumed her work on the *Sunday Times* and then on the *New York World*, which her husband also joined. In 1860, she became editor of *Demorest's Monthly Magazine*, retaining this post until 1887 and writing a column in most issues until 1889. She also wrote for a number of other journals, including *Godey's* and the *Home-Maker*. Her work was syndicated, and thus she was read in many parts of the country.

This energetic woman also wrote a number of books. Some of these, like many of her columns, dealt with conventional "women's issues." For example, Jane wrote a cookbook ("a good, practical cook-book" emphasizing simple recipes), which went through a number of editions.[3] In this work, Jennie offered a number of hints about "household management," as well as recipes. Jane Croly also wrote books on knitting and crocheting and on needlework. Some of her more domestic *Demorest's* columns were also collected in 1864 and published.[4]

However, Jane Croly's interests went well beyond the conventional definition of a woman's place, and her involvement in contemporary political and economic issues was a central part of life in the Croly family. The issue of the suffrage was to become the central question for many women, but that happened slowly. In the years immediately after the Civil War, Jane Croly seems to have generally favored women's suffrage, but without making it her central concern.[5] For example, in an 1866 *Demorest's* column, in an argument echoed by many suffragists, she observed that the issue had taken on new life with the demand for "negro" suffrage. She asked whether white women were less able politically than negro men. At the same time, she noted as a factual matter that most women did not yet desire the vote. Indeed, Croly argued optimistically that if women really came to want the suffrage, they would gain it: "It is sufficient that few women care for it. If they wanted it, they could have it at once; if half of them wanted it they could have it; if a tenth part of them went to work energetically they could obtain it easily for the whole."[6] When women did vote, it must be on "terms of equality with intelligent American men: it must be, not as a royal gift extended to them by man, but an act of justice—of restitution." Jane Croly thus supported the suffrage without making it her major priority. She was more concerned with the practical economic situation of American women: "The right that women most want in this country is the right to work, without feeling that it is a degradation. . . . Women will work for their husbands without feeling themselves lowered by it; why not for themselves?"[7]

Jane Croly returned to both issues—suffrage and economic independence—at regular intervals in her writings. For example, in an 1875 column she declared that "there is no position in this world which does not require money."[8] She went on to argue against laws that deprived women of control of their own earnings and inheritances. At the same time, she argued more strongly for the suffrage, claiming that disenfranchising women marked them as inferior or unworthy, whatever the intention of men, and issuing an eloquent plea: "Where, in the domain of thought, can be found an intelligent reason for giving an ignorant man, just landed on our shores, and only one remove from barbarism, the right of suffrage, the right of a voice in the councils of the nation, and refusing it to American women, the mothers of the republic, the cultivated wives and daughters of American men?"[9] Croly rejected the idea that men can reasonably speak for women in politics and concluded that if the state persisted in treating women as wards of men, it had the obligation, at the least, to provide them shelter, education, and employment when men failed to do so.

Several years later, in a book on marriage, Jane Croly tied the suffrage issue to a broader view of women's rights. The "Women's Movement," she argued, was changing domestic relations in fundamental ways. Formerly, women had been content to be subordinate to their husbands, "but the modern theory of individual rights demands that a woman shall be free to live her life as well as a man is." Stating a strongly liberal argument, Jane Croly continued, men's and women's "separate individualities are superior to, instead of subordinated by, the duties and claims of the family." She noted that the "state of warfare" that was sometimes needed to achieve these rights was unfortunate, but was the result of "the appropriative, masterful, and tyrannical spirit of men" and would continue "until justice, or at least partial justice, has been done." She again noted that the ballot would not solve all social problems, but went on to argue that the suffrage movement itself was developing women's abilities: "But the effort to obtain [the vote], to lift themselves to a higher place, to take a part in the public interests and activities of life, will educate and ennoble women."[10]

Jane Croly's feminism was expressed in a different political context in the 1884 presidential election. Writing in *Demorest's* (and noting that she was normally reluctant to mention politics in "the quiet pages of a family magazine"), Jennie June argued that from a woman's point of view it was most appropriate that the issue of Grover Cleveland's fathering of an illegitimate child had been raised in the campaign: "If this is true . . . it is a high compliment to the morality of the age that a crime toward a woman has at last been made a reason why a man should not be available for honorable office, or considered fit to represent loyal men and good citizens."[11] These were strong words for the time.

Jane Croly diverged again from the generally domestic emphasis of *Demorest's* when she devoted an extensive article to "the industrial question," the growing conflicts between capital and labor.[12] Knowing no doubt that her readers would be interested in this question because of the enormous growth of labor unions and labor strife in these years, Croly noted that people were beginning to pay more attention to the quality of work and to the importance of education (both of which she greatly valued), but that these advances would not bear fruit until the "vexed questions in regard to labor" could be solved. This long article briefly reviewed the theories of Owen and Fourier, which Croly felt had failed because they assumed the perfectibility of human beings. Croly recommended instead a cooperative, profit-sharing arrangement developed by a French entrepreneur, Edme Jean Le Claire, who had organized a "Mutual Aid Society" for his workers in 1838. Le Claire had developed pension and life insurance arrangements, as well as placing half the profits of his business in a fund for the workers. In Jane Croly's view, the success of the plan seemed to prove the power of "associated instead of divided interest." Le Claire had hastened the "extinction of poverty and pauperism, simply by the application of the co-operative principle between employer and employed" and had revealed that "the great secret was, and is, that *each* must work for *all*."[13] These ideas of a cooperative control of industry would later echo in her son's writings.

On more specifically feminist issues, Jane undertook her own empirical research on the condition of women in England, France, and Germany during an 1885 trip. She reported that women were taking a more assertive role in all these societies and were winning passage of such legislation as the Women's Property Act in England, which gave married women the right to their own earnings. She concluded that "women abroad have grown tired of nursing a wretched and dependent gentility, and find the world is as much their oyster as that of a man, if they use it so. The *role* of the victim has ceased to be interesting, and does not apply to any independent, self-reliant woman."[14] American women should take note!

Jane Croly also wrote a book to advise the "new woman" who found she had to work (or who wanted to do so). Her message was to work hard and carefully, to pay attention to quality, and especially to demand control of her own resources: "Mind your own business, keep control of your own money affairs . . . and if you have anything to give, give it; do not allow it to be tricked out of you, or give away the most precious result of your efforts—your independence."[15] In this book, she again considered the larger economic picture. The concentration of business in larger enterprises was "law," she argued, in words that again could later have been written by her son, and was "the natural result of growth and expansion." Women had to adapt to these changed economic conditions, just as men did. But workers—men and women—must be aided, as society owed much to them. Jane argued for "changing [the] working environment, by improving living conditions; by creating and giving access, out of working hours, to libraries, galleries, museums, botanic gardens, and halls where good music can be heard."[16] She was optimistic that these reforms could be advanced in America as they had been in England.

Jane Croly worked for women's causes in several areas besides her writings. Most importantly, she was a leader in the women's club movement. Indeed, she is known as the "Mother of Women's Clubs" to the club movement today.[17] Jane was the moving spirit behind the founding of the women's club of New York, Sorosis, in 1868.[18] In her specialized field of journalism, Jane Croly also founded the New York Women's Press Club in 1889. In 1890, Sorosis, under her leadership, took the initiative in establishing the General Federation of Women's Clubs, which grew rapidly into a major national organization. (By 1896, the General Federation included 1,425 clubs.) [19] Jane Croly also owned and edited the *Woman's Cycle*, the journal of the club movement. In her last years, she wrote a vast work (running 1,184 pages), *The History of the Woman's Club Movement in America*.[20] In her handwritten dedication, she wrote that the work was intended for the "Twentieth Century Woman by one who has seen, and shared in the struggles, hopes, and aspirations of the woman of the Nineteenth Century."

For Jane Croly, the women's club was one way for women to overcome their previous isolation. The club movement brought together women from many backgrounds—from different classes and geographical areas—"to perfect within its own membership that unity in diversity which is the basis of its life."[21] In a letter written just a month before her death on December 23, 1901, she noted that a club should help women develop "the modern co-operative spirit."[22]

However, the club movement should not only aid the members. One of Jane Croly's arguments for the establishment of the General Federation was that a national organization would allow a more effective national presence. "There is a vast work for clubs to do throughout the country in the investigation of moral and social questions, in the reformation of abuses, in the cultivation of best influences;—not the influence of class or clique or party, but a wide, liberalizing, educational influence."[23] Many clubs began to emphasize social problems in the late 1880s, and the establishment of state and local federations enabled them to cooperate on these issues.[24]

What influences, then, could this energetic and prominent woman have had on her son? Herbert rarely wrote about his mother in future years, and it is clear that he was not as close to her as to his father. To some observers, this indicated a lack of maternal concern. Herbert's wife, Louise

Emory Croly, encouraged this conclusion when she wrote to Felix Frank-furter shortly after Herbert's death that Jane Croly "was very clever, am-bitious—and a tremendous worker—and not in the least domestic." Lou-ise judged that her mother-in-law "simply didn't know what it was to be maternal."[25] A partial rebuttal to this picture of Jane Croly can be found in a moving reminiscence that Croly's sister, Vida Croly Sidney, wrote for the Golden Jubilee of Sorosis. She remembered attending meetings with her mother and recalled Sunday teas and dinners with Jane's friends visiting their home. Vida also pointed out that Jane "ran a large house, superin-tended the care of four children," and that she "carried on a voluminous correspondence with many friends."[26]

Maternal care aside, what might Herbert Croly have *learned* from his mother? Living with Jane Croly, he would have been encouraged—even forced—to develop an interest in political and social issues. Strangely, Herbert never showed any particular interest in women's issues, but his mother's concern for individual rights, an important concept in liberal political thought, was surely impressed on him. Jane Croly's interest in economic issues and her rejection of both laissez-faire and radical social-ism were no doubt suggestive to her son. Her emphasis on the possibili-ties of cooperative endeavors to solve "the industrial question," and her club emphasis on "unity in diversity," would have encouraged in him a sense of social solidarity. Jane's concern to use the General Federation as a political pressure group for a broad range of social reforms would also have communicated a public-spirited concern for social improvement. The large numbers of visitors (both men and women) who came to tea or dinner would have opened the mind of the young man at home. Finally, a basic influence is surely Jane's concern to solve current social issues through *writing* about them.

HERBERT CROLY's father encouraged him in many of the same directions, including the career of journalism. David Goodman Croly was born in Ireland in 1829 and came to the United States while still an infant.[27] After his marriage, and the brief experiment in Rockford, David Croly became first city editor and then managing editor of the *New York World*, a new, strongly Democratic paper. David held this position until late 1872 and was presumably fully involved in local and national politics. He then joined another new paper, the *Daily Graphic*, and continued as editor there until 1878.

In 1868, while on the *World*, David Croly became involved in a project that provided important financial support for him and later for Herbert. With an associate, he founded the *Real Estate Record and Builders' Guide*, which summarized real estate transactions in the rapidly growing New York market. Croly wrote for the *Record and Guide* for several years, giving up an active involvement in 1873, but rejoining in 1880. From then until his death in 1889, he wrote a weekly column, "Our Prophetic Department," in which he commented on a wide range of economic—and political—issues.[28]

Like his wife, David Croly wrote a number of books while engaged in daily journalism. A notable early work, published anonymously in 1864, was *Miscegenation*, in which Croly probably coined the term. This work seemed to approve of racial intermarriage: the author claimed to muster the forces of "Christianity, democracy, and science" to "teach that a people to become great, must become composite."[29] However, the book was a hoax, designed to stir up Northern anxieties about race relations for the benefit of the Democratic party in the election of 1864.[30] Like many Democrats, indeed many Americans, of the period, David Croly was something of a racist, and this view, too, would influence his son.

David's more nonpolitical projects included a book, *The Truth about Love*, drawn from Croly's *World* writings, which argued for considerably freer sexual practices than were common.[31] Late in his life, he also collected some of his *Guide* prophecies into *Glimpses of the Future*, which he noted was "to be read now and judged in the Year 2000."[32] David Croly also founded a periodical in the early 1870s, with the boast that it was neither a monthly nor a quarterly, but "a periodical with no assured periodicity." Each article in this unique journal was published on paper of a different color, with type of various sizes and ink of various tints.[33] Two or three issues appeared.

Jane Croly wrote of her husband that "he hated the obvious way of saying or doing a thing. He cultivated the 'unexpected' almost to a fault, and always gave a touch of originality even to the commonplace."[34] Years later, Herbert echoed this judgment: "He was a man of enormous fertility of mind. He could, I think, originate more ideas in less time than any man I ever met." Even the loyal son was forced to admit, however, that "his disposition to criticize his own ideas was not as well developed as his power of originating them."[35]

The cause that most inspired David Croly was the advancement in the United States of the philosophy of Auguste Comte. Early in their life together, Jane Croly seems to have been committed to Comte's Positivism also, and Herbert later wrote that he had been baptized into the Comtean "Religion of Humanity" as a child.[36] Jane's commitment to positivism was apparently somewhat transient, but David remained a strong partisan for the rest of his life.[37]

The most complete expression of David Croly's positivism was a book, *A Positivist Primer*, of 1871, in which he tried to make Comtean ideas accessible to Americans. In this work, David Croly presented an optimistic picture of the "religion of humanity." The human condition, he wrote, "is constantly growing better, constantly improving, and its future will be as much more glorious than its present as its present is superior to its past, and that this may be accomplished, depends entirely upon the willing activities of those who now form the visible side of her existence." Reflecting the Comtean rejection of traditional religion, he wrote: "The only heaven that we recognize is the heaven that can be realized on this earth by intelligent human effort."[38] This religion of humanity would "set to work, consciously to subordinate this egoism, as he [Comte] called it, to unselfishness or altruism." To the convinced positivist follower, this "perpetual act of devotion to our fellow-men" was "no mere sentiment generated by an illusory enthusiasm, but . . . a scientific verity, a fact."[39]

For David Croly, society was an organism, and individuals were not free and independent agents. "The peculiarity of our whole scheme of man's life . . . is that we regard humanity as a whole, and reject the so-called sovereignty of the individual. The individual, with us, is an abstraction—he does not exist, he is a mere cell in the entire organism." From this argument he derived an ugly metaphor: "The bees in the hive represent the Positivist conception of government; if it is necessary for the good of the hive that the drones should be killed, killed they must be; they but live for the community, the community does not exist for them."[40] In David Croly's understanding of the Comtean scheme, government was to arise out of the people and was to act strictly in support of the collective good. But if it was government of and for the people, it was not government by them, as actual control was to be exercised by an elite "composed mainly of the philosophers, scientists, and artists."[41]

Finally, in the field of economics, David Croly joined his wife in observing that "in noting the progress of modern society, one remarkable tendency has not escaped us. It is the great concentration of wealth into few hands, this tendency to concentration keeping pace with its aggregation. . . . It is our belief that nothing can stop this tendency of wealth to concentrate in individual hands." It must be controlled, then, by a power "which we now vaguely apprehend as public opinion. We know how powerful this is, even in its present unorganized state. . . . A Vanderbilt, fifty years from now, will be an impossibility."[42] This belief, that economic power needed to be controlled by public opinion, and thus by government, was crucial in Herbert's later elaboration of reform liberalism.

David Croly continued to express these arguments for the next two

decades, and he particularly tried to communicate his Comtean enthusiasm to Herbert, who recalled after his father's death in 1889:

> From my earliest years it was his endeavor to teach me to understand
> and believe in the religion of Auguste Comte. One of my first recol-
> lections is that of an excursion to Central Park on one bright Sunday
> afternoon in the spring; there, sitting under the trees he talked to me
> on the theme which lay always nearest his heart—that of the solidar-
> ity of mankind. There never, indeed, was a time throughout my
> whole youth, when we were alone together, that he did not return to
> the same text and impress upon me that a selfish life was no life at
> all. . . . His desire to impress upon me a belief which he held himself
> with all the force of a religious conviction led him to attempt expla-
> nations which the mind of a child could neither grasp nor retain. He
> even discussed, for my benefit, theoretical questions as to the exist-
> ence and nature of the Supreme Being; discussions, of course, that I
> could so little understand that it was like pouring water on a flat
> board. . . . I should have full opportunity to compare the Positivist
> *Grand Etre* with the Christian Cross. Under such instruction it was not
> strange that in time I dropped insensibly into his mode of thinking,
> or, more correctly, into his mode of believing.[43]

These family teachings would soon be challenged.

HERBERT'S EARLY formal schooling was in J. H. Morse's English, Classical
and Mathematical School for Boys in New York. In 1884, he began to take
classes at the City College of New York while living at home. In September
1886, however, Herbert left New York to enroll at Harvard as a freshman
special student.[44] In his first year in Cambridge, aside from French and
English, Croly took a history course, "Constitutional Government in
England and America," and a course in political economy, "The Economic History of Europe and the United States since 1763." Most importantly for his future interests, he enrolled in "The History of Philosophy"
with George Herbert Palmer and "Logic and Psychology" with William
James.[45]

Herbert kept in close touch with his family and particularly his father.
Several years later, he wrote to his fiancée, Louise Emory, that "[I] used to
send him packets of thirty or forty pages every other day—which he used
to answer with marvelous regularity and unfailing kindness in spite of the
fact that he detested letter-writing. My own letters I have destroyed; his I
have kept, but I never have the courage to read them."[46] Louise did read

them after Herbert's death, and she gathered some of David Croly's letters together as a record of these years.

The early letters were full of typical, if severe, fatherly advice: "Do try and form methodical habits." "Be careful not to get tangled up with young women of any kind." And a message from the practical Jane: "Your mother still finds fault with your penmanship. It is not legible from a printer's point of view."[47] But it was soon clear that more serious issues were at stake: Herbert was straying from the fatherly teaching: "My Dear Boy—you said something about the divergence between my ideas and those of the philosophers whose works you are reading at College," David wrote in late October. "Let me beg of you to form your own judgment on all of the higher themes—religion included—without any reference to what I may have said. All I ask is that you keep your mind open and unpredisposed."[48] At the same time, however, the father urged an extensive reading list on his son, one heavily weighted with Comteans. David recommended that Herbert read Harriet Martineau's translation of Comte, the works of Comte's English editor, Frederick Harrison, and no fewer than three other English positivists. David Croly also recommended Herbert Spencer, arguing that Herbert would note Spencer's debt to Comte. Perhaps most significant, he asked Herbert to read John Stuart Mill's "Estimate of Comte's Life and Works" (including as well a positivist rebuttal of Mill).

David Croly continued to urge Mill on Herbert, and when he likely took the advice, the result must have been eye-opening, for in Mill's commentary on Comte, Herbert Croly would have encountered one of the most devastating philosophical critiques ever written. Mill's *Auguste Comte and Positivism* distinguishes between Comte's early work, primarily derived from the *Cours de philosophie positive* of 1830–1842, and the "later speculations of M. Comte," primarily the *Système de politique positive* of 1851–1854. Mill writes approvingly of major parts of the early work—the logic, the theory of the sciences, and the philosophy of history. However, he is satirically critical of the political system proposed in the early work and even more savagely critical of the moral theory, and particularly the "Religion of Humanity," of the late work.[49] Mill's treatment of Comte's disciples, especially those who resolutely followed the master to a number of absurd positions, would probably have been particularly painful to Herbert.[50]

We don't *know* that Herbert Croly read Mill. But it *is* clear that his horizons were greatly widened at Harvard, even as a freshman and sophomore. It seems apparent that as he thought about philosophy and read more widely, Herbert rejected a narrow Comtean focus. He would also have realized from reading Mill and other works that his father's Comteanism was not fully representative of Comte's theory, emphasizing more fully the religious views than the logic or scientific aspects of the theory. Herbert made this evolution clear in the testimonial he wrote in 1889 after his father's death. After having noted that he had fallen into David's "mode of believing," he added:

> While I was at college I was surrounded by other influences, and while retaining everything that was positive and constructive in his teaching, I dropped the negative cloth in which it was shrouded. My change in opinion was a bitter disappointment to him, as several letters which he wrote at the time testify. But intense as was his disappointment, it never took the form of a reproach. This is very remarkable when we consider what an essential part of his character his beliefs constituted.[51]

This comment seems to say that it was especially the Comtean religion that Herbert rejected in his first years at Harvard, but it also suggests a more thorough questioning of his father's assumptions.

This process of Herbert's intellectual redefinition was gradual, however, and David Goodman Croly continued to press his views. In early November 1886, for instance, he wrote: "Do not become bewitched by brilliant or showy paradoxes. Reject anything that runs counter to the common sense of the average man. There was something in your long letter recently received about the 'becoming' which had a flavour of Hegel. Beware of metaphysics, my son. We live in a real world and should not be fooled by words." In the spring, he asked whether it is "worthwhile to thoroughly understand Descartes, Spinoza or any of the metaphysical philosophers? The ones to be constantly studied, to my mind, are Kant, Hume, Berkely [*sic*], J. S. Mill, H. Spencer, but life is too short to master the unfruitful thinkers such as Hegel."[52]

David Croly also gave advice on politics and economics to his son. He urged: "Do not commit yourself against state socialism. There is a good deal to be said for government ownership of natural monopolies, such as telegraph, railroad, etc."[53] He doubted that Herbert would get proper training in these fields: "I almost dread your going through a course of Political Economy at Harvard, the theories which prevail there are . . . a quarter of a century behind the age."[54] He asked if Herbert would prefer to spend a term at Johns Hopkins instead: "I judge there is more advanced thinking among the professors there than at Harvard."[55] David also urged his son to take up the study of sociology (the last of the sciences, according to Comte), noting that "so far the foundation of this noblest of sciences has not been laid. Why not make it the work of your life? . . . Society is an organism controlled by laws of development which when discovered can be modified by man himself. Here is a career for you, my son, a noble one."[56]

These letters are also revealing of the personal circumstances of father and son. Perhaps realizing that he was by now quite ill, David Croly thanked Herbert for returning some money, adding: "Realizing the shortness of my own life I care nothing for the money myself . . . nor am I anxious to pile it up for you and your sisters as I hope you will have an honorable ambition to make your own living."[57]

In his second year at Harvard (1887-1888), Herbert began to develop an interest in religion, taking a course in comparative religion (which apparently focused on Christianity). His major work was again in political economy and philosophy.[58]

The basic political economy course was taught by J. Laurence Laughlin in the first semester and Frank W. Taussig in the second.[59] Laughlin (1850-1933) had just brought out an edition of Mill's *Principles of Political Economy*, which the students presumably read. He had also recently prepared a short book, *The Study of Political Economy: Hints to Students and Teachers*, about how to study the subject. This work probably formed the basis of his own teaching. In it, Laughlin recommends the standard works of classical economists, but also critics of that approach (for example, Henry George—though not Karl Marx).[60] The recommended approach is historical, and Laughlin emphasizes that the Civil War has brought major changes in the American economy. He attacks socialism as a doctrine, but recommends using socialist writings in classes.[61] The major point of the book is that dramatic changes in the nation's economy have created the need for the study of economics, presumably urging his students to take up the challenge. Laughlin also emphasizes the connections of economics to the law, to the ministry, and to journalism, emphasizing the latter's influence on public opinion.[62] Overall, Laughlin seems to have been fairly conservative in his economics, but his emphasis on the need for different points of view, his emphasis on the rate of change in American society, and his praise of journalism as a career might well have made his sophomore listener pay attention.

Frank Taussig (1859-1946) was younger, just at the start of a long and illustrious career at Harvard. His area of expertise was the tariff and international economics. Most of his writings came later, and it is difficult to estimate what he taught in the spring of 1888. One evaluation of his overall career emphasizes his sympathy to English classical economics, but also his own theoretical innovations on that tradition.[63] Another judgment, by Joseph Schumpeter, is that Taussig's writings on wages and capital grew out of a new current in American economics that was running strongly in the 1880s, and Schumpeter identifies this work with that of Francis A. Walker and John B. Clark.[64] Yet another estimate, by Talcott Parsons, emphasizes Taussig's search for a "middle path" between the dogmatism of left and right, and Parsons judges the work "ethically and politically in the best traditions of a tolerant liberalism, which above all was not deaf to the cry for social justice and the corresponding indictment of certain features of the existing order. . . . Professor Taussig has been in his generation the leading exponent of the same admirable tradition as John Stuart Mill."[65] Parsons went on to note that the growth of state control over the economy was accepted by Taussig, but that he had been concerned with the "extreme difficulty, especially perhaps under modern democratic conditions, of guaranteeing that this control shall in fact be used impartially."[66]

Harvard's economists thus exposed Herbert Croly to classical economics, but also to new approaches and new questions as their discipline changed rapidly in the 1880s.[67] Most important, the work with Taussig probably encouraged Croly to connect economic questions with broader moral and political issues.

David Croly remained skeptical about this preparation: "What I dread is that your political economy course will give you a bias towards believing that what is, is right. You ought to reread Comte on Political Economy in his Positive Philosophy. You should also read Bridges, Marx and the Socialist writers, not that they are right but that they are the most recent studies on the wealth and labour problems."[68]

David Croly also had doubts about Herbert's work in philosophy, which included "English Ethics" with Palmer, and a course in "Monism and the Theory of Evolution in Their Relation to the Philosophy of Nature" with Josiah Royce.[69] David Croly seems to have been particularly bothered by the former: "I am just a little dubious as to the wisdom of spending so much effort to set forth the ethical theories of these 17th century moralists. I wish your studies were more in the direction of modern scientific thought."[70] Despite these fatherly doubts, it is clear that Harvard's philosophers and political economists were having a major impact on Herbert Croly's mind.

THIS IS NOT THE PLACE for a full examination of the teachings of the Harvard Philosophy Department in Croly's years. Bruce Kuklick's work covers that ground very thoroughly.[71] In his first two years, Croly took two courses with George Herbert Palmer, in the history of philosophy and in English ethical philosophy. Not an important original philosopher, Palmer called himself a "moderate idealist" and had done work with an associate of the English idealist T. H. Green, noted for his Hegelianism but also for his reformulation of English liberal political theory.[72] His major influence on Croly would probably have been as a teacher rather than an original mind, although it would be very interesting to know if he talked about Green's political theory.

William James was quite the opposite—a searching mind, working out a number of original positions. In his earlier years at Harvard, James had been involved with Charles Peirce and others in working out the origins of pragmatism—the argument that belief must be defined by practice. James was to develop this doctrine in his later *Pragmatism* (1907), but in the late 1880s he was very much under the influence of Royce on philosophic questions and preferred to teach primarily psychology, which is what Croly took.[73] In the late 1880s, James was at work on *The Principles of Psychology* (1890). This sprawling work of 1,400 pages covered a wide range of issues, but it did not come to firm conclusions. Rather, as Kuklick argues, James "half-heartedly defended a scientific psychology and a metaphysical idealism, neither of which satisfied him; and he half-heartedly defended a distinction between the two which he did not believe."[74] James was always very open about his own uncertainties, and it is likely that his students were exposed to many diverse arguments in the course of his teaching.[75]

Josiah Royce was the third philosopher with whom Croly studied in this period. His was a powerful mind, espousing an "absolute idealism" and arguing for the centrality of God in human affairs. But Royce also argued a form of voluntarism or free will, showing perhaps one influence that James had on Royce.[76] In 1885, Royce had published his first major work, *The Religious Aspect of Philosophy.* His religious views assumed a monistic vision of a divine unity, and this was the vision no doubt imparted to Herbert Croly and protested by David Croly. In a later writing, *The Problem of Christianity* (1913), Royce made this vision more explicitly Christian, arguing that communities (such as the church, but also political bodies) were defined by a particular purpose—that of the church being redemption. This explicitly Christian framework was probably not so clear when Croly first studied with Royce, but the emphasis on unity and on the concepts of community and purpose would have been clear.[77] Croly would use all of these ideas in his own theory.

What was perhaps most apparent to Herbert Croly in 1886–1888 was that Auguste Comte was no longer relevant to modern philosophy. An earlier member of the Harvard department, John Fiske, had attacked Comte and advanced instead Herbert Spencer, but Fiske had not been given a permanent appointment, and by the time Croly came to study philosophy, Comte was simply no longer studied.[78]

Croly left Harvard in June 1888, after his second year. David Croly's health was steadily worsening, and he died less than a year later, in April 1889. In that year, Herbert served as secretary to his father and must have worked with him on the *Record and Guide*. Some years later, confusing his chronology a bit (or perhaps counting summer vacations), Herbert wrote: "When he was not well, after I left college, I was his constant companion for about three or four years. I used to act as his amanuensis and we used to have long discussions about every aspect of modern literature, economics, and politics. I was very much amused when it suddenly occurred to me after I had written 'The Promise of American Life,' how many of its leading trends of thought I could trace back to these discussions and which were directly promoted by things he had said."[79]

A number of David Croly's columns in the *Record and Guide* in the 1880s had commented on the need for government to take a more active role in controlling monopolies. To assume this role, government would need to be reorganized, and this would in turn demand that Americans get over their fear of it. The Jeffersonian heritage of minimal government needed to be abandoned.[80] David Croly presumably urged Herbert to adopt these and similar views during their conversations in the last year of his life.

At David Croly's death, Herbert inherited a share in the *Real Estate Record and Builders' Guide*, and he served as editor and wrote unsigned pieces for the journal for two years, while living at home with his mother and sisters. These editorial comments addressed a wide range of current social issues, but concentrated particularly on economic questions. One topic was the trusts, which Croly (following both his father and mother) argued were inevitable and were likely to prove beneficial in terms of economic efficiency, though not without dangers to society as well. These dangers, he argued, must be controlled by government.[81]

An 1890 column advanced a theme that Croly used in many later works—the idea that the modern world had resulted from religious and political revolutions in the last several centuries and was now undergoing an industrial revolution. "That the outcome of [this revolution] will be exactly what either Capital or Labor expects is scarcely probable. Some middle way between the clash of interests will no doubt be found to the advantage of all concerned."[82] This search for a "middle way" was a theme familiar to Croly from his mother, probably from his economics course with Taussig, and perhaps from his father. It would be a major theme fifteen years later when Croly sat down to write *The Promise of American Life*.

But Herbert did not immediately pursue his interest in politics and economics. Instead, the publishers of the *Record and Guide* started a new periodical in mid-1891, the *Architectural Record*, and Herbert joined the staff for a year. His first signed article was a venture (not terribly successful) in popular aesthetics. Croly assured his readers of the value of art ("an indispensable element in the matured and perfect life"). However, displaying a democratic temper probably acquired from his mother and some of his Harvard studies, he was equally sure that art would not be successful apart from a popular and widely shared culture: "If you mistake it to be the patented possession of a cultured few . . . it will make you exacting, finical and even querulous."[83]

Croly did not immediately continue in his cultural career either, as he was married in May 1892 to Louise Emory. Louise was from an upper-middle-class Baltimore family, and Herbert had met her while he was studying at Harvard and she at what would soon be called Radcliffe College. Herbert and Louise decided that he needed to return to Harvard to finish his education.

In the fall semester of 1892, Herbert again registered for an English course, this time in advanced writing (Croly's later style is convincing evidence of the futility of trying to teach good writing). As before, he concentrated in economics and philosophy.

Louise Croly later wrote that Herbert "was greatly interested in Edward Cummings's course in Social Science."[84] Cummings's interests are clear in articles he published in the period in the *Quarterly Journal of Economics*.[85] One topic that he had written about, and that presumably formed a central part of the course, was the role of the state in regulating industry, particularly disputes between capital and labor. In 1887, Cummings had written approvingly of state experimentation in this area (particularly citing commissions in New York and Massachusetts) in enforcing industrial arbitration.[86] Some years later, just after Croly took his course, Cummings followed this with another article on national regulation, as under the Interstate Commerce Act of 1887. Cummings wrote approvingly of this development of national power and also of the role that unions played in rationalizing the economic situation.[87]

Another topic of research was unions themselves. Cummings particularly focused on developments in England, but also compared English unionists to the Knights of Labor. He emphasized that unions performed many benefits for their members and argued that their success was watched with fear by the more "militant socialists" who benefited from industrial strife and despair.[88] This moderate position would have appealed to Croly, who had himself argued the year previously for a "middle way" in industrial relations.

Yet another topic that Cummings had researched was cooperative societies in Europe and in America. In an article written two years before

Herbert sat before him, Cummings had summarized the work of European cooperatives. These differed, he explained, some being initiated by unions, others by employers; some of each kind were successful, others not. One of the successful employer cooperatives that Cummings emphasized was the very Maison Leclaire that Jane Croly had written about in 1886. Using virtually her words, Cummings argued that cooperatives were a promising way to solve "the industrial problem."[89] Cummings's conclusion was very favorable to cooperatives: "I have no hesitancy in welcoming profit-sharing as the next great phase of industry"; and he called cooperatives a mean between the extremes of laissez-faire and radicalism.[90]

Cummings may also have begun to introduce his students to Fabian socialist thought. This is not reflected in his writings in the early 1890s in particular, but in 1899 he published a long article on Beatrice and Sidney Webb's writings on British trade unions. The bulk of this article is a factual presentation, but Cummings points out that trade unionists were like all other humans—that there were many points of view expressed in the labor movement. He noted that the Webbs emphasized the nationalization of public services and also the growth of cooperatives and called their theory "the new collectivist philosophy of Trade Unionism, and, incidentally, of society in general."[91] Cummings left his own evaluation ambiguous, but he did argue that the Webbs were trying to develop a new approach—opposed to classical economics, to "that obsolete abstraction known as the individual," and also to the "old-fashioned bias" of Karl Marx. Rather, he saw them as emphasizing the "bias of that new and true collectivist socialism."[92] These topics that Croly absorbed in Cummings's classroom would all be suggestive for the future political theorist. Thus it is clear that Croly was taught much more than classical laissez-faire economic theory at Harvard; he was exposed to many of the newer economic currents, most of which emphasized an increased role for the government.

On his return to Cambridge, Croly also took philosophy courses with two of Harvard's stars, Royce, again, in a course in cosmology, and George Santayana in a course on aesthetics.[93] Santayana had graduated from Harvard in 1886, studied abroad, and then completed a Harvard Ph.D. in 1889, also becoming a faculty member. In his early philosophical positions he was under the influence of James's psychology[94] and was probably not yet the dominant influence he later became when Walter Lippmann studied in the same department.[95] When Croly was in his class, he was presumably at work on the book published in 1896 as *The Sense of Beauty.* This work explored the relation between aesthetic sensations and the order imposed on them by our intelligence.[96] Croly, who had already written on art, was no doubt involved in exploring the more philosophic dimensions of aesthetics.

Croly had returned to Harvard after his marriage with high hopes of graduating in two more years. However, the semester ended disastrously: he had a nervous breakdown just before exams, and again he withdrew from Harvard.[97]

THIS BREAKDOWN led to the period of Croly's life that we know least about. Herbert and Louise apparently lived in Cambridge and traveled extensively in Europe for the next two years, supported presumably by Jane Croly and/or Louise's parents. They spent summer vacations in Cornish, New Hampshire, and Croly's ties to Cornish were very significant for the rest of his life.[98] This was a summer place that attracted a number of writers, artists, and lawyers, and Croly developed an important series of friends there over the next several years, building his own home in Cornish (financed by Jane Croly) as he developed ties to the area. Among his friends in Cornish were Winston Churchill, the novelist, Norman Hapgood and George Rublee, Croly's classmates who later became public figures, and Philip Littell, who later joined Croly on the *New Republic.* Learned Hand, who became a fast friend, also settled in Cornish.[99]

In September 1895, Croly returned to Cambridge and again reentered Harvard, finally becoming a regular student in 1897. He took a number of courses in these four years, but probably was not a full-time student, for when he left in 1899, Croly still hadn't been awarded the B.A.[100] The degree was finally awarded in 1910, after Croly has become prominent.[101]

Croly's courses were primarily in philosophy in these years. He again took a course with James, one with Palmer, one with Santayana, and two with Royce.[102] This was the period in which James was developing his pragmatic theory further and moving away from Royce's positions. It would have been a stimulating time to study with these two men. For James, of course, pragmatism meant that the "ultimate test" of an idea was the "conduct it dictates or inspires."[103] Experience was crucial in verifying consciousness.

Royce was at work on *The World and the Individual,* delivered first in two series of lectures in 1899 and 1900. It was the "high-water mark of the idealistic tide."[104] Royce had become a more explicitly Christian thinker by now. He had also been working on the notion of self-consciousness, and he was attempting a complete reformulation of his views.[105] Royce noted in his introduction to the first series of these lectures that after a discussion of God and first principles, he would devote the second series "to the application of our fundamental conceptions to the more special problems of the nature of the human Ego, the meaning of the finite realm called the Physical World, and the interpretation of Evolution." He continued: "Having thus sketched our Cosmology . . . we shall conclude the whole understanding by a summary discussion of the problems of Good and Evil, of freedom, of immortality, and of the destiny of the Individual, still reviewing our problems in the light of our general conception of being."[106]

In the two courses he took with Royce in these years, Croly must have been exposed to many aspects of this argument, and he must have watched Royce try to work out his combination of a religiously inspired monistic vision with a sense of the worth of the individual. Royce thought he had proven that such a combination was possible as he made clear in his inspirational close to the first series of lectures: "Therefore are you in action Free and Individual, just because the unity of the divine life, when taken together with the uniqueness of this life, implies in every finite being just such essential originality of meaning as that of which you are conscious. Arise then, freeman, stand forth in thy world. It is God's world. It is also thine."[107] For Royce, these words were a philosophic reconciliation of individual consciousness and a Christian idealism; for Croly, they might already have had more specifically political implications.

Croly's courses in 1895-1899 pointed toward a career in philosophy: in addition to courses in the department, he undertook language preparation in German, in Semitic, and in Greek. However, he also took some more economics, including another course with Cummings, a course in literary criticism, and a course in fine arts with Charles Eliot Norton. Finally, he took a course in Christian theology in the Divinity School and three courses in the History Department in Christian thought and the history of Christianity.[108] This study of Christianity probably put a final end to the Comtean religious theories that Croly had been taught by his father and may also have set the stage for his greatly expanded interest in religion after the First World War. However, in the short run, Herbert's career at Harvard ended abruptly and finally in the spring of 1899, when the Crolys sailed again for Europe, perhaps for Herbert to study philosophy, although it is not clear he ever did.[109]

Fourteen years later, Croly wrote (rather dishonestly) to Felix Frankfurter, whom he had met not long before, that he had "lived in Cambridge for six years as a graduate student with the intention of becoming an instructor in philosophy." He claimed, however, that he found Cambridge "illiberal and petty. . . . While I retained my interest in philosophy itself, the work of a teacher made no appeal."[110] Much later, Croly wrote in private that he had left Harvard and philosophy because he had found himself "the victim of an incoherent eclecticism" and had been unable to work out his own original views among the many influences of his teachers.[111]

Kuklick's research puts Croly's situation in a wider perspective. In previous years, philosophy had encouraged generalists, and even amateur philosophers could be influential. The Ph.D. was also relatively rare. But "by 1900 philosophy was the activity of the professor." Specialized, technical work was becoming the norm.[112] James, Royce, and others of their generation continued to speak to wider concerns, but among the younger members of the profession this public interest and wide scope was becoming rare.[113] Without even a B.A., and with more general interests than a specialized training, Croly was unlikely to get anywhere in philosophy, and he must have realized that in 1899.

His years at Harvard had thus taught Croly much—in history and religion, and particularly in economics and philosophy. Many parallels can be drawn between his studies and his later political theory. But Croly's mind was by no means fully formed in 1899. Harvard had not set Croly in any one direction; rather, he had many different intellectual experiences on which to draw as he turned again to a career in journalism.

THE YEARS FROM 1899, when he left Harvard, to 1905, when he began *The Promise of American Life*, to 1909, when it was published, are the years in which Herbert Croly grew to full intellectual maturity. He had turned away from a career in philosophy and had become a "man of letters" in New York. He was on his own intellectually, and personally as well, after the death of his mother in late 1901.

Croly's writing in this period was largely in the *Architectural Record*, though he wrote a few pieces for other magazines. Most of the *Architectural Record* articles were essentially technical pieces, reviewing recent buildings ("New Theatres of New York," "The Finest Store in the World," "Three New Hotels") or new techniques in building. Croly also published two books on the architecture of personal dwellings in this period.[114] Croly supported himself with this writing and indeed continued to write for the *Architectural Record* until his death, though at a greatly reduced pace after 1909.

It would be nice to know more about Croly's thoughts in these years, but there are no letters surviving from the period. However, we can see the direction of his thinking in some of the less technical pieces in the *Architectural Record*. Several of these mention another influence on his thinking, a novel, *Unleavened Bread*[115] by Robert Grant, which was published in 1900 and which Croly must have read soon after. Croly attested to the importance of Grant's novel in 1910, in a short article he wrote regarding the purpose of *The Promise*:

> The idea which lies at the basis of "The Promise of American Life" first occurred to me about ten years ago, during a reading of Judge Robert Grant's novel "Unleavened Bread." In that story the author has ingeniously wrought out the contradiction subsisting between certain aspects of the American democratic tradition and the methods and aspirations which dominate contemporary American intellectual work.[116]

This was the only influence that Croly mentioned in the article. He also acknowledged the debt to Grant directly, when he later wrote asking him to submit material for the *New Republic*: "You already know how much I owe you personally and how extremely important to the development of my own point of view the reading of your novel 'Unleaven Bread' [*sic*] was."[117]

Unleavened Bread must have appealed to Croly for several reasons, some of them personal. A lot of the action takes place in women's clubs (one scene even at a meeting of the General Federation, founded by Jane Croly ten years earlier), and he would have been familiar with some of the character types (Croly mentions women's clubs in a number of his own writings). Also, part of the novel is set in New York, with the characters buying new real estate "uptown" and trying to decide where the fashionable neighborhoods would be, matters that Croly was familiar with from the *Record and Guide*. More important, a major figure is an architect, Wilbur Littleton, who is committed to work of good quality. He prefers to build honest public buildings such as schools and churches, but his clients usually prefer vulgar residences and the flaunting of private wealth. Worse yet, Wilbur's wife, Selma (the protagonist), sides with the clients in her desire to make money and "get ahead" in the world.

Croly mentioned this novel in several of his articles in the years 1901–1905. One article was a full review in which he argues that Selma, this "troublesome woman," believes that "in a democracy the only qualifications which a specialist needs for his special tasks are untutored enthusiasm, common sense, and a keen eye for the main chance."[118] In Grant's novel, Selma, and not her husband, was the representative American, and Croly criticized the American national tradition "which resents exclusive technical standards and refuses to trust the men who by their thorough training have earned the right authoritatively to represent such standards." Croly would amplify his own view about how standards of quality and specialization could be reconciled with democracy in *The Promise.*

Grant had set his reader thinking, and in another article Croly pronounced *Unleavened Bread* "a novel which throws much more light upon current social tendencies than any American story recently published."[119] Some of the questions in Herbert Croly's mind had to do with the place of culture in American democracy. In his own writings on architecture (perhaps drawing on his work with Santayana), he echoed Wilbur Littleton's complaint: buildings were too often commissioned by tasteless millionaires, and architects were lulled or beaten into accepting materialistic values.[120] Similarly in literature, the average author tried "to be contemporary, representative, popular and vital" more than "well-fashioned, well-observed or well-considered."[121] In short, "while Americans are very much interested in works of art, they have little instinctive love either of the work or the art."[122]

An obvious solution was to divorce art and democracy, and Croly played with this idea: "That the plastic arts in a modern democratic community can ever be both genuinely popular and thoroughly self-respecting is at least a very dubious question."[123] Yet in aesthetics—and, as we shall see, in politics as well—Croly rejected this solution, held back by a commitment to democracy, or at least to its possibilities, and by his earlier judgment that an art that lost touch with popular culture would become effete and "querulous."[124]

But how then could the artist achieve true excellence while retaining popular appeal? To this question, in one formulation or another, Croly returned again and again, in politics as in art. Croly was optimistically uncertain about the possibilities:

> It is by no means necessary to draw an inference . . . that American art will always remain at cross purposes with popular life. The modern national democratic society is a new thing under the sun. Its potentialities are only beginning to be vaguely foreshadowed, and if such an enlarged community can ever get fairly under way, if its numbers can ever become closely united by some dominant and guiding tradition, there is no telling what may come of it. Such a vast source of energy, properly concentrated and guided, might accomplish—well, I do not, at any rate, know what it might not accomplish. . . . All that is, however, a matter of speculation, almost of faith.[125]

In this 1901 article, written for an architectural periodical, Croly already seems more interested in politics than in art. In his reliance on the American people becoming "united by some dominant and guiding tradition," we have an appearance of a major point of *The Promise* and of two concepts central to that work, national community and national purpose. Moreover, Croly has already effected the combination of nationalism and democracy ("modern national democratic society") that is such a central part of the later argument.

Croly amplified these points over the next several years. For example, in 1903, he called for the "infusion of a national organic spirit into the culture" of America, defining this spirit as "the existence of a communicating current of formative ideas and purposes which makes the different part[s] of the social body articulate, and which stamps the mass of its works with a kindred spirit and direction."[126] In a review of Henry James's work, he wrote that "intellectual work of any kind derives much of its momentum and effect from the extent to which it embodies and fulfills a national purpose and tradition."[127] Croly was optimistic about these nationalizing tendencies: as early as June 1902, he wrote that politics and business were undergoing the needed transformation; culture had only to follow: "What the United States needs is a nationalization of their intellectual life comparable to the nationalizing, now under way, of their industry and politics."[128]

Croly's call for a "national organic spirit" certainly reflects the influence of Royce, and perhaps of Comte as well. But it is clear in these *Architectural Record* pieces that Croly was becoming more and more interested in specifically political events. Indeed, when he refers to the "nationalizing" of American industry and politics, it seems clear that he is referring to progressivism. Croly was responding to the national sense that the fabric of American life was rapidly changing in this period—that a new nation was emerging, and that changes were needed in many areas. Industry had developed national trusts in the matter of a few years, and under Theodore Roosevelt's leadership the political system was starting to respond. But where was the "nationalization of intellectual life" to come from, not only in art but also in the more basic philosophic assumptions about American culture in its broadest sense? Croly clearly set out to provide this intellectual program in 1905 when he sat down to write *The Promise of American Life*.

But before examining that work, we should note that there were other aspects of *Unleavened Bread* besides the architectural connection that made Croly think about politics. Grant raised additional issues that were central to the progressive questioning of American life and to Croly's own developing concerns.

A variant on Grant's question of how specialists fit into American culture was his more basic question of what was "truly American" in taste and social values. Grant's characters asked this question often, and all of them valued "American originality." But they couldn't easily define "American." Nor could many Americans easily answer this question in an age when the economy was being transformed before their eyes, when their country had become an international power and had acquired an empire in McKinley's "glorious little war," and when immigration was changing the character of the American population.[129]

Grant also explored issues of social class. The Littletons (Wilbur and his sister, who becomes president of a new women's college) are of "gentle stock." They are middle-class people who are offended by the flashy tastes and superficiality of the nouveau riche businessmen and their wives. This resentment can be compared to the "status consciousness" that Richard Hofstadter has argued was characteristic of progressivism.[130] Many other historians agree that most progressives were usually "old stock" Americans from middle- or upper-middle-class backgrounds.[131]

Grant's novel is an extensive satire of the tastes of "fashionable" society, one of many such works at the time. For example, reading Edith Wharton's *The House of Mirth*, a best-seller in the year Croly started work on *The Promise*, would have recalled a number of Grant's themes in his mind.[132] The contemporary progressive sociologist Thorstein Veblen also explained the behavior of businessmen like Grant's or Wharton's in *The Theory of the Leisure Class* (1899), arguing that wealthy people displayed their social position by such "conspicuous consumption" as that satirized by Grant.

The society of *Unleavened Bread* was thus characterized by growing social divisions, which challenged "the original [American] ideal . . . the illusion that extremes of social condition do not exist." Rather, "society here is divided into sets."[133] Thus Grant was suggesting that the American ideals of equality and fair play and of a common community had been lost; many progressives agreed.

Grant's most obviously political message came in the third part of the novel, in the person of Selma's third husband, Lyons, who is a businessman turned politician. He is extremely successful in politics, elected to Congress, to the governorship, and eventually to the U.S. Senate. But he is also a windbag who (with Selma's encouragement) compromises his own ethical code by taking money from a businessman who wants favorable treatment for his utility company. This entire section of the novel portrays businessmen as unscrupulous and politicians as corrupt, perhaps especially during financial panics, which are shown to be part and parcel of the free enterprise system.[134] The criticism of unregulated laissez-faire practices is crystal clear, as is Grant's call for honorable government regulators and officials.

The corruption of politics by business, and of business itself, was of course a central concern for many progressives. The muckrakers were in the process of sensitizing the American public to precisely the sort of abuses that Grant described—as in Ida Tarbell's exposé of Standard Oil (1904), Upton Sinclair's *The Jungle* (1906), and especially David Graham Phillips's *Treason of the Senate*, the first installment of which appeared in 1906. Richard L. McCormick has shown that the mid-1900s were crucial in the development of progressivism. In New York, for example, a legislative commission with Charles E. Hughes as counsel had exposed the corruption in the utilities industry in 1905. Another investigation into the life insurance industry in the fall of 1905 uncovered the corrupt involvement of Senator Tom Platt and other politicians. These events, in McCormick's view, "pointed to a corrupt alliance between the corporations and all classes of politicians."[135] Living in New York, Croly would have been acutely aware of these developments in the years when he set to work on *The Promise*.

Robert Grant didn't advance many solutions to these problems in his novel, but he did suggest a few directions. For example, a "Reform Club" of the better citizens is organized and tries to introduce a better quality of life into Benham, Grant's fictional city.[136] One of their proposals is to move to an appointed rather than an elected school board, so that qualified individuals ("specialists") can serve, perhaps an intriguing suggestion to the Croly who later came to rely on appointed bureaucracies. As an alternative to "reform," Grant has socialists make a brief appearance to begin to raise embarrassing questions about Lyons's political dealings. Perhaps the message was that if moderate reform didn't succeed, more radical solutions would be sought.

Grant's novel was thus about a lot more than art and architecture. The "current social tendencies" that Croly thought Grant discussed so well involved fundamental issues in American culture and in the American political, economic, and social systems. Many people were beginning to address these issues, and under the inspiration of an activist president a national reform movement was developing. As George Mowry writes, "change was in the air by 1906."[137] *Unleavened Bread* certainly helped Croly focus his ideas, but living in the midst of the developing progressive movement was no doubt what inspired him. Drawing on his own training and education, and on his own mind, he set out to join the progressive debate.

3

Political Theory and "The Promise of American Life"

A desire to address Robert Grant's concern that specialized work was not properly appreciated or encouraged in American culture may have been the proximate cause of Croly's decision to write *The Promise of American Life*. However, once begun, the task grew: "I soon found myself confronted with a much bigger task than I anticipated." The "attempt to justify the specialized contemporary intellectual discipline" that Grant desired led to "the far more complicated and dubious task of giving a consistent account of the group of methods, conventions, and ideas which have been gradually wrought into the fabric of American national self-consciousness." The American people, wrote this architectural critic, needed to be convinced that "the house of the American democracy demands thoroughgoing reconstruction."[1]

Croly's attempt to make a convincing case for "reconstruction" led him to write an important and original work of political theory. To Walter Lippmann, Croly's book was "the political classic which announced the end of the Age of Innocence with its romantic faith in American destiny," establishing its author as "the first important political philosopher who appeared in America in the twentieth century."[2] "Reconstruction" required that Croly give a historical explanation of the origins of contemporary dilemmas such as those Grant had identified, but it also demanded, as it turned out, the elucidation in the American progressive context of central concepts of political theory, such as nationalism, democracy, equality, freedom, and individualism. Moreover, in his attempt to ground his analysis in concrete examples, and to make practical suggestions for reform, Croly came to deal at length with a number of specific policy questions concerning the American political and economic systems and to comment at length on the programs and personalities of the emerging reform movement. It was these specific proposals that probably attracted the most immediate attention for Croly's book, but in the long term it has been his historical analysis and his theoretical discussions that have been the more important parts of the work.

THE PROMISE begins with the argument that Americans need to reject laissez-faire theory and accept the idea of national planning to ensure the "better future." This central argument leads to Croly's theoretical concerns and also to his practical suggestions. At first, however, he is concerned with locating his argument in American history.

Croly admits at once that his message is an unusual one for Americans. Quoting H. G. Wells's *The Future in America*[3] (and anticipating Lippmann's later comment), Croly notes that most Americans think easily and often of "national destiny," but they have been reluctant to conceive that that destiny will not be fulfilled automatically. Clearly evoking the "Manifest Destiny" optimism of the 1840s, Croly agrees with the popular conception that America does indeed have a bright future, but he argues that this future will not come without work—without organization, intellectual effort, and without making reforms in American society. He therefore rejects "destiny" as an appropriate term for America's future, as it is too indicative of the traditional American mixture of "optimism, fatalism, and conservatism," for which he admits "an active and intense dislike." Rather, he suggests two other words as appropriate terminology: "promise" and "purpose."[4]

In Croly's view, a "promise" has to be realized in action, and to be realized it has to be infused with an "ideal" to organize and inspire its followers. Americans may have often thought that their land was one of promise, but they "may never have sufficiently realized that this better future . . . will have to be planned and constructed rather than fulfilled of its own momentum."[5] Croly hoped that Americans would realize that his point was not completely foreign to their history: "In seeking to disentangle and emphasize the ideal implications of the American national Promise, I am not wholly false to the accepted American tradition."[6] In fact, he was optimistic that his argument would be accepted. "New conditions" were causing "an increasing number of Americans" to rethink their nation's promise. The closing of the "virgin wilderness" and the fact that "the Atlantic Ocean has become merely a big channel" were changes bringing home the need for conscious planning, hopefully indicating a popular willingness to accept an ideal that needed to be worked for rather than simply assumed.

In arguing for substituting "purpose" for "destiny," Croly attacked laissez-faire theory and its economic and social effects head-on and in very strong terms: "The existing concentration of wealth and financial power in the hands of a few irresponsible men is the inevitable outcome of the chaotic individualism of our political and economic organization, while at the same time it is inimical to democracy, because it tends to erect political abuses and social inequalities into a system."[7] He argued that the "peculiar freedom which the American tradition and organization have granted to the individual" has resulted in "political corruption" and "unwise economic organization, and the legal support afforded to certain economic privileges . . . due to the malevolent social influence of individual and incorporated American wealth."[8] In perhaps his most bitter attack, he denounced laissez-faire thinkers who "enshrine this American democratic ideal in a temple of canting words which serves merely as a cover for a religion of personal profit."[9]

The political result of these abuses was that "a numerous and powerful group of reformers has been collecting whose whole political policy and action is based on the conviction that the 'common people' have not been getting the Square Deal to which they are entitled under the American system; and these reformers are carrying with them a constantly increasing body of public opinion."[10]

Clearly identifying himself with progressive reform and the attack on corruption in business and politics, and with the 1904 Square Deal campaign of the popular president who had just left office, Croly issued an intellectual call to arms: "The redemption of the national Promise has become a cause for which the good American must fight. . . . The American idea . . . must be propagated by the Word and by that right arm of the Word, which is the Sword."[11] The doctrine of Croly's cause, of the "word" which he presumed to substitute for Manifest Destiny, was "national democracy"—the combination of nationality and democracy, of the Hamiltonian and Jeffersonian traditions in American thought, that is probably the most famous part of his book. Croly hoped that his "constructive relation" of these two ideals would be "in truth equivalent to a new Declaration of Independence."[12]

Before we turn to that combination, however, it may be useful to consider further how Croly came to emphasize the concepts of "promise" and "purpose" that underlie this argument. Where did Croly's faith in a national promise, a common purpose, come from? One answer is simply the events of the time. Croly was attacking laissez-faire theory, the policy of nonintervention in the economy, because he perceived (as so many

Americans did) that it had allowed dramatic changes to occur in American society. In positing a national interest superior to individual selfish interests, he was clearly inspired by the practical example of Theodore Roosevelt, who had articulated the notion of the public interest when, as president, he successfully arbitrated the anthracite coal strike or when he prosecuted the Northern Securities Company under the Sherman Act. Roosevelt's "Square Deal" was a slogan meant to assure all Americans that they would be fairly treated. Croly thought Roosevelt's previous program inadequate, but it did embody the precise combination of democracy and nationalism that he was proposing: Roosevelt's "devotion both to the national and to the democratic ideas is thorough-going and absolute."[13]

However, while the concept of a national purpose was clearly opposed to laissez-faire, it is important to note that it was also clearly opposed to *any* "class-based" ideal, and specifically to socialism. In short, Croly was seeking a "middle-way" between ideological extremes, and he was quite conscious of this intention. The "idea of a constructive relationship between nationality and democracy," he wrote, was "flexible." "It is not a rigid abstract and partial ideal, as is that of an exclusively socialist or an exclusively individualist democracy. Neither is it merely a compromise . . . between individualism and socialism."[14] Croly was clearly trying to create an American ideology that would inspire reform, and it had to be an ideology that appealed to the whole people rather than to any group or class. I believe that this is one element that identifies Croly's thought as liberal from the start, for historically liberal political theory has rejected a class analysis.[15]

Croly was responding to the divisions between capital and labor at the time. However, emerging divisions in American society went even deeper than that. Richard McCormick has pointed out that a host of different interests were organizing in the late 1890s.[16] Professional groups, trade associations, more specialized unions—interest groups were becoming more common and more assertive. Croly had first-hand experience with these forces, as in his mother's organization of the General Federation of Women's Clubs in part for lobbying purposes. In *The Promise*, he was attempting to counter this trend and assert instead the ideal of a single, unified national interest. The high level of immigration at the time may also have encouraged Croly to emphasize the need for a common national purpose.

Additionally, we have seen that Croly's own writings on architecture and American culture, and his reading of Grant's novel, had left him wondering what was distinctively "American." Some ideal was necessary to replace the materialistic ethos so characteristic of modern America. In

The Promise he reached back into American history to find principles that could form the basis of a transformed American culture.

There is another important influence, I think, on Croly's search for a national purpose, and that is the idealism of Josiah Royce. Royce had emphasized unity—a unity of God and man in creation, but also a unity both within and among different "communities," such as churches and particularly nations. For Royce, humans should have a loyalty to their community. Croly had absorbed this teaching from Royce in several classes, but Royce made it even more explicit in a work published the year before Croly's *Promise*. In 1908, Royce wrote that "a spiritual unity of life, which transcends the individual experience of any man, must be real. . . . If loyalty is right, social causes, social organizations, friendships, families, countries, yes, humanity . . . must have the sort of unity of consciousness . . . upon a higher level than that of our ordinary human individuality."[17] In 1909, Croly applied this idealism to a more political arena and argued more specifically for a national ideal. The specifically national focus was Croly's, as Royce had affirmed loyalties to many levels of society ("social organizations," "families," "countries"), but the call for an ideal, a purpose transcending the individual, was derived in part from Royce. For Croly as for Royce, this was a spiritual cause: individuals were to be lifted above their selfish and material interests by a commitment to a higher ideal. The assertion of a public interest was political for Croly, but it was also an intensely moral and even religious statement.

THE CONTENT of the proposed ideal was to be a combination of "nationality" and "democracy," of the Hamiltonian and Jeffersonian traditions in American thought. This combination was not easy or evident, however, and Croly had a somewhat ambivalent view of American ideals and achievements. In his extensive survey of American history, he praised the generation of the Founders as original thinkers, but argued that later figures had not been so original or so clear in their ideas: "For one generation American statesmen were vigorous and fruitful political thinkers; but the time soon came when Americans ceased to criticise their own ideas, and since that time the meaning of many of our fundamental national conceptions has been partly obscured, as well as partly expressed, by the facts of our national growth."[18] Nevertheless, a national ideal, the inspiration of a national promise, had to be derived from its subject, or it would be unconvincing. Whatever their inadequacy, American political ideas and traditions would have to form the basis of the argument: "Such as it is, however, the American people are attached to this national tradition; and no part of it could be suddenly or violently transformed or mutilated without wounding large and important classes among the American people, both in their interests and feelings."[19] Croly also admitted that "in case the proposed conception of the Promise of American life cannot be applied to our political and economic history without essential perversion, it must obviously fall to the ground."[20] Of course, as Croly had remarked earlier, the national tradition couldn't be "violated" in the course of stating the ideal, but it could be "transformed."[21] In Croly's reading of American history, nationalism and democracy were the best candidates for this transformation.[22] We turn first to his understanding of nationalism, or "nationality," as he often called it.

Of the two elements in his ideal, Croly felt more congenial with "nationality" and with its American spokesman, Alexander Hamilton. Croly had remarked at the very beginning of *The Promise* that it was nationality that makes a people "thoroughly alive."[23] He admitted that he admired Hamilton above Jefferson: "I shall not disguise the fact that, on the whole, my own preferences are on the side of Hamilton rather than of Jefferson. He was the sound thinker, the constructive statesman, the candid and honorable, if erring, gentleman."[24] Indeed, ignoring James Madison, James Wilson, and a host of other framers, Croly credited Hamilton with much of the formulation of the "Federal Constitution" itself as well as the legislative program of the Washington administration. His praise of Hamilton's national principle was often laudatory: "On the persistent vitality of Hamilton's national principle depends the safety of the American republic and the fertility of the American idea."[25]

Croly continued this admiration of Hamilton for the rest of his life, writing, for example, to Walter Lippmann in 1921 that Hamilton "was a publicist, a philosopher and a constructor of the whole Federalist point of view; and more than any other single man, the intellectual father of the Republic."[26] Croly shared this enthusiasm for Hamilton with a number of political figures at the time, many of them leading conservatives such as Henry Cabot Lodge and Elihu Root.[27] Most important, he also shared it with Theodore Roosevelt, and it was in his praise of Roosevelt and his linkage of Roosevelt to Hamilton that Croly coined the famous "new Nationalism" phrase, which Roosevelt later used in turn to describe his own program.

In Croly's analysis, Roosevelt was "Hamiltonian with a difference." Hamilton himself had been praiseworthy in emphasizing national cohesion and the need for national programs and power. But Hamilton did not seek a sufficiently broad popular base for the realization of this program. He ignored the other half of the ideal, democracy; he was too fearful of the people. As a result, federalism achieved less than it might have. "It can, I believe, be stated without qualification that wherever the nationalist idea and tendency has been divided from democracy, its achievements have been limited and partially sterilized."[28]

This limitation was emphatically not true of Roosevelt, and Croly pronounced that "the new Federalism or rather new Nationalism is not in any way inimical to democracy. On the contrary, not only does Mr. Roosevelt believe himself to be an unimpeachable democrat in theory, but he has given his fellow-countrymen a useful example of the way in which a college-bred and a well-to-do man can become by somewhat forcible means a good practical democrat." The Harvard man turned cowboy turned Rough Rider had demonstrated that "the whole tendency of his programme is to give a democratic meaning and purpose to the Hamiltonian tradition and method. He proposes to use the power and resources of the Federal government for the purpose of making his countrymen a more complete democracy."[29]

In 1909, Croly was aware (though not as aware as he was later to become) of the dangers of the "national idea." One section of *The Promise* surveyed the possible combination of nationality and democracy in European political systems. In a brief discussion of Bismarck's program, Croly praised the former chancellor for developing the logic of a "national type of political organization" and for transforming his "theory of responsible administrative activity into a comprehensive national policy."[30] But he also faulted Bismarck for "bullying and browbeating" his opponents and noted that he had driven the social democrats into opposition, with the result that the government was "losing touch" with democracy. Croly was not optimistic about Germany's domestic prospects.[31] He also noted that nationalism could lead to war: Europe had "become a vast camp" by 1909. These were examples of the dangers of nationality when it was not combined with "an infusion of democracy."[32]

Despite these reservations, Croly was an enthusiastic nationalist in 1909: "The modern nation, particularly in so far as it is constructively democratic, constitutes the best machinery as yet developed for raising the level of human association."[33] Using phrases that could have been drawn from Josiah Royce, Croly ventured an extended metaphor about the role of "national schools":

> Everybody within the schoolhouse—masters, teachers, pupils and janitors, old pupils and young, good pupils and bad, must feel one to another an indestructible loyalty. Such loyalty is merely the subjective aspect of their inevitable mutual association; it is merely the recognition that as a worldly body they must all live or die and conquer or fail together. The existence of an invincible loyalty is a condition of the perpetuity of the school.[34]

NATIONALITY WAS incomplete without democracy. But what *was* democracy? Croly had a harder time explaining his views on this concept, largely, I think, because he was quite ambivalent in his own mind about democracy. He was genuinely convinced that democracy was a necessary complement to nationality. He also knew that Americans were attached to the concept; if for that reason alone, it would have to be part of the social ideal. But Croly was not an enthusiastic democrat, largely because he was not particularly committed to the concept of equality, which is such a central part of any convincing definition of democracy. Croly's efforts to work out his views on democracy led him into the most theoretically complex parts of his argument.

The historical figure that Croly used to illustrate American democracy was, of course, Thomas Jefferson, and Croly, like his father, did not think highly of the third president. He pronounced that Jefferson did possess "one saving quality which Hamilton himself lacked: Jefferson was filled with a sincere, indiscriminate, and unlimited faith in the American people."[35] This comment was meant as praise, but Croly's reservations are evident. He proceeded to levy more harsh criticisms, terming Jefferson's conception of democracy "meager, narrow, and self-contradictory."[36]

Croly made his criticism more specific by singling out two points. First, he argued that Jefferson was incapable of embodying his theory of democracy "in a set of efficient institutions."[37] This comment was directed primarily at Jefferson the president rather than Jefferson the political theorist. Jefferson's policy, Croly argued, was "the old fatal policy of drift."[38] Jefferson refused to develop governmental institutions because he believed in as little government as possible.

The second major reason for devaluing Jefferson was that his democracy "was tantamount to extreme individualism. He conceived a democratic society to be composed of a collection of individuals, fundamentally alike in their abilities and deserts."[39] Jefferson, to Croly's mind, had not given scope for the more able members of the society to develop their own individual talents—Jefferson's conception of democracy had led to the society that Robert Grant had described, in which "specialists" were not sufficiently valued.

Croly concluded this historical picture by deciding that Jefferson had "sought an essentially equalitarian and even socialistic result by means of an essentially individualistic machinery." He continued: "His theory implied a complete harmony both in logic and in effect between the idea of liberty and the idea of equality; and just in so far as there is any antagonism between those ideas, his whole political system becomes unsound and impracticable." When such an antagonism did develop, in Croly's view, "the Jeffersonian Democrats have been found on the side of equality."[40]

In these passages, we see Croly introducing two other important political concepts, equality and liberty, into his analysis of democracy. In Croly's view, Jefferson had identified democracy too closely with equality, de-emphasizing the importance of liberty. But how could these principles be integrated? What was the proper relation among them? If Jefferson's understanding of democracy was inadequate, what would a more adequate conception involve? These questions—the construction of an adequate understanding of democracy, while giving due account also of the place of equality and liberty in a good political system—brought Croly to central questions of political theory. He tried to make his views clear in a section of *The Promise* entitled "Reconstruction; Its Conditions and Purposes."

Croly begins this argument by positing that democracy "as most frequently understood is essentially and exhaustively defined as a matter of popular government." Contrasting liberty and democracy, he notes that this view has been opposed by "constitutional liberals in England, in France, and in this country [who] have always objected to democracy as so understood, because of the possible sanction it affords for . . . a popular despotism."[41] I think it is significant that Croly does *not* reject this criticism; however, he goes on to say that "ultimate responsibility for the government of a community must reside somewhere." Modern governments require popular sovereignty in some form. In yet another telling passage, Croly again ties democracy to liberty, while suggesting an altered understanding of what liberty might be: "A people, to whom was denied the ultimate responsibility for its welfare, would not have obtained the prime condition of genuine liberty."[42]

Having endorsed popular sovereignty as necessary for democracy and for a good state, Croly at once asserts that this is not a sufficient definition: "If, however, democracy does not mean anything less than popular Sovereignty, it assuredly does mean something more. . . . The assertion of the doctrine of popular Sovereignty is, consequently, rather the beginning than the end of democracy."[43] Croly goes on to explain what else is needed.

The "ordinary American answer" to this question is to cite an aspect of equality as central, specifically "equal rights under the law." As Croly presents this typical answer: "If any citizen or any group of citizens enjoys by virtue of the law any advantage over their fellow-citizens, then the most sacred principle of democracy is violated. On the other hand, a community in which no man or no group of men are granted by law any advantage over their fellow-citizens is the type of the perfect and fruitful democratic state."[44]

Croly is convinced that this is the common American view of democracy. Individuals would enjoy equal liberties under this principle, and a reconciliation of individual and social interests would be effected. "The divergent demands of the individual and the social interest can be reconciled by grafting the principle of equality on the thrifty tree of individual rights, and the ripe fruit thereof can be gathered merely by shaking the tree."[45] Croly's metaphor here evokes, of course, the "old fatal policy of drift," the prevailing laissez-faire assumptions. So the common American definition of democracy is wrong; Croly's earlier statement of the need for a national *purpose* was meant to demonstrate the inadequacy of this very view. The ideal of democracy would need to be further reconstructed.

Croly begins this process by making a bow to equal rights: "It must be immediately admitted . . . that the principle of equal rights, like the principle of ultimate popular political responsibility is the expression of an essential aspect of democracy."[46] However, there are two major problems with this principle: first, it is illogical and inconsistent, and second, it doesn't give adequate scope to the truly able individual. Thus Croly is asking for conceptual clarification, but he is also saying that he has doubts about an emphasis on equality. He is trying to develop a conception of democracy while de-emphasizing equality—not an easy argument to make.

Croly turns first to the conceptual clarification. "Equal rights" has meant two different things to Americans, he argues, which we might call today equality of *rights* or equality of *opportunity.* An emphasis on rights has led inevitably to an emphasis on property in the American system. Yet, in the very same breath that Americans defend property rights, they also argue that their system allows equality of opportunity. Croly thought that most Americans had so far failed to perceive that the logic and particularly the practical effects of these two understandings of "equality" are contradictory: people who begin the "race of life" with property are at a substantial advantage, and there is, in fact, no true equality of opportunity present in the system.

> The democratic principle requires an equal start in the race, while expecting at the same time an unequal finish. But Americans who talk in this way seem wholly blind to the fact that under a legal system which holds private property sacred there may be equal rights, but there cannot possibly be any equal opportunities for exercising such rights. The chance which the individual has to compete with his fellows and take a prize in the race is vitally affected by material conditions over which he has no control. . . . Those who have enjoyed the benefits of wealth and thorough education start with

an advantage which can be overcome only by very exceptional men.[47]

This argument was a strong challenge to laissez-faire, a challenge as powerful in theory as Croly's criticism of the social effects of laissez-faire had been in more practical terms. His conclusion was that Americans had not "readjusted their political ideas to the teaching of their political and economic experience."[48] American opinion would have to admit that allegiance simply to "equality of rights" would not do, that "continued loyalty to a contradictory principle is destructive of a wholesome public sentiment and opinion." The principle of equal rights, as Americans had stated it, was "confusing, distracting, and at worst, disintegrating." Instead, America needed a theory that was "binding and healing and unifying."[49]

Croly tried to furnish this theory as he turned to the second objection to the common view, that it doesn't give adequate scope to able individuals. As he begins this theoretical construction, Croly makes clear once again his own doubts about another fundamental understanding of equality, the idea that humans have equal abilities. He argues immediately that some people are more able than others, and a political system must give able individuals space to achieve their potential. Indeed, this would be a true equality of opportunity, and in the sphere of intellect and political leadership, not material advantage. It is interesting to note that Croly thus was pointing out the importance of personal liberties like freedom of speech and de-emphasizing economic liberty. Of course, to this faithful student of Royce individual potential in any field must be achieved *within the social ideal*, within the common good. It can't be an individual, selfish potential. Croly thus posits a conception of a democratic community, the "national democracy" that will allow a true equality of opportunity for able individuals to achieve their full development.

This is the conception that Croly thinks Jefferson overlooked. When Jefferson "and his followers" have referred to "the people," they have meant "the people in so far as they could be generalized and reduced to an average. The interests of this class were conceived as inimical to any discrimination which tended to select peculiarly efficient individuals or those who were peculiarly capable of social service."[50]

This was an inaccurate characterization of Jefferson's own views. Perhaps Herbert Croly was following his father's views rather than reading Jefferson on his own. If he had read further, he would have found that Jefferson did indeed identify a "natural aristocracy" as an important element in a society, and did hope (for Jefferson there was no institutional guarantee) that a democratic electorate would often trust in these able leaders.[51] Perhaps Croly was really thinking more of the Jacksonians, or perhaps he was writing against the contemporary invocation of Jefferson as a theorist of laissez-faire. In any case, he thought the effect of this "Jeffersonian" view was to "discriminate in favor of the average or indiscriminate individual," and this had "succeeded at the expense of individual liberty, efficiency, and distinction."[52] Croly also meant to suggest that a true democracy was less a matter of popular will than popular deliberation that was to be guided by the more able—in which argument he was closer to Jefferson than he realized.

One way to save individual liberty and distinction was that of "Hamilton and the constitutional liberals," who argued that the "state should interfere exclusively on behalf of individual liberty."[53] Again significantly, Croly does not reject this view as wrong, but he does find it inadequate. As he had already argued, this was not a possible answer in a democracy. A "constitutional liberal" state (Croly uses the example of the "Orleans Monarchy" in France) "might well give its citizens fairly good government," but it "could not arouse vital popular interest and support."[54]

In his own theory, then, Croly rejects a limitation on the suffrage, appealing as this answer might be (he writes it "has the appearance of being reasonable; and it has made a strong appeal to those statesmen and thinkers who believed in the political leadership of intelligent and educated men").[55] On the other hand, the able must be given a leading role in a democracy, which must thus "encourage the political leadership of experienced, educated, and well-trained men, but only on the express condition that their power is . . . used . . . for the benefit of the people as a whole."[56]

Croly had earlier argued that a democracy "cannot afford to give any one class of its citizens a *permanent* advantage. . . . It ceases to be a democracy, just as soon as any *permanent* privileges are conferred by its institutions or its laws."[57] This clearly suggests that able individuals should be able to earn temporary distinctions. Indeed, a "well-governed state will use its power to promote edifying and desirable discriminations." Such "advantageous discriminations," when "properly selected," contribute "both to individual and to social efficiency." But they must not be allowed to "outlast their own utility."[58] He concludes that "the individual is merged in the mass, unless he is enabled to exercise efficiently and independently his own private and special purposes."[59] At the same time, "transformed" democracy "must cease to be a democracy of indiscriminate individualism, and become one of selected individuals who are obliged constantly to justify their selection; and its members must be united . . . by a sense of joint responsibility for the success of their political and social ideal."[60]

Croly thought he was now ready to "venture upon a more fruitful definition of democracy." It does not mean, he wrote, "merely government by the people, or majority rule, or universal suffrage." These are indeed part of its "necessary organization," but democracy's essence is

> to promote some salutary and formative purpose. The really formative purpose is not exclusively a matter of individual liberty, although it must give individual liberty abundant scope. Neither is it a matter of equal rights alone, although it must always cherish the social bond which that principle represents. The salutary and formative democratic purpose consists in using the democratic organization for the joint benefit of individual distinction and social improvement.[61]

This is a very interesting formulation. On a formal level, Croly has identified the elements that are normally viewed as essential to democratic theory.[62] He has assumed majority rule and universal suffrage. He has seen that individual freedoms are a part of democracy, though he has not emphasized the direct connection to the democratic process of such freedoms as freedom of speech or freedom of the press. He has also seen that equality is a necessary part of democracy, though he has de-emphasized equality substantially at the same time. On the other hand, Croly's delineation of reconstructed democracy has elevated the role of the able individual—of the elite, if you will—more than we normally see in a "democratic" theory. Admittedly, he has tried to make it clear that this must be an elite of talent and not of birth or money (again, he was much closer to Jefferson here than he knew), and it could not be permanent.[63] Still, his theory is meant to give considerable scope to a political and intellectual elite—within the limited framework of popular sovereignty. Croly here shows himself to be *not* an egalitarian, even as he tries to be a democrat. It was a difficult position to sustain, as he found out in future years.

THE PROPOSED construction of a polity that gave adequate scope to a political and intellectual elite while remaining democratic was optimistic, Croly realized, and he searched for examples that would prove the point. He found one in American history and one in contemporary politics.

The historical example was Abraham Lincoln, and Croly devoted a ten-page section of his historical analysis to the topic "Lincoln as More Than an American." In a generally gloomy survey of American history (particularly after the founding period), Lincoln stood out. His fame came, of course, from abolishing slavery and saving the union, but Croly went well beyond these points. "The life of no other American," he judged, "has revealed with anything like the same completeness the peculiar moral promise of genuine democracy." Lincoln's was the "kind of excellence which a political and social democracy may and should fashion."[64]

Lincoln's particular virtue was to be a man of the people. He could sit in the "corner grocery store" and swap stories with all classes of people. But he was also a man who exhibited "high and disinterested intellectual culture," unlike the ordinary American who "subordinated his intelligence to certain dominant practical interests."[65] Lincoln read widely and trained his mind effectively. He was personally humble, politically magnanimous, yet "intellectually candid." Above all, he was not afraid to use national power when it was needed. "He became the individual instrument whereby an essential and salutary national purpose was fulfilled."[66]

The contemporary example of Croly's national democracy was, of course, Theodore Roosevelt. Croly judged that "more than any other American political leader, except Lincoln, his devotion both to the national and to the democratic ideas is thorough-going and absolute." Roosevelt was not perfect—his program needed reconstruction. Even so, Croly believed that Roosevelt had combined democracy with the requisite emphasis on a disinterested elite: "Mr. Roosevelt has exhibited his genuinely national spirit in nothing so clearly as in his endeavor to give to men of special ability, training, and eminence a better opportunity to serve the public."[67]

The ideal of a national democracy was thus possible. Yet it would not be easy to develop fully the sense of national purpose that Croly knew would be necessary to hold the good society together. To assume that this ideal could be realized was something of a matter of faith as well as political planning.[68]

Croly realized how optimistic some of his assumptions were. He wrote at the beginning of his last chapter that "in the course of this discussion, it has been taken for granted that the American people under competent and responsible leadership could deliberately plan a policy of individual and social improvement." This in turn implied that "human nature can be raised to a higher level by an improvement in institutions and laws."[69] Croly admitted that many readers probably would have thought this point "overworked," and he also admitted that in his understanding "human nature is composed of most rebellious material, and that the extent to which it can be modified by social and political institutions of any kind is, at best, extremely small."[70] However, Croly went on essentially to admit the charge: "Democracy must stand or fall on a platform of possible human perfectibility. If human nature cannot be improved by institutions, democracy is at best a more than usually safe form of political organization." And in his concluding paragraph, he quoted Montesquieu to the effect that "the principle of democracy is virtue."[71]

As we have seen, an important influence on Croly's idea of a national purpose was Josiah Royce's idealism. Royce had conveyed to his pupil a philosophic, yet also a religious, vision of a community united by loyalty to an ideal. This philosophy *cum* religion taught Croly that moral improvement or "regeneration" (one of his favorite words)[72] was possible. We have seen the influence of this view in such passages as Croly's extended metaphor of the national schoolhouse. Another discussion in which Croly's faith is evident is his treatment of "Tolstoyan democracy." Here he writes that "the idea that a higher type of associated life can be immediately realized by a supreme act of faith must always be tempting to men who unite social aspirations with deep religious faith."[73] He judges this a "more worthy and profound conception of democracy than the conventional American one of a system of legally constituted and equally exercised rights, fatally resulting in material prosperity."[74]

Nevertheless, Croly realizes this view is unrealistic and impossible of practical realization. It may be possible to change small groups of "unregenerate men from a condition of violence, selfishness, and sin into a condition of beatitude and brotherly love," but such an exclusive idea will never do for a national organization. "In this world faith cannot dispense with power and organization. . . . But with the help of efficient organization it may possibly survive, whereas in the absence of such a worldly body, it must in a worldly sense inevitably perish. Democracy as a living movement in the direction of human brotherhood has required, like other faiths, an efficient organization."[75]

In this passage, we see only a partial triumph of the social theorist and political realist over the religious believer. Nevertheless, the theme of "brotherhood" is never far from the surface, and a full understanding of Croly's conception of "national democracy" must take account of this dimension of his thought.

Brotherhood or fraternity (to use what Croly considered a synonym) was tied to democracy in another discussion, which follows immediately on Croly's "fruitful definition of democracy" that we have just discussed. Here Croly draws on a work by a French writer, Emile Faguet, who seems in turn to be discussing Tocqueville. Faguet had written that liberty and equality were contradictory, indeed were exclusive of one another—the famous Tocqueville argument. But Faguet went on to claim that fraternity could conciliate these principles, indeed could stimulate them to be more productive. Croly takes this French triad and reinterprets it slightly: "The two subordinate principles, that is, one representing the individual [liberty] and the other the social interest [equality], can by their subordination to the principle of human brotherhood, be made in the long run mutually helpful." He adds: "The foregoing definition of the democratic purpose is the only one which can entitle democracy to an essential superiority to other forms of political organization."[76] Croly's national democracy was thus grounded in American history, but it was also based on a moral vision of what a good human community must be.

IN THE COURSE of discussing "national democracy," Croly often explored the concepts of "rights" and "freedom." Yet he did not emphasize these concepts in *The Promise*. At first glance, this de-emphasis, of freedom particularly, is strange, since freedom and rights have always been central in American thought about politics. However, the point is less strange when we remember the political context within which Croly was writing. Conservative theorists strongly emphasized property rights in this period. Indeed, the decision of the Supreme Court in *Lochner v. New York* (198 U.S. 45)—one of the high points in the theory of substantive due process, the theory essentially enshrining property rights in the Fourteenth Amendment—had been handed down in 1905, the year Croly began writing. The theory of rights was thus often equated with a conservative emphasis on property. Freedom as a concept was less clearly identified with conservative policies. Nevertheless, substantive due process included such understandings as "freedom of contract," which was a foundation of the theory of property and of laissez-faire generally.

While Croly does not emphasize the concepts of rights and freedom, he does deal with them, and they are important to his thought. Indeed, I think that his reconceptualization of freedom in *The Promise*, while not fully developed, is one of the central aspects of his political theory. Together with his writing on the idea of individualism, his ideas about freedom are central to the reconstruction of American liberal political theory that Croly was shaping.

In *The Promise*, Croly resisted any idea that the concept of rights was the foundation of a good political system. He thought that rights overemphasized the divisions within a polity, rather than its unity. He wrote that when liberties and rights were "abstractly considered," they tended to "conflict both one with another and, perhaps, with the common weal." If the chief purpose of a democracy was the preservation of rights, "local, factional, and individual ambitions" would be overly encouraged.[77] A "right" was also too absolute for Croly—it implied too strong a restriction on the ability of the government to act in the national interest. For these same reasons, Croly resisted using a social contract understanding of the origin of government. A country was not the result of a "necessary but hazardous surrender of certain rights and liberties in order that other rights might be preserved." On the contrary, "the nationalized political organization constitutes the proper structure and veritable life of the American democracy."[78] In this rejection of social contract theory and the conception of an isolated individual armed with abstract "rights," Croly was in agreement with much of the developing progressive theory of the time.[79]

As he traced these arguments in American history, Croly thought that the federalists had mistakenly overemphasized property rights. They "sought to surround private property, freedom of contract, and personal liberty with an impregnable legal fortress." The antifederalists were also to blame in seeking to require "a still more stringent bill of individual and state rights."[80] Croly was by no means completely opposed to these arguments. He wrote that these "legal restrictions" had their "value"; they were even "the expression of an essential element in the composition and the ideal of the American nation. The security of private property and personal liberty . . . demanded at that time, and within limits still demand, adequate legal guarantees."[81] So Croly was not opposed to individual rights and liberties or to private property *per se.*

However, he did oppose an overemphasis on these concepts. He thought the American system had gone too far in guaranteeing rights against the democratic principle. In Croly's view, "every popular government should in the end, and after a necessarily prolonged deliberation, possess the power of taking any action, which, in the opinion of a decisive majority of the people, is demanded by the public welfare."[82] No doubt thinking about Court decisions such as *Lochner,* Croly occasionally stated his anger at the enshrinement of absolute property rights in more extreme terms: "The time may come when the fulfillment of a justifiable democratic purpose may demand the limitation of certain rights, to which the Constitution affords such absolute guarantees; and in that case the American democracy might be forced to seek by revolutionary means the accomplishment of a result which should be attainable under the law."[83] However, he normally expressed himself more moderately. The fault in the current understanding of rights lay in the "practical immutability of the Constitution." Supporting in effect an easier process of amendment, Croly argued that if the Constitution "could be altered whenever a sufficiently large body of public opinion has demanded a change for a sufficiently long time, the American democracy would have much more to gain than to fear from the independence of the Federal judiciary."[84]

I think it is inaccurate to conclude that Croly was opposed to individual rights. However, it is accurate to say that in *The Promise* he resisted a conceptualization of "natural rights": any area of behavior to be reserved to the individual was the result of a social determination, not an abstract principle.

It is also the case that Croly was not very interested in causes that would later become important "civil rights" issues. For example, he did not concern himself with issues of racial equality. The National Association for the Advancement of Colored People (NAACP) was founded in 1909, the year Croly's book was published, and some of his fellow progressives were involved.[85] But Croly was not. Indeed, several passages in *The Promise* make it clear that Croly was racist in some of his conceptions. For example, in his historical analysis, while opposing slavery he wrote of southern slaveholders that they were right "in believing that the negroes were a race possessed of moral and intellectual qualities inferior to those of the white man."[86] Croly was not alone in these attitudes, but it is clear that his concern for "regeneration" was culturally somewhat limited.

More surprising because of his own upbringing was Croly's entire omission of the topic of women's suffrage and more generally of women's rights. Despite having a leading feminist for a mother, Herbert Croly displayed no concern for women's issues, nor does his writing on democracy in *The Promise* ever deal with the issue of suffrage restriction because of sex.

It would seem that the reasons for these omissions lie primarily in Croly's sense of national unity and in his strong opposition to any appeal for the interests (whether or not these were couched in the language of "rights") of any group within the national democracy. The sense of national unity, of a national community, is a dominant theme of *The Promise*, and it prevented Croly from being as sympathetic as he would become to group arguments for equality or rights within this community. It is also true that Croly (probably largely because of his personal background) was not an egalitarian—he was not a defender of the poor or the oppressed, despite his emphasis on democracy.

IN EXAMINING Croly's views on the concept of freedom, it may be useful to establish immediately that "freedom" or "liberty" (I use the words as synonyms) have several meanings. Isaiah Berlin has distinguished between "negative" and "positive" freedom.[87] In addition, the concept of "positive freedom" has two somewhat different meanings, one suggestive of a moral freedom and one describing a social or economic sufficiency that is necessary for freedom in practical terms. These distinctions are useful in understanding Croly's conception of freedom.

Berlin's "negative freedom" is the classic liberal emphasis on freedom *from* the control of others; it maximizes the domain of individual choice.[88] Leading theorists of this persuasion would be John Locke, Benjamin Constant, and in most respects John Stuart Mill. This is the sense of liberty emphasized in classic liberal theory. It is what we have seen Croly describe as the position of the "constitutional liberals." I have argued that this traditional understanding of liberty was important to Croly, but it was a partial, "limited" truth and was too often opposed to democracy.

Croly argues that this understanding of liberty is distinctively English; indeed, the "idea of liberty" is called the "great formative English political idea."[89] However, in English politics this idea came to stand for the property rights of the English upper classes, with the result that the English political leaders "abandoned . . . leadership in economic affairs and allowed a merely individualistic liberalism complete control of the fiscal and economic policy of the country."[90]

Croly hoped that Englishmen would "come to understand the need of dissociating their national idea from its existing encumbrances of political privilege and social favoritism."[91] In other words, liberty needed to be extricated from laissez-faire economics. Pressing his own view of the American "national ideal" on them, Croly thought that Englishmen also would need to accept a greater degree of democracy. This would not, however, be easy given the English economic system. In short, negative liberty of the English or "constitutional liberal" variety was important for Croly, but it was not sufficient.

Isaiah Berlin describes "positive freedom" (in the first of the senses we mentioned, that of freedom as a moral imperative) as an idea that humans are free when they live according to the dictates of a "latent rational will, or their 'true' purpose."[92] This is freedom *to* lead a good, moral life. It is this sense of the concept that we find in Rousseau's *Social Contract* where he urges us to exchange natural freedom (negative freedom) for civil or moral freedom (positive freedom). This is also the freedom of Kant, and particularly of Hegel, for whom we are free within the nation-state. It is also the freedom of Auguste Comte.[93]

We might expect, particularly in view of David Croly's positivism, that this view of freedom could be found in Herbert Croly's writings. His training in Royce's idealism might also be thought to dispose Croly to this argument. In fact, however, this understanding of freedom is not present in any substantial sense in Croly's thought. Croly does hope that when individuals live according to a national ideal they will be inspired to a more moral life, but he does not argue that this is "freedom." The argument of *The Promise* does not lead to a theory of positive freedom in this sense. One reason it does not is that Royce's influence on Croly led only very partially in this direction, and, of course, Royce's thought was only one of many influences that can be found in *The Promise*. Rather, Royce, while he certainly drew from Hegel, drew more strongly from English idealism, and English idealists had introduced crucial distinctions into their thought, including a distinction between "society" and "the state" and a much stronger emphasis on individualism.[94]

In fact, English idealism led in the direction of our second understanding of positive freedom, that of freedom as an economic sufficiency allowing a practical enjoyment of individualism or freedom. I think that this understanding of freedom can be found in Croly's thought—indeed, that he is one of the first Americans to use this sense of positive freedom.

This second understanding of positive freedom is hard to define. It is essentially the argument that humans need economic security and other social conditions (normally provided, at least in part, by the state) that will allow us to develop our individuality without finding our lives controlled by others because of economic privations. The idea is nicely expressed in Franklin D. Roosevelt's "Four Freedoms" speech, in which he spells out four essential freedoms in the world: freedom of speech, freedom of religion, "freedom from want," and "freedom from fear." The first two are negative freedoms; the last two point in the direction of this understanding of positive freedom.[95]

The seminal statement of this position was by the English idealist T. H. Green (1836–1882), whose theory Croly could well have studied with Palmer and Royce. In a lecture on "Liberal Legislation and Freedom of Contract" in 1880, Green had argued that freedom was not "merely freedom from restraint and compulsion." Rather, "when we speak of freedom . . . we mean a positive power of doing or enjoying something worth doing or enjoying. . . . We mean by it a power which each man exercises through the help or security given him by his fellow-men. . . ."[96] Green went on to say that "the ideal of true freedom is the maximum of power for all members of human society alike to make the best of themselves. . . ." For him, this was "freedom in the positive sense."[97]

Later English writers drew from Green, arguing both that they were adapting the older liberal theory to new conditions, and that they were maintaining the central emphasis on liberty. For example, in *Liberalism* (1911), Leonard Hobhouse wrote that new liberals regarded "the State as one among many forms of human association for the maintenance and improvement of life . . . and this is the point at which we stand furthest from the older Liberalism." However, Hobhouse went on to claim that there was "some reason for thinking that the older doctrines led, when carefully examined, to a more enlarged conception of State action . . . and we shall see more fully before we have done that the 'positive' conception of the State which we have now reached not only involves no conflict with the true principle of personal liberty, but is necessary to its effective realization."[98] He later expands on the argument that "there is no intrinsic and inevitable conflict between liberty and [state] compulsion, but at bottom a mutual need. The object of compulsion is to secure the most favourable external conditions of inward growth and happiness so far as these conditions depend on combined action. . . . The sphere of liberty is the sphere of growth itself. There is no true opposition between liberty as such and control as such."[99]

Croly did not make the connection to classical liberal theory quite so explicit, but it seems clear that his argument is virtually the same as Hobhouse's. For example, Croly writes that a "wholesome democracy should seek to guarantee to every male adult a certain minimum of economic power and responsibility. . . . The individuals constituting a democracy lack the first essential of individual freedom when they cannot escape from a condition of economic dependence."[100] Such dependence is contrary to all understanding of the American promise, both the popular belief in economic prosperity and Croly's own ideal of national democracy.

Croly makes the restrictive, liberty-denying nature of laissez-faire clear when he writes that "Americans have always associated individual freedom with the unlimited popular enjoyment of all available economic opportunities. Yet it would be far more true to say that the popular enjoyment of practically unrestricted economic opportunities is precisely the condition which makes for individual bondage."[101] State action to lend assistance to the "workingman to raise his standard of living" would "increase the amount of economic independence enjoyed by the average laborer . . . and intensify his importance to himself as an individual. It would in every way help to make the individual workingman more of an individual."[102]

These statements are not a fully explicit statement of positive freedom, but the direction in which Croly was seeking to "transform" or "reconstruct" the idea of liberty is, I think, clear. Croly had not yet adopted the "liberal" label, as Hobhouse and Green had, but he had established some of the conditions for doing so.

BEFORE WE CAN talk of Croly being a liberal, we must consider one more concept—that of individualism. This idea is rightly considered the touchstone of liberalism—no theorist can be considered a liberal who is not concerned to enunciate a theory of individualism.

Croly had, as we have seen, renounced the traditional American ideal of an isolated individual, armed with rights and facing a hostile world. Rather he had described a human being who was social and shared in a common national purpose. At the same time, Croly had been sensitized by his reading of Grant to the argument that able individuals (specialists) should develop their own particular abilities rather than being limited by the prevailing values of the society. As in his delineation of a national idea that rejected both laissez-faire and socialism, Croly was thus trying to find a middle position on the individual-community balance.

This middle position is evident throughout *The Promise*. For example, in the chapter in which he is most theoretically detailed, Croly writes that it is the function of the democratic state "to represent the whole community; and the whole community includes the individual as well as the mass, the many as well as the few. The individual is merged in the mass, unless he is enabled to exercise efficiently and independently his own private and special purposes."[103]

Croly considers the question of individualism in a number of other passages. For example, his discussion of positive freedom, just considered, had argued that state action to help free workers from economic coercions would intensify their individualism. The major explication of the concept of individualism, however, occurs in the long final chapter of *The Promise*, which is entitled "Conclusions—the Individual and the National Purpose." This chapter is often diffuse, but Croly attempts to bring his criticisms of American culture together with a focus on individualism. He argues that America in its policy of "drift" has really not "encouraged individualism at all." It has not encouraged specialists and the full development of individual capacities. This would be true individualism: "Individuality is necessarily based on genuine discrimination."[104] Emphasizing his previous theme of a common national purpose, Croly tries to tie his points together:

> A national structure which encourages individuality as opposed to mere particularity is one which creates innumerable special niches, adapted to all degrees and kinds of individual development. The individual becomes a nation in miniature, but devoted to the loyal realization of a purpose peculiar to himself. The nation becomes an enlarged individual whose special purpose is that of human amelioration, and in whose life every individual should find some particular but essential function.[105]

This passage clearly seeks to have it both ways—Croly refuses to sacrifice either the individual or the community. There is certainly a suggestion of the Hegelian nation, but the theme of individualism is distinctively liberal and American. Indeed, the passage is very different from the metaphor of the beehive that we saw David Croly using, in which he argued that the bees "but live for the community, the community does not exist for them."[106] Rather, Herbert is much closer to Jane Croly's "unity in diversity." At the same time, it is clear that Croly had not yet reached a fully consistent position. For example, was this able individual to act in his own interest or *only* in the national interest? This passage does not provide a full answer.

As he struggled to bring his argument to conclusion, Croly sought to bridge or reconcile this division between the individual's own goals and the community, and he did this by invoking religious imagery and the concept of brotherhood or fraternity. Just as he had sought to conciliate freedom and equality by invoking brotherhood, so Croly now sought to conciliate the individual and society: "It has been admitted throughout [the book] that the task of individual and social regeneration must remain incomplete and impoverished, until the conviction and the feeling of human brotherhood enters into possession of the human spirit."[107]

Croly ends by drawing explicitly on an argument by George Santayana. He quotes Santayana as saying that in a democracy "the common citizen must be something of a saint and something of a hero."[108] But Croly changes this emphasis in his own conclusion, moving away from the emphasis on democracy and equality and instead emphasizing Grant's specialists once again: "The common citizen can become something of a saint and something of a hero, not by growing to heroic proportions in his own person, but by the sincere and enthusiastic imitation of heroes and saints, and whether or not he will ever come to such imitation will depend upon the ability of his exceptional fellow-countrymen to offer him acceptable examples of heroism and saintliness."[109]

I think this final emphasis on the development of the able *individual* as a model for the democracy shows where the balance (slight though it is) lies in Croly's thought. The passage clearly establishes that despite his reluctance to emphasize liberty as the formative American principle, Croly was clearly transforming *liberal* theory. There is a continued emphasis on the individual in *The Promise*, an emphasis that coexists somewhat uneasily with the emphasis on "national democracy" but which nevertheless is a basic point in Croly's political theory.

In a broader perspective, Croly is in the very difficult position of trying to hold to several principles at once and to work out an acceptable reconciliation among them. He is emphasizing individualism—but making it clear that this is not the individualism of laissez-faire theory. He is accepting the value of negative freedom—while again refusing to take it as far, particularly in the economic area, as laissez-faire did. He is working toward a new understanding of "positive freedom." He is emphasizing democracy—in part because he believes in it, but even more because Americans will insist on a democratic component in the national ideal. He is aware that equality is a part of democracy—but he is not an enthusiastic egalitarian. Finally, he is committed to the idea that a national purpose can be made explicit, to provide a sense of community, of brotherhood even, to conciliate the individual aspirations of its members.

Put this way, it is clear that *The Promise of American Life* was an extraordinary theoretical achievement for someone who had not written about politics before. It was original, suggestive ("fruitful" as Croly would put it), rich in detailed argument and conceptual explication. However, it is also clear that the argument was not fully clarified—or rather, that Croly did not want to choose among his many somewhat contradictory emphases.

The conciliation of different emphases is characteristic of much of modern liberal thought. For example, John Stuart Mill defended the principle of democracy in *Considerations on Representative Government*, worried about democracy and argued for the primacy of liberty in *On Liberty*, and argued for equality in *The Subjection of Women*. Leonard Hobhouse, in words very similar to Croly's, argued for a "common good [which] includes every individual. It . . . postulates free scope for the development of personality in each member of the community."[110] Hobhouse also wrote that "individuals will contribute to the social will in very varying degrees. . . ."[111] More recently, John Rawls tries to reconcile a priority for liberty (but with equal rights to this liberty) with social and economic inequalities when these work to the advantage of the least favored, at the same time writing of "the idea of social union."[112]

In Croly's case (and presumably in all these liberal theories) the essence of the argument was the search for a middle way—as in Croly's reconciliation of Hamilton and Jefferson and the repudiation of both socialism and laissez-faire. The precise point was that Croly did not want to ally himself with any preexisting point of view. He was trying to develop a new, centrist position that would command wide support in American politics—wide support for a position that would be truly reformist but not revolutionary, a position that could speak for the progressive movement.

4

"The Promise" and Reform Politics

In *The Promise of American Life*, Herbert Croly developed a theoretical understanding of politics, but he also applied that understanding to most of the political and economic issues that were central in the period. In the course of discussing these issues, Croly established his place among progressive reformers, while also differing with several progressive positions. He evaluated the contributions of a number of leading reformers to the movement, further consciously positioning his own book in the diverse set of reform impulses that was progressivism.[1] An examination of Croly's views on these issues provides an interesting comparison to the more theoretical chapters of *The Promise*.

Croly's most insistent recommendation was that American institutions needed to emphasize the principle of nationality. Nationality was a perspective, not a specific institution. Even so, if a common national purpose was to be achieved, there would have to be a concrete vehicle developed to embody this purpose, and in Croly's view that could only mean an emphasis on the federal government. Federal leaders had not always thought in national terms, as Jefferson showed. Still, given the conditions of the time, Croly concluded that "the national advance of the American democracy does demand an increasing amount of centralized action and responsibility."[2] In Croly's historical analysis, the Civil War had shown the weakness of the original national structure, and Lincoln's combination of democracy with national power had shown the possibilities. It was time to develop these possibilities and finally to carry through on this institutionalization of the national promise.[3]

Croly did not describe in detail the powers that the national government should have, but he did specify "the regulation of commerce, the organization of labor, and the increasing control over property in the public interest" as powers "assuredly to be included."[4] Croly thought that his proposals would be resisted as "injurious to certain aspects of traditional American democracy." However, he was sure of the safety of his proposed combination of nationality and democracy. Fears about centralization just illustrated the faults in previous formulations of the American democratic ideal. When properly conceived, democracy should welcome nationalism.[5] In *The Promise*, Croly trusted explicitly in the power of public opinion to control national power, making this clear in a comparison of the reform potential of the national government as opposed to the state governments: "The Federal government belongs to the American people even more completely than do the state governments, because a general current of public opinion can act much more effectively on the single Federal authority than it can upon the many separate state authorities. Popular interests have nothing to fear from a measure of Federal centralization."[6]

It seems clear that Croly was encouraged in this optimism by the strong reform currents running throughout American politics in the years in which he was writing. Richard McCormick has pointed out that "progressivism was the first . . . reform movement to be experienced by the whole nation."[7] Mass-circulation newspapers and muckraking magazines were bringing the cause of reform into every household, giving progressivism a popular base that certainly encouraged Croly's optimism about the role of public opinion. The national government could overcome local allegiances and partial appeals and speak for the American nation as a whole.

WITHIN THE NATIONAL government, Croly recommended strong presidential leadership. Indeed, he relied on executive leadership at all levels of government, judging that "our legislatures were and still are the strongholds of special and local interests, and anything which undermines executive authority in this country seriously threatens our national integrity and balance."[8] Certainly Croly was encouraged in this belief by the example of Theodore Roosevelt, who claimed he had tried to use the powers of his office fully: "While President, I have *been* President. . . . I have used every ounce of power there was in the office."[9] Thus inspired by Lincoln and Roosevelt, Croly was reasonably optimistic that the U.S. Constitution gave the president ample power to provide leadership for the federal government and the nation as a whole.

However, he was less optimistic about the state governors. In fact, the bulk of Croly's writing about the executive in *The Promise* consists of a proposed model of state executive power. The governor, Croly proposed, was to be given the dominant, although not the exclusive, power to introduce legislation and was thus responsible for providing a coherent program for his state. These proposals could be accepted or rejected by the legislature, but if rejected they would be "submitted to popular vote."[10] The legislature itself was to be reconstituted to resemble a "legislative and administrative council or commission" in that it was to be a small body of experts who could deal with the details of legislation, the whole to be "tantamount to a scientific organization of the legislative committees."[11]

This projected executive would indeed have been a powerful, almost dictatorial figure. Croly partially balanced this Hamiltonian executive with the requirement that democratic control of this process be secured by the popular progressive device of the recall. He admitted that recall as currently implemented sometimes had the appearance of "depriving an elected official of the sense of independence and security which he may derive from his term of office." However, when officials were elected for longer terms, "the recall is for this purpose a useful and legitimate political device."[12]

This plan, sketchy as it is, clearly shows the application of Croly's principles of "national democracy" to the specific problem of reforming state governments. The governor would be the able individual, the political generalist, who would display expertise in leadership, but who would also speak for the whole state, just as the president would speak for the nation. Democratic controls would be loose and would be exercised by the people of the state through the recall. Of course, in arguing for the recall Croly was identifying himself with a popular progressive cause, although he did not accept the whole rationale for that device.

Allied to a reliance on the executive leader, in Croly's view, was an increase in the role of the executive bureaucracy, a group of specialists reporting to the generalist governor. Civil service reform had been a progressive step, but while patronage abuses were reduced in the state governments, efficiency had not noticeably increased. Croly called for a further depoliticization and an increased professionalization of the bureaucracy. In his scheme, department heads would continue to be political appointees, but they should "exercise their authority through permanent departmental chiefs," as in the English system. Croly admitted that some critics might worry about bureaucratic usurpation of power, but he was optimistic that administrators could be "disinterested." He observed that if policy was not carried out by officials "who were disinterestedly and intelligently working in the public interest, it would be bound to fail; but so would any method of political organization."[13]

In these proposals, Croly was clearly reacting to the revelations about corruption in the political system which, McCormick has argued, were a precipitating factor in the growth of progressive reform in the first years of the century.[14] In Croly's view, the "professional politician," the boss, would not be needed if a disinterested administrative corps could be created. The boss had evolved to deal with the complexity of government, but in Croly's view administrative reform would bring a general simplification of politics. The voters would choose among the leaders, and a professional administrative elite would run the rest. "The professional politician would be left without a profession."[15]

Croly's stress on the administrative specialist, and his concomitant hope that the "professional politician" would be weakened or eliminated, clearly resembled important features of Bismarck's Germany. However, these arguments were also quite representative of a broad tendency in much of progressivism. Robert H. Wiebe has written that "progressivism was the central force in a revolution that fundamentally altered the structure of politics and government early in the twentieth century."[16] In Wiebe's interpretation, this development of a bureaucratic political system emphasized "continuity." The common assumption was that "trained, professional servants would staff a government broadly and continuously involved in society's operations. . . . [T]hese officials should hold flexible mandates, ones that perforce would blur the conventional distinctions among executive, legislature, and judiciary. Above them stood the public man, a unique and indispensable leader. Although learned enough to comprehend the details of a modern, specialized government, he was much more than an expert among experts. His vision encompassed the entire nation."[17]

This was almost precisely Croly's view, and the political leader he usually had in mind was Theodore Roosevelt. However, Croly could have been thinking of other reform leaders as well. For example, Charles Evans Hughes had won election as governor of New York on a platform of fighting corruption, of administrative reform, and of government regulation of the economy.[18] Hughes had been a leader in investigating corrupt business practices and in attempting to weaken the bosses, such as Senator Platt, who were the model of Croly's "professional politician." He would have provided Croly with a good example of a "disinterested" leader relying on administrative reform measures.

Croly's writings on administrative reorganization were thus typical of a major thrust of at least the eastern, urban wing of the progressive movement. He didn't originate these arguments, but his integration of the theory of administrative reform into a more broad theoretical framework would have been influential on those readers who were already predisposed to seek "good government" through administrative means.[19]

It is also important to note that Croly's writings on administration probably affected his thinking about democratic theory. At the end of the section on administrative reform in *The Promise*, Croly observed that "a democracy has no interest in making good government complicated, difficult, and costly. It has, on the contrary, every interest in so simplifying its machinery that only decisive decisions and choices are submitted to the voter. . . . The cost of government in time, ability, training, and energy should fall not upon the followers but upon the leaders."[20] This statement is consistent with Croly's general emphasis on the able leader, but the phrasing also suggests the development of what political scientists later came to call an "elite theory of democracy"—the argument that the requirements of democracy are satisfied when the people choose between contending elites.[21] Croly does not make this fully explicit, but it seems that a de-emphasis of the popular role in a democracy is clearly implied in these sections of *The Promise*.

Croly continued, indeed sharpened, his reliance on a trained bureaucracy over the next few years. In 1910, seeing the need to train able administrators, he proposed the formation of a national School of Political Science, to be located in Washington and modeled after the École des Sciences Politiques in Paris. The school would be "designated as the crowning member of the departments of political science in the several universities. . . . Its chief object should be to turn out men equipped— either as administrators or legislators—for public life." The school would also encourage national awareness of public policy innovations: "The prosperous future of a democratic nation depends upon the foundation and diffusion of sound, progressive ideas and authentic information."[22] Thus we see that Croly's "able individual" would be trained to develop his own abilities, but that these abilities would in turn be put to work for the nation. The theory of *The Promise* found substance in Croly's proposed institutional reforms.

Here again, Croly was typical of progressivism generally, as much of the movement relied on the deployment of scientific expertise to solve the nation's problems. As McCormick points out, social science disciplines emerged in the period 1880–1910, and their "methods inspired elements common to nearly every reform of the age: the investigation of facts, the application of social-scientific knowledge, the entrusting of trained experts to decide what should be done, and the authorization of governmental officials to take the steps that science suggested."[23] The modern administrative state was emerging, and Croly was optimistic about its future.

Laissez-faire policies would be replaced by concerted national action, based on an explicit national ideal and spearheaded by a trained administrative elite.

AS WE HAVE SEEN, Croly was suspicious about the legislative branch of the government. Congress was usually too representative of local interests and was thus unable to take a national perspective. The state legislatures were no better. They were often corrupt and incompetent. If reorganized and given clearer responsibilities, they might perform better service, but Croly was not optimistic.[24]

We have also seen that Croly's political theory did not emphasize the concept of rights. In practical terms, this perspective included a suspicion of the role of the courts and of "government by lawyers." In Croly's view, the American system too often focused on issues of constitutionality rather than principle. He noted sarcastically that "the lawyer, when consecrated as Justice of the Supreme Court, has become the High Priest of our political faith. He sits in the sanctuary and guards the sacred rights which have been enshrined in the ark of the Constitution."[25]

Croly wished to reduce the authority of lawyers in the American system, doubting their ability to act in a disinterested fashion: "When they talk about a government by law, they really mean a government by lawyers."[26] However, his comments in *The Promise* on the Supreme Court itself were more moderate. In Croly's view, the Constitution was "an ambiguous document which might have been interpreted along several different lines."[27] He believed that the Court much too easily read its own views into its interpretations, and these views in turn often reflected the opinions of the bar. Therefore, it was crucial to reform the legal profession. In Croly's opinion, "the tendency of the legally trained mind is inevitably and extremely conservative."[28] This tendency had been heightened, he feared, in the last decades of the nineteenth century. Croly hoped that this tendency could be counteracted by the development of the new sense of national purpose, but he was not noticeably optimistic that this was likely.

Croly's specific recommendations on the courts in *The Promise* are ambiguous and inconclusive. In this respect, he was not very responsive to the progressive agitation about the role of the courts in blocking reform legislation and in protecting property rights. For instance, one of the main reasons for the progressive faith in the device of the recall was to be able to control at least those judges who were popularly elected.[29] Croly endorsed recall of executive officials in certain cases, as we have seen, but he did not extend this recommendation to the recall of judges.

The progressive devices of initiative and referendum did not stir

Croly's enthusiasm either. He wrote that he understood why these proposals were popular. "American legislatures have betrayed the interests of their constituents, and have been systematically passing laws for the benefit of corrupt and special interests." The popular assumption was therefore that the people must "take back the trust" that had been "delegated to representative bodies."[30] However, Croly was not at all sure that this was the correct answer. Both initiative and referendum were fundamental alterations to the political system, in large part abandoning the notion of representative democracy and returning to direct democracy. "Such a fundamental principle and tradition as that of representation should not be thrown away, unless the change can be justified by a specific, comprehensive, and conclusive analysis of the causes of the failure of the state governments."[31]

Several pages later, Croly returned to the issue of referendum, but again he was ambiguous in his judgment. The principle of letting voters pass on measures voted by their representative "cannot be disputed by any loyal democrat." However, while "the principle upon which the referendum is based is unimpeachable . . . a question remains as to the manner in which [it] . . . can be best embodied."[32] Croly immediately invoked the principle of specialization and expertise: "There is a large part of the work of government, which must be delegated by the people to select individuals, because it can be efficiently exercised only by peculiarly experienced or competent men."[33] Croly concluded with a lukewarm approval of some uses of the initiative and referendum, as in Oregon, where "the power of initiating and consummating legislation is bestowed on the electorate without being taken away from the legislature." But he warned that any further weakening of the state legislatures would mean that they "will probably exercise their remaining functions with even greater incompetence."[34]

We can see in this discussion that Croly's emphasis in *The Promise* on the importance of expertise set him apart from some of the popular progressive political causes. He was sympathetic to the aspect of progressivism that emphasized the importance of the administrative state, but he was clearly uncomfortable with (though not totally hostile to) the aspects of progressivism that emphasized the principles of popular control over the government. That is, he was sympathetic to the Roosevelt vision of executive leadership, but less so to the Western progressive vision of democracy. One is reminded of H. L. Mencken's comment that Roosevelt "didn't believe in democracy; he believed simply in government."[35] That is too strong a comment for Croly, but we *can* see that Croly's commitment to "nationality" was stronger than his commitment to "democracy."

Another issue on which Croly's *Promise* was somewhat outside popular progressivism concerned the place of political parties in the political system. The progressive years were a time of enormous change in the American party system.[36] Voters became considerably less loyal to "their party" in this period, and voter turnout also dropped. Many progressive measures were aimed specifically at weakening the power of party leaders, or "bosses," and some had that effect, if not in exactly the ways sought by the reformers. In addition, two of the most successful third parties in American history, the Socialists and the Progressives, flourished and then died in the years between 1900 and 1920.

Croly's attitude to parties was one of skepticism. He usually viewed political parties negatively: they were divisive agencies within the nation, clearly interested in local issues and too often involved in corrupt practices. In this perception, particularly regarding corruption, most progressives probably agreed with Croly, for it is clear that there was a widespread skepticism of the two national parties, a skepticism quite evident, for example, in the 1906 elections.[37]

However, Croly did not agree with the usual progressive prescription: the direct primary. Primaries were extremely popular with progressives as a means of weakening the control of the bosses over the nominations of candidates and thus over the government generally. Even so conservative a progressive as Charles Evans Hughes committed a lot of his prestige as governor to fight for a direct primary in New York in 1909.[38] Croly was skeptical about the primary, and while he admitted the popularity of this remedy as a medicine for political corruption, he worried that "this device will in the long run merely emphasize the evil which it is intended to abate." Croly observed that the number of elections would be increased significantly under a primary system. Primaries would weaken boss control "whenever public opinion was aroused. . . . But whenever public interest flags,—and it is bound to flag under such an absurd multiplication of elections and under such a complication of electoral machinery,—the politicians can easily nominate their own candidates."[39] In these comments, Croly was an extremely perceptive political observer, but he was not a committed progressive.

Once again, we see that in *The Promise* Croly did not rely on an aroused democracy. He didn't like the effect of parties on the political system, but attempting to democratize them to increase popular participation was neither desirable nor likely to be effective. Croly's sympathies clearly lay in the direction of administrative reform.

THIS RELIANCE on administration was evident in the most famous and important of Croly's specific proposals—his extensive commentary on the need for government regulation of the large corporations that had developed in the American economy, as opposed to simply breaking them up by application of the Sherman Antitrust Act. This issue was *the* dominant issue of the day. The "trusts" had been developing since the Civil War, and by the mid–1880s there was considerable public pressure for government to act.

One answer was to break up business combinations, and that was the avenue taken in the Sherman Antitrust Act of 1890. However, that act was vague and difficult to enforce, and it did little to restrain the growth and further consolidation of business. It became increasingly clear to many Americans that the concentration of economic power was not an easy problem to solve.

Another answer was to emphasize government regulation of business, not by breaking it up but by controlling its practices. This answer was suggested by such state regulatory bodies as the Massachusetts Board of Railroad Commissioners.[40] Support for federal regulation grew after Supreme Court decisions of the mid–1880s greatly limited state regulatory powers. In 1887, Congress created the Interstate Commerce Commission (ICC), charged with determining that railroad rates be "just and reasonable" and forbidding various monopolistic practices. However, by the late 1890s, the judiciary had restricted the powers of the ICC as well.[41]

It is important for our understanding of Herbert Croly's arguments for federal regulation to note that a new movement toward such regulation began in the early 1900s, partly under Theodore Roosevelt's leadership. Important legislative achievements included the Elkins Act of 1903, which outlawed the railroads' practice of illegal rebates to large customers, and the stronger Hepburn Act of 1906, which gave the ICC power to fix maximum railroad rates and strengthened the commission in other ways. The Mann-Elkins Act of 1910 further strengthened the ICC.[42]

This increased regulation of the railroads was also reflected in other industries. Most significantly, Congress enacted the Pure Food and Drug Act in 1906, setting up the Food and Drug Administration (FDA) to regulate meatpacking and other industries. There were various forces behind the enactment of this act. Certainly the publicity that Upton Sinclair (in *The Jungle*) and other muckrakers brought to the issue helped. Many progressives were also involved in the campaign for food and drug regulation, including Croly's Cornish neighbor, Norman Hapgood, the editor of *Collier's*. Theodore Roosevelt's participation was crucial, and Croly would certainly have been thinking of Roosevelt as he developed his ideas about regulation. Roosevelt thought that the muckrakers were excessive in their vitriol (as was evident in his April 1906 speech in which he coined the term "muckraker"). Even so, he supported the legislation, and the final outcome owed much to his political support.[43] However, some middle-class interest groups also worked hard for the FDA, including Jane Croly's Women's Club movement, consumer groups, and the American Medical Association (AMA).[44] And not only reform groups pushed for this legislation. As David Vogel argues, "at the time of its enactment, the Pure Food and Drug Act was not even considered by industry to be consumer legislation; its real purpose was to abolish unfair competition in trade. The driving forces behind passage of the law were various farm and industry groups that wanted protection from adulterers and debasers."[45] Thus there were many groups and many motivations behind the movement for greater regulation of industry.

For Herbert Croly, Theodore Roosevelt's position was probably dominant. Roosevelt soon moved beyond simply providing political support, and in his last years as president he began to enunciate more coherent principles of regulation. For example, in his 1906 Annual Message to Congress, he argued that the attempt to break up large corporations was "noxious where it is not ineffective. Combination of capital like combination of labor is a necessary element of our present industrial system."[46] For Roosevelt, the "effort should be not so much to prevent consolidation as such, but so to supervise and control it as to see that it results in no harm to the people."[47] Roosevelt also gave some indication of at least one motivation behind his policy, to head off more extreme calls for socialization of industry: "The best way to arrest the very undesirable move for the government ownership of railways is to secure by the government on behalf of the people . . . such adequate control and regulation . . . as will do away with the evils which give rise to the agitation."[48] However, Roosevelt could also attack business, and in 1907 he heightened his rhetoric, criticizing "certain malefactors of great wealth" who were profiting from the current business panic. In January 1908 he went even further, calling for federal regulation of the stock market, and in very strong terms he attacked the railroads in particular for dishonest practices, as well as attacking the courts for their support of business.[49]

CROLY WAS AWARE of these developments as he examined the question of regulation in *The Promise,* and he sought to present the issue in all its complexity. For example, he noted that more corporate managers saw that they would have to submit to either state or federal regulation, and that the latter promised a more predictable business climate.[50] Croly was also struck by the legal complexities. Not much progress could be made until the courts interpreted the power of Congress to regulate interstate commerce more broadly, or until a constitutional amendment allowing wider regulation was passed. In addition, he was convinced that the problem of the trusts was part of a wider problem; it would lead inevitably to consideration of a much larger issue, that of distribution of wealth in American society.[51]

As with the rest of his theory, Croly sought to present his economic thought in a historical framework, both in *The Promise* and in his biography of Mark Hanna written two years later.[52] That this biography is generally sympathetic is sometimes cited as evidence of a pro-business and essentially conservative trend in Croly's thought.[53] But such an interpretation is misleading, for Croly does not admire Hanna, but rather presents him as representative of a limited period of American history. Hanna flourished in a time when the country first entered upon industrialization—when its natural resources had to be developed, and when "individual and social profits" were "combined and confused." Laissez-faire was appropriate in those years.[54] However, as natural resources are developed, society profits less and less from the benefits "which the state [is] showering upon the individual." Businesses take short cuts and become corrupt. Also, the original business pioneers pass from the scene, and great wealth is given to men of lesser ability who have not earned it. In Croly's view, this last point was particularly important: it was morally reprehensible, both intrinsically and because it eliminated the rough equality of opportunity that had prevailed. By the early years of the new century, the system appropriate to Hanna's day had to be reformed and replaced by a new economic system.[55]

Croly was convinced that any plan must necessarily be tentative. Much of his conviction that large-scale industry must be regulated depended on the presumed efficiency of the new, larger units. Yet Croly was unsure that a sufficiently long period had elapsed to settle this question. His skepticism was still evident two years later in a letter to Learned Hand: "The proper course is to let large scale and small scale production fight it out. The question is not yet settled how far and in what industries each is more efficient, and it should not be pre-judged. In the meantime the large corporation will have to be regulated."[56] Croly was willing to predict that a substantial percentage of American industry would be more efficient in larger units, but the present lack of evidence suggested the wisdom of plans that could be reversed if the opposite proved true. Because of the complexities involved, Croly's proposals have a dual long-run and short-run nature, which must be recognized if they are to be correctly understood.

Croly sought to develop a plan that would in the short run control some of the abuses of the trusts, but also permit these organizations to continue in existence, allowing the country to profit from their assumed efficiency. He admitted that his policy left the trusts "in possession of those fundamental economic advantages, dependent on terminals, large capital, and natural resources, which place them beyond effective competition."[57] Added to these natural advantages would be legal recognition through a mandatory federal incorporation act. State regulation would consequently be greatly reduced. The only alternative to this regulation of big business was to invoke the Sherman Act, which Croly strongly opposed. Deliberately to undo corporations would "constitute a step backward in the process of economic and social advance." Industrial organization should be "allowed to work itself out."[58]

The corporations would thus benefit from recognition. On the other hand, they would also face stringent regulation in the public interest. Croly considered that there were two broad types of regulation. The first was to legislate a detailed list of unacceptable business practices. This was not feasible. The second was to create a flexible commission with sufficient power to control business. This was Croly's choice, but again there were several possible models. One model was the ICC, but Croly felt this was too limited—it had not proved effective, even with the recent strengthening legislation (though that and the FDA were very promising initiatives).[59] Another model was the New York State Public Service Commission, which had the power to regulate utilities in New York, passing on all mergers, all issuance of securities, and all changes in rates and services.[60]

Croly approved of New York's effort, seeing it as "the first emphatic recognition in American political and economic organization of a manifest public responsibility." Yet he wondered if such detailed regulation, if extended nationally, would not impair the efficiency of the regulated corporation.[61] Croly found his solution in a combination of the ICC and public service commission models: a commission that would set forth broad principles without interfering at every step and turn. Thus the regulatory law should define what kinds of securities could be issued, it could review (but not set) rates, and it should have the power to investigate corporate finances. At the same time, the corporation would retain substantial autonomy in making business decisions, such as the actual setting of prices.[62]

If this was the whole of the short-term plan, it might not have made too many enemies among corporate managers. However, Croly made it clear that even in the short run two supplementary measures were necessary. The first of these was simply to note that some few corporations (such as the railroads) were likely to be so set on gouging the public that more radical steps would be necessary, even in the short run: "If the interest of a corporation is so essentially hostile to the public interest . . . the logical inference therefrom is not a system of semi-official and semi-private management, but a system of exclusively public management. The logical inference therefrom is public ownership, if not actual public operation."[63]

In his second proposal, Croly turned explicitly to deal with the "social question," the distribution of wealth in society, and with corporations that turned in "excessive profits" because of monopolistic or oligopolistic control of their industry. In quite a radical proposal, Croly called for a "system of taxation, in respect to the semi-monopolistic corporations, which would deprive them of the fruits of an excessively large margin [of profit]."[64] The effect, he hoped, would be to encourage management to think of long-term efficiency rather than short-term profits. If the scale of taxation of profits could be properly graduated, business initiative could be preserved. In any case, the state would be entitled to a certain percentage of the profits in return for legal recognition, a percentage that might rise as high as seventy-five percent in industries that were strongly monopolistic.[65] This proposal would not have been happily received by the businessmen of Croly's day!

It must be remembered that these are all short-term proposals. Croly stressed that this plan of "automatically regulated recognition of semi-monopolistic corporations would be intended only as a transitional measure. Its object would be to give these somewhat novel industrial agents a more prolonged and thorough test than any they have yet received."[66]

Croly's recommendations for the long run were necessarily more vague because he refused to predict economic developments with any certainty. However, two factors rendered the system of "regulated recognition" less desirable in the long run. In the first place, financial profits that businessmen would be able to reap still rendered their interest "different from that of the community as a whole." Mere regulation would not ensure that their efforts were directed to the common purpose that Croly was urging on his readers. Secondly, as the country grew, regulated corporations were virtually guaranteed an expanding market, an increment that would be achieved through no real effort on their part. Croly's judgment was that this was wrong. Consequently, he proposed a long-run plan in which large corporations that maintained a dominant position in their industry (which was likely, given government recognition and regulation) would gradually be taken over by the government:

If they survived for some generations and increased in efficiency and strength, it could only be because the advantages they enjoyed in the way of natural resources, abundant capital, organization, terminals, and responsible management were decisive and permanent. . . . Just in so far, that is, as a monopoly or a semi-monopoly succeeded in surviving and growing, it would partake of the character of a natural monopoly, and would be in a position to profit beyond its deserts from the growth of the community. In that event a community which had any idea of making economic responsibility commensurate with power would be obliged to adopt a policy of gradual appropriation.[67]

Croly believed that the primitive form of this policy could already be seen in the way municipalities were dealing with public service corporations. They were learning to restrict the franchises they granted to a limited term of years, "and the tendency is towards a constant reduction of the length of such leases and towards the retention of the right of purchase, exercisable at all or at certain stated times."[68] Precisely the same situation did not yet exist nationally, but Croly suggested that the railroad system of the country was close to the point where its possession of natural monopolistic advantages suggested public ownership and operation, or public ownership and private operation. Carrying the argument further, he suggested that "whenever the conditions, obtaining in the case of railroad and public service corporations, are duplicated in that of an industrial corporation, a genuinely national economic system would demand the adoption of similar measures."[69]

Such were Croly's short-range and long-range proposals to reform the industrial system. They would, if implemented, "convert to the service of a national democratic economic system the industrial organization which has gradually been built up in this country."[70] The debt that the short-term plans owed to Roosevelt and to the developments in government regulation of the early 1900s was obvious. Croly was trying to build on these developments and to present the case for regulation in the context of his more general argument for a national democracy and a Hamiltonian central government.

However, the long-term suggestions went substantially beyond Roosevelt's program and beyond any proposal that corporate executives were likely to support. They would, in fact, have set him apart from most progressives, who continued to favor regulation when they were willing to go beyond the Sherman Act at all. Croly's positions were actually closer to the socialists and to such writers as Richard Ely and Walter Rauschenbusch.[71] There are also substantial similarities between Croly's proposals and a centralized Hegelian state. In these proposals, we also see Croly's deeper moral ideas—for example, his dislike of individual profit resulting from common efforts and his strong emphasis on a national community and the religious idea of brotherhood.

THE PROMISE ALSO contained an analysis of the conditions of unions in the United States and proposals about how the government should control the distribution of wealth through the tax system.

As regards unions, Croly took a somewhat ambivalent position. He had many criticisms to offer, and yet his recommendations were fundamentally sympathetic. The major criticism concerned a tendency in unions to subvert the individuality of their members by encouraging all workers to work the same number of hours, for the same wages, and produce the same quality finished product. Croly's liberal theory and his emphasis on the development of a true individual specialization are evident in his rejection of these standards. Even more disturbing was the degree of loyalty that a union required of its members, making union allegiance the "most important attachment of his [a member's] life—more important in most cases than his attachment to the American ideal and to the national interest."[72] Croly the nationalist and communitarian could not regard this condition with equanimity. He was also alarmed at the frequency with which the more militant unionists resorted to "mob-violence," especially because these actions encouraged what he took to be the false belief that the existing political system was incapable of effective reform.[73]

Yet Croly's recommendations were favorable, for he urged that labor unions be accorded legal recognition. Such a step would amount to some "discrimination" by the government in their favor and against the non-union laborer, whom Croly termed an "industrial derelict" who had the effect of forcing down wages, thus preventing his fellows from achieving any real independence (an echo of the theory of positive freedom). Unions, Croly argued, "deserve to be favored, because they are the most effective machinery which has as yet been forged for the economic and social amelioration of the laboring class."[74]

As regards tax policy and the distribution of income generally, we have already seen that Croly tied social reform to industrial reorganization. Similarly, he favored the recognition of unions as a way of bringing a larger measure of social justice to workers. These were but partial measures, however, affecting limited segments of the population. Many poor people would not benefit greatly from either industrial reorganization or the advancement of unions. However, Croly was convinced that "any considerable amount of grinding poverty constitute[s] a grave social danger in a democratic state." This point was related to his embryonic conception of positive freedom: a "prudent democracy" would not necessarily seek to equalize wealth fully, but it should seek to guarantee "a certain minimum of economic power and responsibility."[75] Croly's insistence that the "national interest of a democratic state is essentially concerned with the distribution of wealth" was a central point throughout The Promise.[76]

The device that Croly supported to mitigate the inequalities of wealth was a graduated inheritance tax, to be imposed entirely by the federal government. This tax would have the effect of slowly decreasing the large fortunes built up by preceding generations and would prevent people from having the use of wealth they had not earned.[77]

Strangely, and perhaps a bit naively in view of the rather far-reaching redistribution of wealth he professed to seek, Croly refused to go beyond the inheritance tax and support a graduated income tax (despite Roosevelt's having called for both in late 1907). This to him was both a less efficient and less equitable means for achieving his end.[78] Perhaps he worried that an income tax would reduce the incentive of the most able Americans to develop their full capacities. In this judgment, Croly is perhaps open to the criticism that his suggestions were not adequate to do much to achieve social justice, that his admiration of the able took precedence. Yet it should be remembered that he did seek to use the "excess profits" corporation tax to limit profits to socially acceptable levels, and this was another reason for his rejection of the income tax—it would in a sense be superfluous when the total income of business (and thus businessmen) was already controlled.

There are two other issues on which we need to compare Croly's *Promise* to progressivism: municipal reform and foreign policy. On neither was he entirely representative.

Municipal reform was a central concern of the progressive movement, and many leading progressives came out of city halls. In addition, several movements allied with progressivism, such as the settlement house movement, were focused on urban problems.[79] Croly wrote indirectly about cities when he proposed state political reform, but *The Promise* substantially ignores the whole urban scene, a curious omission for a native New Yorker. The omission was no doubt puzzling as well to Croly's progressive readers, and it must have suggested that his book was somewhat removed from their central concerns.

Historians differ as to the general position of the progressive movement on foreign policy issues, a topic to which Croly devoted significantly more attention. In John Thompson's view, most progressives did not pay much attention to foreign affairs in the years prior to World War I. On the specific question of America's expansionism, Thompson writes that "the predispositions of most progressives were anti-imperialist."[80] On the other hand, William E. Leuchtenburg has argued that progressives were largely supportive, or at least accepting, of "the imperialist surge" in American foreign policy during and after the Spanish-American War.[81] In part, this was because of Theodore Roosevelt's strong interest in foreign policy and his support of imperialism. As Leuchtenburg argues, the "remarkable hold" that Roosevelt had on his supporters swung many of them to the cause of an assertive foreign policy.[82] In Leuchtenburg's view, Croly's *Promise* (which he claims "influenced the Progressive movement more profoundly than any other book") bears out this "close link between progressivism and imperialism."[83] I think Leuchtenburg's is a correct reading of Croly's views, on balance, but there are some qualifications that should be noted.

Croly's basic point is that an assertion of American nationality must require a more active foreign policy. "The American nation, just in so far as it believes in its nationality and is ready to become more of a nation, must assume a more definite and a more responsible place in the international system."[84] It is also clear that Croly saw the United States as being in a political but primarily an economic competition with the European powers. If it was not well organized and efficient in its practices (hence a need for reform at home), the United States would lose ground.[85]

On the specific issue of imperialism and the colonies acquired in the Spanish-American War, Croly took a more equivocal position. He supported "the validity of colonial expansion even for a democracy," but "always assuming that the people whose independence is thereby diminished are incapable of efficient national organization." He also wrote that the United States had been justified in protecting Cuba against Spain and also in assuming "its much more abundant responsibilities in respect to Porto Rico."[86]

On the other hand, Croly argued that a democratic nation had "an unusually high standard of obligation for the welfare of its colonial population." This included providing for economic prosperity and for "their educational discipline and social improvement." He was very doubtful that these requirements were being met in the Philippines, where the shedding of much blood "constitutes a grave responsibility" and where the Filipinos had enjoyed a "comparatively moderate benefit" from American colonization.[87] (Croly also noted that the United States might be overextended in the Pacific, and that the Philippines would be very hard to defend against Japan.)

In international as in domestic affairs, Croly thus sought to unite nationalism with democracy. Nationalism meant a strong, responsible foreign policy. Democracy implied at least some concern for the benefit of local populations. Croly was optimistic the combination could be achieved: "The United States must by every practical means encourage the spread of democratic methods and ideas. As much in foreign as in domestic affairs must the American people seek to unite national efficiency with democratic idealism."[88]

In reviewing the various areas of the world, Croly expressed reservations about the "dangerously militant tendency" of the Monroe Doctrine, but he still urged that the United States try to create a "stable American international system." We might, he suggested, have to undertake "tasks" in other Latin American countries as we had in Cuba, and he urged that the United States try to "introduce a little order into the affairs of the turbulent Central American republics." Still, Croly claimed to reject a policy of "political aggrandizement in the Western hemisphere" and called for cooperation with Mexico in Central American affairs.[89] He urged the creation of stable relations with Canada as a major priority, and he was guardedly optimistic about American relations with Europe. Croly thought that "the emancipated and nationalized European states of today, so far from being essentially antagonistic to the American democratic nation, are constantly tending towards a . . . more fruitful association." At the same time, the European system was too "organized for aggressive war" and the United States needed to keep her distance.[90]

Croly was of several minds about Asian policy and particularly about China. The United States should try to protect the territorial integrity of China (a good national principle). However, Croly also expressed an interest in the "free commercial development" of China. These aims would not be easily achieved, he feared.[91] These positions were close to Roosevelt's.[92]

Foreign policy was thus an area where Croly took a wider view than many progressives. He was supportive of many positions held by Theodore Roosevelt. At the same time, this section of *The Promise* does not contain the almost fulsome praise of Roosevelt that one finds elsewhere. This is a significant omission, because an energetic foreign policy was one of Roosevelt's major emphases as president. Croly's cool tone probably indicated a reservation about too nationalistic a foreign policy, a reservation that in future years would help lead Croly to a reassessment of Roosevelt. Croly thought that an important responsibility of the democratic United States was to play a leading role in developing a stable international political and economic system, to parallel the national system to be developed at home. His liberalism was internationalist even in this first formulation.

THIS COOLNESS toward Roosevelt on foreign policy was unusual in *The Promise*; by and large, Croly was enormously admiring of the former president. This is most clear in the section of the work in which Croly criticized various progressive leaders. Several, including William Jennings Bryan ("ill-conceived" program, not a nationalist); William Travers Jerome, nonpartisan New York district attorney (no "independent thought on our fundamental political problems"); and William Randolph Hearst, 1906 Democratic candidate for governor of New York ("unscrupulous expression of the radical element in the Jeffersonian tradition") were found wanting.[93] However, Roosevelt was strongly praised: "It is fortunate, consequently, that one reformer can be named whose work has tended to give reform the dignity of a constructive mission." Of course, T.R.'s program, too, needed to be "reformed": "Mr. Roosevelt's reconstructive policy does not go very far in purpose or achievement, but limited as it is, it does tend to give the agitation for reform the benefit of a much more positive significant and a much more dignified task."[94]

We have seen that Croly's views were typical of progressive arguments in many areas (insofar as we can generalize about a diverse movement). On the other hand, his stands on such progressive staples as the initiative and referendum and the direct primary and his lack of interest in municipal affairs set him apart from the mainstream of the movement. In part, this may be because Croly *wasn't* typical of progressives in terms of his personal and intellectual background. Robert Crunden has argued that in his research on the background of progressives, he found that the "typical" progressive was (among other points) raised in a devout, evangelical protestant home, a supporter of the "early Republican Party, free soil, and the Union cause," devoted to Lincoln, restless in his career, educated at a small, denominational college, and often involved in journalism, settlement house work, or higher education.[95] Croly fit some of these characteristics but not all, and particularly not the religious criterion. Indeed, Crunden specifically mentions Croly as an outsider in the movement and argues that he should be called an "urban liberal" rather than a "progressive" largely because of the religious factor.[96] It would also seem likely that Croly was something of an outsider because of his education, particularly his philosophic training. Moreover, in *The Promise* he *sought* to be outside—to be a critic of progressive assumptions as well as a supporter of many aspects of reform.

However, while Croly maintained a polite distance from many progressives, he was very close intellectually to Roosevelt. On many aspects of his theory, Croly was inspired by Roosevelt, and often he patterned his specific recommendations after Roosevelt's general positions, although not always in all details. Croly at times went beyond Roosevelt, as in his long-range economic proposals, and he sometimes took a more moderate stance, as in foreign policy. Still, it would have been clear to all readers that Croly was in the Roosevelt wing of the progressive movement.

On the publication of *The Promise of American Life* in the fall of 1909, Croly sought to make this identification personal as well as intellectual. He asked his friend Learned Hand (or Hand volunteered) to send a copy of *The Promise* to Roosevelt. Accordingly, Hand wrote to Roosevelt: "I think that Croly has succeeded in stating . . . the bases and prospective growth of a set of political ideas which can be fairly described as Neo-Hamiltonian, and whose promise is due more to you, as I believe, than to anyone else."[97] Roosevelt replied on April 22, 1910, acknowledging the receipt of the book.[98] Then Croly and Hand waited.

Some months later the desired result occurred. Roosevelt wrote to Croly:

My dear Mr. Croly: I do not know when I have read a book which I felt profited me as much as your book on American life. There are a few points on which I do not entirely agree with you, yet even as to these my disagreement is on minor matters. . . . I shall use your ideas freely in speeches I intend to make. I know you won't object to my doing so, because, my dear sir, I can see that your purpose is to do your share in any way for the betterment of our national life. . . . Can't you come in to see me at the Outlook office? I want very much to have a chance to talk to you.[99]

The political theory of *The Promise of American Life* was launched into national politics.

5

Progressivism and "Progressive Democracy"

Croly's *The Promise of American Life* was well received. The book never sold particularly strongly, but it became well-known in just the circles that Croly sought to influence—the political and intellectual leaders of the country, and particularly those committed to reform.[1] As Alvin Johnson, an associate of Croly's on the *New Republic*, later wrote: "It was a powerful book, powerfully hard to read; but if one worked one's way through the involved sentences and the long-worded abstractions, one found a real philosophy of American progressivism."[2]

Many other readers came to the same conclusion over the next several years, especially after Theodore Roosevelt had praised *The Promise* as "the most profound and illuminating study of our national conditions which has appeared for many years." Croly would perhaps have been slightly less pleased with Roosevelt's conclusion that "especial emphasis is laid on the assertion that the whole point of our government experiment lies in the fact that it is a genuine effort to achieve true democracy."[3] But he was no doubt most happy that Roosevelt adopted his "New Nationalism" terminology in a series of speeches he made in the later summer of 1910. This association with Roosevelt propelled Croly into a national spotlight. Indeed, Learned Hand wrote to Croly in February 1911: "My dear friend, you are becoming an authority. I have no doubt that in a few years, myths will be established about you. Perhaps you will take on the form of the Sun-God. . . . What with the Colonel giving you such a splendid send-off, and a second edition coming out, you are quite the rage."[4] The years 1910 to 1914 were thus years of political involvement for Herbert Croly.

These were also years of intellectual growth and development. Croly's views on both theoretical and practical issues changed, partly, I think, because of the political successes of progressivism, and partly because of his own reading and thinking about politics. By early 1911, Croly had concluded that *The Promise* was "out of date" and must be "practically rewritten in case it is to have any permanent value."[5] It was also the case that while Croly was enormously pleased with Roosevelt's use of his ideas and became a close supporter, he was also uneasy about some of Roosevelt's formulations of progressivism and about the way politics distorted theoretical positions. Some of his writing in the period was thus meant to "rescue the features of the New Nationalism from the disfigurement that infant received at the hands of T. R. and his critics." In the course of this rescue, Croly developed "some new stuff" that would form the basis of a more elaborate treatment of politics.[6]

The result of this rethinking and reformulation was Croly's second major work of original political theory, *Progressive Democracy*, which was first delivered as the Godkin Lectures at Harvard in 1913–1914 and then published in late 1914. A reformulation of Croly's political theory in some crucial areas, this book also showed Croly to be more fully committed to the progressive version of reform than in *The Promise*. *Progressive Democracy* is written much more from "within" progressivism, and it both benefits and suffers from that identification.

Another aspect of Croly's life in the years from 1910 to 1914 needs to be mentioned. Croly gained prominence from *The Promise*, but the book didn't make him rich. To support himself, he continued to write articles for the *Architectural Record*. He also undertook an authorized biography of Mark Hanna with the intellectual and financial support of the Hanna family, particularly Hanna's progressive son, Dan. Even with these means of support, Croly's finances were often precarious, and this was one factor that encouraged him to accept the post of editor of the *New Republic* in 1914. While this decision to "hitch myself to a desk in New York," as Croly described it to Hand,[7] gave him an unparalleled opportunity to write for a large weekly audience, it also marked an end to a period in which Croly had the freedom to develop his theory in a more leisurely or disinterested fashion. It is to the elaboration of Croly's thought in the years 1910 to 1914 that we now turn.

CROLY'S FIRST political writing after the appearance of *The Promise* was an article on the current political scene in the May 1910 *North American Review*.[8] In *The Promise*, Croly had avoided too many explicit comments on the political parties (as opposed to the party system). Still, it was clear where his allegiances lay. The Democratic party, he had written, was confused by trying to incorporate both the populist William Jennings Bryan and the conservative Alton B. Parker. Democrats were still too tied to local interests—the "party of secession" hadn't adopted a national perspective, they had never really developed a "progressive national idea." (Interestingly, in this discussion, Croly came very close to linking "progressive" and "liberal." The specific subject was William Travers Jerome, the Democratic district attorney, who had claimed that the Democrats were the party of "liberal ideas." Croly disagreed: "If by 'liberal' we mean, not merely radical and subversive, but progressive national ideas, the application of the adjective to the Democratic party is attended with certain difficulties.")[9]

On the other hand, Theodore Roosevelt had restored the Republican party "to some sense of its historic position and purpose." However, "the Republican party is still very far from being a wholly sincere agent of the national reform interest."[10] So neither party was pictured as ideal in *The Promise*, but the Republicans had more possibilities.

In the *North American Review*, Croly stressed that "new economic and political conditions" required a close evaluation of the extent to which either party could be "responsible for the formulation and execution of a national policy."[11] His conclusions still favored the Republicans. They were judged "more national," whereas the "tendency of irresponsible individualist Democracy is factious and distracting."[12]

However, the bulk of the article is a more subtle analysis of the ability of the Republicans to undertake reform. The party had built a hugely successful economic system in the late nineteenth century (a theme Croly was to elaborate shortly in his biography of Hanna). However, economic privilege had gotten out of hand, and an "artificial and overheated" economy had developed, which the Republicans were foolishly trying to protect. Two contemporary policies confirmed this judgment in Croly's view. First, the Payne-Aldrich Tariff of 1909 was an attempt to safeguard the "domestic capitalists" in their "home market."[13] Second, Croly argued that "any permanent and dangerous economic privileges enjoyed by individuals or corporations must depend upon the appropriation of certain natural resources." This Republican policy of fueling economic development by "giving away" national property primarily for the benefit of the few "could not last."[14] Severe changes thus were called for in the economy and particularly in the tariff and conservation areas. However, the Republican party was not responding and was therefore "facing one of the most difficult and dangerous crises of its career." It was a party "committed by its traditions" to a national view, but it wasn't adapting quickly enough to new circumstances. Instead, it was splintering into two wings, "regular

Republicans" and "Insurgents." The "regular Republicans" around Taft were competent "public-spirited administrators." But public opinion had moved much faster than they had.[15] National policies were not forthcoming from this group.

Croly was ambivalent about the insurgents. They were not always very national in their perspective either: "They are suspicious of the East . . . suspicious of much in contemporary economic and political life, which is essential to American national efficiency. They have made a bugbear of monopolies. . . . They have not as yet thought out either the meaning of their insurrection, the consequences of their reforms or the principles which underlie their programme." Still, they were "fighting for certain reforms, the adoption of which is essential both to the redemption of the traditional responsibility of the Republican party and to the economic welfare of the American people."[16] On balance, Croly was negative: the insurgents had "all the earmarks of agitators rather than statesmen, and not one of them can be named (unless Theodore Roosevelt is still to be classed as an insurgent) who is capable of inspiring general confidence and becoming a national political leader."[17] Croly's hopes clearly lay with Roosevelt.

This is an interesting article in a number of respects. It continues much of Croly's nationalist emphasis. On the other hand, it suggests a more radical vocabulary. Croly had previously not used such terms as "capitalist" with quite the same tone. Perhaps the Payne-Aldrich Tariff made him more cynical about business. Croly's emphasis on the conservation issue and his linkage of that issue to a change in the economy in recent years was also new. Of course, conservation was particularly identified with Theodore Roosevelt, and Croly was in this sense signaling his support of T.R. In Roosevelt's last years as president he had appointed the National Conservation Commission, with Gifford Pinchot as chair, to survey America's natural resources. The commission had reported in December 1908, after surviving hamstringing by Congress (perhaps confirming Croly's low view of a legislature's ability to take a national view). Even as Croly was writing his article, the Ballinger-Pinchot affair, which drove a further wedge between Taft and Roosevelt, was coming to a head.[18] Croly's emphasis on the conservation issue very clearly tied his analysis to these specific political events, as well as to the Roosevelt cause.

We might note that Croly's connection of the importance of the exploitation of resources to the growth of monopolies in an "overheated" economy, and hence the connection of conservation to broader changes in economic policy, was a common theme in the period. For example, some months later, the historian Frederick Jackson Turner delivered a presidential address to the American Historical Association in which he argued that in the generation since the closing of the frontier, America had witnessed a tremendous change: "a wonderful chapter, this final rush of American energy upon the remaining wilderness." The country had gained enormous industrial production in a very short time, but it was also "peculiarly the era when competitive individualism in the midst of vast unappropriated opportunities changed into the monopoly of the fundamental industrial processes by huge aggregations of capital as the free lands disappeared."[19] In Turner's analysis, the political system had responded with such federal programs as the conservation movement, the strengthening of the ICC, and the "recent legislation for pure food and meat inspection." This impulse was continuing in current politics: "We have the voice of the insurgent West, recently given utterance in the New Nationalism of ex-President Roosevelt, demanding increase of federal authority to curb the special interests, the powerful industrial organizations, and the monopolies, for the sake of the conservation of our natural resources and the preservation of American democracy."[20] Aside from the more favorable tone toward insurgency (which Croly might have accepted somewhat more fully after Roosevelt's western tour in support of many insurgents), Croly would have agreed completely with Turner and would, of course, have been pleased to see his "New Nationalism" phrase in common use.

CROLY'S OWN article in the May *North American Review* had only mentioned Roosevelt (who was hunting in Africa while Croly was writing) in passing. However, Roosevelt's return the following month and his subsequent letter to Croly indicating that he would use Croly's ideas and then Roosevelt's dramatic series of speeches on his Western tour in August and September brought Croly to a more complete commitment to the Roosevelt cause.

Roosevelt's speeches were meant to support various western Republican candidates, most of them insurgents in the view of Taft and his allies (though Roosevelt's association with the insurgents was incomplete; witness his refusal to visit Wisconsin or support Robert M. LaFollette). As John M. Cooper has pointed out, Roosevelt in 1910 was not constrained by office or personal candidacy.[21] Hence he was free to speak out, and he did so in a systematic series of speeches that quickly became known as the "New Nationalism."[22] The most famous of the speeches was given at Osawatomie, Kansas, on August 31, 1910. Here, in the peroration of the speech, Roosevelt declaimed that "the American people are right in demanding that New Nationalism, without which we cannot hope to deal with new problems. The New Nationalism puts the national need before sectional or personal advantage. . . . This New Nationalism regards the executive power as the steward of the public welfare."[23]

The phrase "New Nationalism" was Croly's, and there seems little doubt that Roosevelt had taken it from *The Promise*. But what else did Roosevelt borrow? What other ideas did he use "freely in speeches I intend to make"? Historians have differed substantially on this question.[24]

Roosevelt's own view of the origins of his "New Nationalism" was clear in a speech he gave in Syracuse, New York, just after the western tour. Roosevelt responded to the severe criticism the Eastern establishment had made of his speeches by arguing that "the New Nationalism really means nothing but an application to new conditions of certain old and fundamental moralities. . . . In my western speeches I said chiefly what I again and again said in messages to Congress when I was President. I very slightly developed the doctrines contained in these presidential addresses in order to meet the development of the new conditions."[25]

David Levy argues that Croly actually helped Roosevelt work on the Osawatomie speech.[26] Whether or not this is so, I do think there are some instances in which Croly's thought can be discerned in Roosevelt's arguments. Croly's ideas seem particularly present in those parts of the speeches dealing with economic regulation. Yet, as we have seen, a great many of Croly's views were based on Roosevelt's policies and even sometimes on his messages. The phrasing about "combinations in industry" and particularly the "commission principle" could have come from Croly, but much of the substance of even these arguments had indeed been part of Roosevelt's policies earlier. There is also a lot of phrasing in the speeches, even on topics that Croly covered, that does not use terms that Croly commonly used. For example, Roosevelt argued in Syracuse that "we believe also in steadily using the power of the government to secure economic democracy as well as political democracy."[27] Croly would have agreed, but he did not use this terminology in *The Promise*. In short, it seems that there was some influence from Croly on Roosevelt, but it is more clear that Roosevelt had earlier influenced Croly. It is also clear that Roosevelt was correct when he said that he was drawing primarily on his own previous policies. Perhaps reading Croly had helped in the "development" of T.R.'s ideas, but the bulk of the influence ran the other way.

It should be remembered that the ideas about economics that Roosevelt likely borrowed from Croly were Croly's *short-term* suggestions—and not all of these. For example, Roosevelt didn't mention Croly's short-run "excess profits" tax. More importantly, Roosevelt steered away from any mention of such long-term solutions as nationalization of semimonopolistic industries in the New Nationalism. For this reason, Croly would have thought Roosevelt's formulation inadequate.

Indeed, Croly had some private reservations about T.R.'s 1910 speeches. For instance, he remarked to Hand that Roosevelt wasn't displaying the "qualities of patience and forbearance" that were necessary for leadership.[28] He also wrote that "the more I watch the effect of T.R. on different classes of men, the more it looks to me as if his particular influence was really trembling in the balance. He has to go about things differently, and if I get the chance, I shall tell him so. *Me Big Injun*."[29] Hand agreed: "Really if we are to have our New Nationalism with no more light than this, it's doubtful whether we want it at all!"[30] It's impossible to know exactly what features of Roosevelt's speeches were bothering Croly and Hand. Roosevelt had articulated progressive positions, but he also had tried to avoid a full break with Taft and the regular Republicans. This straddling could certainly have led Croly to think Roosevelt inconsistent. In any event, it is clear that Croly was not fully satisfied with either the program or more particularly the politics of the first statement of the New Nationalism.

In fact, the 1910 elections didn't turn out especially well in either Croly's or Roosevelt's opinion. The Democrats gained control of the House of Representative and many governorships. While the Republicans retained control of the Senate, they were dependent on the western insurgents for their majority, which was an unstable situation. Some candidates that Roosevelt had endorsed had done well, but others such as Henry L. Stimson in New York and Albert J. Beveridge in Indiana had lost.[31] As Croly remarked to Hand, "it is all going to be an awful mess for the next few years." But he did admit that the Democrats "are entitled to their innings. Let us see what they can do."[32]

The 1910 election might in fact have shown that progressive reform was changing and deepening in ways that Croly did not immediately appreciate. Some historians have suggested that if progressivism was indeed primarily a middle-class, "native stock" movement in its origins (and even that is questionable in some interpretations), many different progressivisms soon emerged. One of the strongest of these newer reform currents was an "urban liberalism" primarily supported by "new stock" men who were Democrats. In this view, other groups were becoming progressive and turning to the Democratic party as an acceptable vehicle for reform. Thus John Buenker argues that "urban liberalism ... provides much of the explanation for the resurgence of the Democratic party in the north-eastern industrial states."[33] These changes were positive additions to progressivism. The diffusion of a reform impulse through many groups in American society would clearly strengthen progressivism. In addition, most of the national progressive legislative triumphs would be achieved by the Democrat Woodrow Wilson, who entered the national scene on his election as governor of New Jersey in 1910. However, these developments lay in the future. Croly was not optimistic about the reform possibilities of "the Democracy" in 1910–1911.

THE POLITICAL SITUATION from the 1910 elections to the summer of 1912 was "a mess" as Croly had predicted. Pressure built on Roosevelt to run for the Republican nomination against Taft, but he resisted that pressure until early 1912. Croly made it clear that he would be in the Roosevelt camp if one formed, but in the meantime he continued to develop his ideas and to work on the Hanna biography.

One of Croly's interesting contacts with other progressives in this period was with the Oregon leader William S. U'Ren, who had been active since 1900 in pushing for the initiative, referendum, and recall. Modified versions of the initiative and referendum had been accepted in Oregon in the early years of the century, and in 1908 U'Ren's People's Power League had successfully fought for a state constitutional amendment implementing the recall of all elected officials (apparently including at least some judges).[34] In late 1911, U'Ren wrote to Croly that he had "read your 'Promise of American Life' a couple of weeks ago with much interest and pleasure. Also with profit. In nearly all of it I am in accord with your views."[35] Of course, Croly's views on direct democracy had been at best lukewarm in *The Promise*, but he *had* singled out Oregon's as an intelligent attempt to combine these measures with the principle of executive authority.

The specific occasion of the correspondence with U'Ren was a meeting of the American Political Science Association in late December 1911, at which Croly presented a paper on "State Political Reorganization" and U'Ren served as a discussant. In this paper, Croly indicated a change in his position on direct democracy from the doubt of *The Promise* to a more enthusiastic acceptance. While Croly repeated some previous reservations, he now argued that direct democracy was a valuable way to get around the responsiveness of state legislatures to "special interests" as opposed to the interest of the whole people. The tone of Croly's remarks was much more welcoming to the progressive initiatives.[36] Croly now celebrated the democratic virtues of citizen involvement more strongly than in *The Promise*. Noting that "during the past decade a decided change has taken place in the public attitude," he proclaimed that "the watchword of the 'Progressives,' has become 'trust in the people' and such a trust constitutes manifestly the only possible foundation on which a democracy can erect an enduring superstructure of political institutions."[37]

Croly also continued to urge that executive responsibility be strengthened, even as the recall served as a democratic check on executive power.

He argued that initiatives and referenda should be limited in number so as not to confuse the voters. However, Croly specifically approved U'Ren's People's Power League proposals to combine a strengthened executive (and a reconstituted legislature) with direct democracy.[38] In Croly's view (adopting the phrase he would use as the theme of his next book), a "progressive democracy is bound to be as much interested in efficient administration as it is in reconstructive legislation."[39]

In his response, U'Ren reacted positively to Croly's arguments for executive responsibility, but he strongly defended direct democracy as necessary to control corruption and overthrow "government by plutocracy in the American states and cities." He asked Eastern progressives like Croly to trust that Oregonians were not going too far too fast. Direct democracy was not an end; however, it was a necessary means to achieve the end of progressive reform.[40]

Another discussant of Croly's paper was Chester H. Rowell, a California progressive. He did not comment very specifically on Croly's points, but rather argued the more general case that progressivism was by now a dominant political movement that took many forms. Rowell endorsed the initiative, referendum, and recall, but he argued that progressivism was more than direct democracy and that Croly had taken too narrow a view of the subject. In what was perhaps a criticism of Croly for not getting more involved in politics, Rowell noted that "the philosophic analyst is not a good soldier. He reads papers before the Political Science Association, for the delectation of posterity."[41] From his involvement with Roosevelt, Croly no doubt already was aware of these tensions between participating in reform and keeping one's distance to allow sufficient perspective.

For the moment, Croly chose to remain the outsider. Indeed, his major work in 1911 was the Hanna biography. However, even this work continued some contact with progressives. Most importantly, Croly met and corresponded several times with Roosevelt to get his perspective on T.R.'s vice presidential nomination in 1900 (the biography quotes Roosevelt at length).[42] Croly also spent time in Cleveland, meeting with Mark Hanna's former associates but also with his son, Dan, an Ohio progressive, and he traveled to California in February 1911 and met with William Hunt and other progressives.[43]

Croly's biography is largely a straight recounting of Hanna's life, which is presented favorably, although as representative of a different historical period. Croly makes some of his own views clear, as in commenting that by 1900 "the ordinary patriotic American was inclined to accept the process of consolidation [of business] as inevitable and desirable."[44] In a discussion of Hanna's effectiveness at raising campaign contributions from corporations, Croly somewhat excuses Hanna's practices, saying that he developed the technique and "removed from it, so far as possible, the taint of ordinary corruption."[45] Moreover, in Croly's argument, Hanna pushed this practice so far that the political system had rebelled against it, so that by 1912 the "prevailing tendency of politics [is] to ignore business in the treatment of business questions."[46] Both of these points were optimistic conclusions for the time, and they reflect Croly's larger optimism that a disinterested government could effectively regulate giant corporations without business being able in turn to control the regulation process.

Croly's central argument is that Hanna was the creature of his time, that his dealings were honorable given current political morality. This judgment fits into Croly's own overall analysis of American history, as developed in *The Promise*, but the verdict on Hanna must have seemed rather too favorable to a number of progressive readers.[47]

The years 1910 and 1911 were thus a period of political transition for Croly. The publication of *The Promise* had brought considerable political prominence, but Croly's personality was such that he was distinctly uncomfortable taking a leading political position. Probably for this reason, because he needed to complete *Hanna* for financial reasons, because he preferred his role as a critic, and because the political situation was too cloudy, Croly didn't attempt to convert his new prominence into a political career. At the same time, he did establish closer ties with several leading progressives, ties that influenced his evolving theory. In particular, the developing strength of the progressive movement began to confirm Croly's earlier hope that progressivism could serve as a vehicle for the implementation of "national democratic" reform. For this reform to work, however, a forceful leader was necessary. Croly continued to cast Roosevelt in this role.

BY FEBRUARY 1912 Croly had finished *Marcus Alonzo Hanna*, and the political situation was close to a decisive development. Croly and Hand had been speculating about Roosevelt's intentions for several months, and each had met with Roosevelt to discuss politics. Croly was unsure if Roosevelt would be successful in gaining the nomination over Taft, but his own support was clear: "If he does run, a good strong argument can be made on his behalf."[48] On February 22, Roosevelt announced that he was indeed going to run for the Republican nomination, and Croly immediately pledged his support.[49]

Croly was in contact with Roosevelt during the spring and sent him some proposals about state administrative reform and about the direct democracy issue.[50] However, he was not actively involved in Roosevelt's campaign for the Republican nomination. However, once Roosevelt was denied the nomination and bolted the convention to form the Progressive party, Croly was an enthusiastic supporter. The new party, he wrote to Hand in July, "contains more promise for future good government than any recent movement in American politics. You will find it driven by the logic of its own . . . situation towards nationalism." Roosevelt and his supporters were "the men who want to do something and who are willing to use the agency of the government for the realization of their program." On the other side, while Wilson could make claims to being a progressive, his party could not: "You will find the Democracy gradually pushed into a dogmatic states-rights position."[51]

Croly met with Roosevelt during the campaign,[52] but aside from private advice his most visible public support was an article arguing the Progressive cause that appeared just before the election in the *American Magazine*.[53] Identified in large print by the magazine as "The Man From Whom Col. Roosevelt Got His 'New Nationalism,' " Croly wrote with authority and passion for the Roosevelt camp. His thesis was that Roosevelt was the leading progressive political figure and deserved the support of all progressives for his past accomplishments. Croly was at pains to argue that progressives should not support Wilson because his party would limit any possibility of reform. On the contrary, "a thoroughly progressive party and a thoroughly progressive platform call more loudly for allegiance than can any single leader."[54] In phrases that T.R. himself might have regretted, Croly declared that Roosevelt's "leadership is indispensable just at present. . . . But in the long run a national party waxes as big as its purpose and program."[55]

Croly's article only slightly reworked some old themes from *The Promise*, but he also used some interesting new language. The Progressive party, he wrote, "takes over the Democratic tradition of popular rule; it takes over the Republican tradition of national responsibility; and by virtue of a combination of the two principles it will hereafter make the American nation expressly responsible for the realization of a social democratic ideal."[56] Croly's use of "social democratic" probably shouldn't be emphasized, but it did suggest an interesting evolution in his thought. The article also combined Croly's own themes of a purpose and of faith and brotherhood with the religious imagery of progressivism. Roosevelt's speech to the August Progressive convention had been entitled "A Confession of Faith," and Croly echoed that theme in his appeal to all progressives to unite behind T.R.: "Those who lack the faith, let them remain outside; but if a man has seen the light and shared the faith, the National Progressive party has a right to claim him as its own."[57] Croly had signed on to the cause.

THE OTHER AREA in which Croly contributed to the Progressive campaign concerned the central issue of the regulation of business. This issue was a difficult one for both the Progressives and the Democrats in 1912. The Progressives were split between two contrasting views—the position that the Sherman Antitrust Act should be strengthened, and the position that bigness was inevitable and that national regulation of corporations was the answer. In this division, Croly was clearly in the latter camp. But translating these arguments into attractive party positions proved difficult.

The political difficulties within the Progressive party were evident in the platform hearings in early August. A number of proposed planks had been submitted calling for regulation by what was coming to be called a federal trade commission, including planks by Croly, Learned Hand, and their friend George Rublee.[58] But other drafts had stressed the trust-busting approach. Roosevelt tried to compromise these approaches, supporting a full plank on regulation but also allowing a short paragraph that called for strengthening the Sherman Act. Political confusion ensued when these statements were read at the convention. George W. Perkins, the Morgan partner who was a major financial backer, left the hall protesting that the Sherman Act paragraph shouldn't have been included. After quite a furor, the platform committee agreed it should have been omitted, and the short paragraph was dropped from the written text. Several days after the convention, most members of the platform committee, on further reflection, thought they had in fact approved it.[59]

The political fallout from this confusion was very harmful to the Progressives. Many people assumed that Perkins had dictated the removal of the paragraph, and this only strengthened the impression that the House of Morgan was supporting Roosevelt. In fact this was not true, as Perkins was acting quite on his own and against J. P. Morgan, Jr.'s wishes, but the impression persisted.[60]

Compounding the confusion, Roosevelt repeated a compromise position in his early campaign speeches. For example, in his "Confession of Faith" he argued that the "antitrust law must be kept on our statute-books, and . . . rendered more effective."[61] But Roosevelt also went on to argue that the concentration of industry was inevitable and economically advantageous. "It is utterly hopeless to control the trusts merely by the antitrust law."[62]

From the start of the campaign, then, Croly was getting a painful lesson in how politics and politicians could distort a theoretical argument. The later weeks of the campaign proved yet more difficult, as even Roosevelt's compromise position was attacked by Wilson and his supporters as a position in favor of "monopoly," without any acknowledgment of the qualifications that Croly would have wished to emphasize.

Wilson's own "New Freedom" position was also somewhat unclear. For instance, he could assert (on September 17): "I am for big business and I am against the trusts."[63] Louis Brandeis soon became Wilson's main adviser on economic issues, and Brandeis furnished Wilson with much material emphasizing the importance of competition. However, later in his campaign Wilson usually spoke not simply of competition but of the "regulation of competition," comparing his position to what he said was Roosevelt's call for "regulated monopoly." The Wilson camp tried to suggest a larger difference than probably existed between the "New Freedom" and the "New Nationalism."

Brandeis also published a series of politically effective articles in Norman Hapgood's *Collier's Weekly*, arguing his position on competition. He even wrote editorials for Hapgood to publish praising his own articles![64]

Croly and Hand tried to furnish material to Roosevelt to rebut the Wilson-Brandeis arguments. Hand wrote to Frankfurter that he and Croly were "each independently trying to say something about the trust plank to meet Brandeis's effort to throw us into the camp of the monopolists."[65] Unfortunately, we don't have copies of Croly's suggestions. However, it is unlikely they had much effect, for Roosevelt continued to straddle the issue, for instance writing to *Collier's* that "I am not for monopoly. We intend to restore competition."[66] In the emotional speech he made in Milwaukee on October 14 after having been shot, Roosevelt emphasized his performance as president in reviving *both* the Sherman Act and the Interstate Commerce Act—neatly having it both ways.[67]

In another major theme of the campaign, Wilson attacked Roosevelt as proposing a paternalistic "government of experts." Roosevelt countered this accusation by terming Wilson's statement that "the history of liberty is a history of the limitation of governmental power, not the increase of it" as "outworn academic doctrine. . . . It is simply the *laissez-faire* doctrine of . . . three-quarters of a century ago."[68] Croly would have agreed with Roosevelt's comments (though Wilson's statement was hardly typical of his position), but Wilson's charges were perhaps uncomfortably close politically to being an accurate representation of *The Promise of American Life*. Croly probably saw in this campaign that some of his ideas were not as feasible politically as they were convincing in a more complete theoretical presentation.

The outcome of the 1912 election was clear by the last weeks of October. Wilson had successfully portrayed himself as a progressive and indeed had attracted some substantial progressive support, especially in Eastern urban areas.[69] Croly's appeal to all progressives to become Progressives was heeded by too few voters. Wilson had also gained the support of organized labor, in fact distorting the Progressive position as opposed to the right to organize, despite Roosevelt's protestations to the contrary. Most important, Wilson held his party together, and while he didn't win by a majority of the popular vote, he had a healthy plurality and a large majority in the Electoral College, as well as a Democratic Congress.

Croly's own reaction to the election is not recorded, but he must have been severely disappointed. He must also have been frustrated at the degree to which his ideas had been distorted in the political arena. Roosevelt had spoken for regulation, but the New Nationalism as preached on the stump had been quite different from the New Nationalism of Croly's book. Wilson's attacks on monopolies and paternalism had also been clever political distortions of the Progressive position. Of course, if Croly could have seen how the Wilson administration would develop, he might have been encouraged by the new president's acceptance of the need to "regulate competition." As Thomas McGraw has argued, this statement "did not reflect a coherent strategy or a detailed program." Nevertheless, it was an opening, and in 1914 Wilson developed it into a proposal for a Federal Trade Commission.[70] Perhaps the Progressive insistence on a regulatory commission was ultimately to bear fruit, but that result lay in the future.

Croly's own immediate future lay in writing. After the election, Roosevelt offered Croly a position in the new Progressive party offices, but Croly refused. We don't have Croly's letter, but Roosevelt's response admitted that Croly's writing "will have more weight if you are not an officer of the Progressive Party."[71] Croly soon moved to Washington for the winter of 1913 and took up the work that became *Progressive Democracy.*

PROGRESSIVE DEMOCRACY is quite a different book from *The Promise of American Life*. It strongly reflects Croly's participation in progressive politics, and while the book treats both theoretical and policy issues, it often emphasizes the latter, whereas *The Promise* had been more strongly theoretical. As *Progressive Democracy* was clearly meant to speak directly to the progressive movement, and even for the Progressive party, it is appropriate to begin with Croly's partisan positions and then consider the theory and the policy recommendations that flow from the theory.

Croly begins with the assertion that since the 1912 election, "a movement of public opinion, which believes itself to be and calls itself essentially progressive, has become the dominant formative influence in American political life."[72] Even as late as 1904, when Mark Hanna died, "standpattism" was in control, but in the intervening ten years progressivism has become a systematic and "self-conscious" force that has gone well beyond such "superseded reform movements" as populism.[73] Progressivism has shown that America can still renew herself: "Progressivism testifies and insists that the national will . . . has not been enfeebled."[74] In short, Croly is most optimistic about the potential of the progressive movement.

The initial success of the movement was due largely to Theodore Roosevelt: "More than any other single leader, Theodore Roosevelt contributed decisively to the combination of political with social reform and to the building up of a body of national public opinion behind the combination. Under his leadership as President, reform began to assume the characteristics, if not the name, of progressivism."[75] That initial impetus has been continued by the Progressive party, which "has done more to make the progressive idea count at its proper value in American public opinion, and to make possible the realization of a certain portion of the progressive program, than has any other agency of progressive expression."[76] The Progressive party has thus been the most full expression of the movement, which "needed a partisan organization whose dominant purpose was the advancement of progressive policies."[77] Croly even argues that the creation of the Progressive party has forced the Democrats leftward and has strengthened the progressive cause within Wilson's party.[78]

Croly's opinion of Wilson was ambiguous in 1914 and in fact seems to change in the course of the writing. Early in *Progressive Democracy,* Croly calls Wilson "sincere" in his progressivism but charges that Wilson has tried to keep his commitment vague. He also supports Roosevelt's campaign charge that Wilson's statements are laissez-faire theory warmed over. Continuing his earlier emphasis on the need for a collective purpose, but now increasingly using "social" rather than "national," Croly wrote: "Not a word that President Wilson uttered during or since the campaign indicated any tendency on his part to substitute for an automatic competitive economic regime one in which a conscious social purpose . . . was to play a decisive part. The 'New Freedom' looks in general like a revival of Jeffersonian individualism."[79]

However, later in his analysis, Croly is distinctly more favorable. He terms the Underwood Tariff of 1913 "the only tariff bill of the last seventy years which represented an honest attempt to subordinate special interests to the national economic welfare."[80] Croly also praises Wilson personally as a "wise, firm, yet conciliatory man"[81] (in words he would retract in

1919!). However, Croly's conclusion is still negative. Wilson has been trying to "persuade the American people that the Democracy is peculiarly
entitled to be the instrument of progressivism." Yet he has too often
"placed an interpretation on progressivism which associates it with a revival of the old Jeffersonian individualism and expressly distinguishes it
from a social democracy." Croly admits that "in practice the 'New Freedom' has approximated in certain respects to the 'New Nationalism.' "[82]
But he is convinced that Wilson's ties to his party will ultimately limit his
success.

Croly did see that if Wilson "succeeds for a sufficiently long time in
keeping the leadership of the Democratic progressives without breaking
with the Democratic conservatives, he will make the position of the Progressive party extremely precarious. It may fall to pieces."[83] His point was
prophetic, but despite these worries Croly was optimistic about the Progressive party—and with some reason. It should be remembered that in
spite of their defeat in 1912, the Progressives had done quite well in many
parts of the country in the fall of 1913. For example, they had elected
twenty-three legislators in New York as opposed to four in 1912. Croly
and many other Progressives were optimistic that such successes would
continue.[84]

CROLY THUS SUPPORTED the Progressive party in his new book. However, his
major purpose in writing *Progressive Democracy* was to provide a program
for the progressive movement as a whole and also to explain the political
theory of reform to those not yet committed. In his view, many Americans
still clung to outdated conceptions, and they deserved a complete explication of progressive values. If "progressivism is to be constructive . . . it
must be prepared to replace the old order with a new social bond. . . . The
new system must provide . . . a new faith, upon the rock of which may
be built a better structure of individual and social life." Croly hoped that
the "value of the book" would lie in the "spirit which characterizes the
attempt" to define this new program for supporters and potential supporters.[85]

In *The Promise*, the basis of Croly's social ideal had been a combination of nationality and democracy. In *Progressive Democracy,* both of these
elements are still present, but they are redefined and the balance between
them is altered. Croly has a new understanding of society, and hence of a
nation, and he is much more committed to democracy.

Croly still occasionally uses the term "national democracy,"[86] but
particularly as his analysis proceeds the "faith" that Croly provides for
progressivism is described as a "progressive democratic ideal" or a "pro-

gressive democratic faith."[87] Croly's imagery is often heavily religious—
even more so than in *The Promise*. For example, the analogy of the nation
as a schoolhouse, in which everyone had a role, is now replaced by a
Calvinist religious analogy of "individual and social life" as a "journey of
a company of pilgrims in the dark over a rough and dangerous country."[88]
Progressive democracy is the faith that ties these pilgrims together.

However, a closer look at this "pilgrim analogy" reveals a very significant change in Croly's thought. In *The Promise*, he had written of individuals and of their commitment to national democracy. But *Progressive Democracy* emphasizes that the pilgrims often form groups: "Individual
pilgrims or groups of individual pilgrims can live spiritually upon the will
to realize some specific social program and purpose."[89] Thus groups have
purposes too, and these can be beneficial to the overall community so long
as they don't "allow the competition fundamentally to divide them one
from another. Their rivalry [must] be subordinated to a sense of unity
derived from their faith in the holiness of the city."[90] Thus the faith of
progressive democracy "makes not for an indiscriminate fusion, but for a
genuinely social union, constituted both by individuals and by those
smaller social groups which give direction to so much of individual life."[91]

When he moves out of this analogy, Croly addresses this change in
his theoretical assumptions quite explicitly. He notes that "one particular
school of philosophical idealists had always been attributing, on what
were essentially pragmatic grounds, this kind of reality to social combinations. Society was as real to certain of the idealists as were individuals."[92]
I think Croly is referring here to Josiah Royce and George Herbert Palmer, and particularly to T. H. Green. He is perhaps remembering that in
talking of loyalty to communities Royce had argued that humans joined
many such communities, not only the nation that Croly had previously
emphasized.

However, it is not primarily his idealist training that has brought
Croly to a pluralist position. Rather, "it has been reserved for recent social
psychologists to give a concrete account of the way social minds are
formed." Croly has now learned that society is "made up of an innumer-
able number of smaller societies. Men and women become associated
together for the accomplishing of an infinitely large and various number
of purposes, and each of these different associations constitutes a society. . . . Every church, every club, every political and military organization,
every labor union, every family . . . constitutes a society."[93]

Croly was no doubt influenced by reading social psychologists. But
his political experiences of the last few years had also convinced him of
the importance of groups in American politics. Considering primarily reform groups, Croly noted that "the number of civic societies, voters'

leagues, ballot associations, woman's suffrage unions, single-tax clubs and the like are increasing steadily and are exercising more and more influence upon the political action of their members."[94] Indeed, his lengthy consideration of William U'Ren's Oregon program in *Progressive Democracy*, which we will consider in connection with his other policy recommendations, involved Croly in a complex interweaving of group allegiances, executive responsibility, and elements of direct democracy. Thus Croly's views changed because of his reading and reflection about politics, but also because of his involvement with progressive reform and simply because of his observation of changes in American society.

We must remember that at the same time that he accepts pluralism, Croly does not want to abandon the nation. In his view, groups "necessarily seek some form of mutual accommodation and adjustment. . . . Out of these joint responsibilities and common purposes a social ideal gradually emerges. Society comes to be conceived as a whole . . . into which the different centres of association must be fitted."[95]

Croly's democratic theory also evolved in very significant ways, for *Progressive Democracy* is much more enthusiastic about democracy than *The Promise* had been. Even Croly's historical analysis (which is less incisive than in the earlier book) now finds democracy to be the single dominant theme of the American nation. For example, Croly now emphasizes New England town meetings ("importance . . . can scarcely be overestimated") whereas he had previously ignored this tradition of direct democracy.[96] Jefferson is not Croly's hero (there are no real heroes in *Progressive Democracy*—even Lincoln is ignored), but the Republicans under Jefferson are praised for accepting the federalist political structure. Croly almost credits Jefferson with fusing democracy and nationalism![97]

As in *The Promise*, Croly is convinced that the American people are committed to democracy,[98] and it must be a part of the ideal for that reason alone. But where in the earlier book his own sympathies lay with nationality, Croly is now a committed democrat. Indeed, his optimism about democracy was such that Holmes wrote that he was "moved and cheered by your hopefulness," also noting: "I don't care so much for morals as an end as you seem to."[99] Holmes was accurate in his understanding both of Croly's optimism and his faith.

In *The Promise*, Croly had tried to develop a theoretically sophisticated understanding of democracy and of the relation to democratic theory of majority rule, equality, and freedom. *Progressive Democracy* does not develop these arguments further. Rather, Croly is content to assert that "democracy does not consist of a devouring popular sovereignty to which all limitations are essentially obnoxious. Many severe limitations are imposed upon it as a condition of its own self-expression."[100] At the same time, there can't be limitations on the suffrage; everyone must vote: "Democracy is not government by peculiarly qualified people or by a peculiarly qualified part of the people. It is or it should be government in which the largest possible proportion of the adult citizenship of the country effectively participate."[101] These passages point in different directions. They could be reconciled, but Croly never really resolves them—he simply assumes that democracy is something close to majority rule, with some restrictions which he doesn't spell out.

What *is* crucial in Croly's democratic understanding is what is left out from his previous formulation. In *The Promise*, Croly had obviously been uncomfortable with democracy and particularly with the related concept of equality. While he did endorse a limited understanding of equality, he emphasized the special role of able individuals within a generally democratic nation. We even suggested that Croly could be said to hold a theory of "democratic elitism." In *Progressive Democracy*, the emphasis on able individuals has vanished. There is simply no indication that Croly believes anyone is more able than anyone else.[102] Croly has thus come to a very significant acceptance of equality, though without any explicit argument for or definition of that concept. The theory in essence *assumes* democratic principles and virtually assumes a definition of democracy as so obvious that it doesn't need explication.

A central question is how this change came about in Croly's thought. Since Croly doesn't signal the change, he doesn't supply an answer, but one supposition would be that his reading of other progressives such as John Dewey would have influenced Croly to a more democratic position.[103] Since Croly refers to Dewey in the closing section of *Progressive Democracy*, this suggestion is certainly plausible. Croly was also acquainted with Walter Weyl, who would join him on the *New Republic* and whose *New Democracy* had been published in 1912. Croly could have been influenced to a greater acceptance of democracy by Weyl's emphasis on democracy, especially industrial democracy.[104]

My own sense is that Croly primarily accepted democracy because he was so optimistic about progressivism and about the popular support that he saw growing for progressive reform. He assumed that Americans were committed forever to the progressive faith, and he in turn committed to a conception of a pluralist, democratic state. He might also have reflected that a Woodrow Wilson would have a harder time attacking this new message than the elitism of *The Promise*!

Six years later, when he reflected on the progressive movement with a hindsight born of a war and its attendant experiences, Croly ruefully remarked that he and all progressives had been incredibly optimistic not to worry about the danger posed by the state.[105] But, of course, he *had* worried about the state—he had insisted that it be democratic. What he really hadn't worried enough about or thought through fully enough was whether a *democratic* state needed to be restrained in some form.

PERHAPS THIS CHARGE is not fully accurate, because there are other concepts that we need to examine, the concepts of rights, freedom, and individualism. Croly does not usually link these explicitly to his democratic theory in *Progressive Democracy*, but they are important both in themselves and in relation to his democratic positions.

We saw that Croly had not emphasized the concept of "rights" in *The Promise*. While he hadn't been opposed to personal or even to property rights when limited, this concept was so identified with conservative arguments at the time that Croly did not emphasize it. In another important evolution in his thought, *Progressive Democracy* is significantly more open to the concept of rights.

This openness can be seen in Croly's historical analysis, in which he acknowledges that "early American democratic law-givers" were as committed to the conception of individual rights as they were to democracy: "Both the political experience of their own forbears and a radical analysis of the origin and meaning of society demonstrated the existence of certain individual rights as incontestable, indefeasible and inalienable as the right of the people to institute and alter their form of government."[106] He goes on to admit that "thus the definition and fortification of a bill of civil rights constituted the core of any stable and fruitful system of popular government."[107] This is essentially an argument that early Americans were both liberal and democratic, a very substantially different historical picture from *The Promise*.

However, Croly soon returns to an earlier theme. These rights were important, but they became rigid and were made to stand against rather than with democracy. "At this point the inalienable right of the people to institute governments began to conflict with the equally inalienable liberties of the individual. . . . The indefeasible popular political rights were contradicted by the equally indefeasible popular civil rights."[108] Given this choice, Croly regrets that America too often chose a rigid conception of individual rights, but he certainly does not totally reject the need for rights.

Croly returns to this choice—which is, of course, a central question in much of American political thought—in his discussion of the progressive conception of "popular sovereignty." Here he identifies rights with "constitutionalism" and again denies that progressive democracy should be totally opposed: "The new assertion of popular political power and responsibility is not equivalent to the substitution of democratic absolutism for democratic constitutionalism. Constitutionalism necessarily remains; but the constitutions are intrusted frankly to the people instead of the people to the constitutions."[109] When democracy and rights are pushed to extremes, then, Croly picks democracy—but he would like to hold to both values.

Two more brief points are relevant to Croly's conception of rights. We saw in *The Promise* that Croly was not strongly committed to issues of racial or gender equality. This is substantially true also of *Progressive Democracy*; however, he does write with considerably more fervor about the evils of slavery as a violation of human rights, and he also seems to accept women's suffrage as imminent.[110] Secondly, Croly specifically endorses the concept of private property and just as specifically calls for its modification. "But to modify is not to eliminate."[111]

In *Progressive Democracy*, Croly does not emphasize the concept of freedom as fully as he did in *The Promise*. An acceptance of negative freedom (which is close to the concept of rights) is implied in several passages.[112] The references to positive freedom are just slightly more extensive. For example, Croly recognizes that economic deprivation limits freedom: "If wage-earners are to become free men, the condition of freedom must somehow be introduced in the wage system itself."[113] He also writes: "Upon the rich have been conferred the opportunity and the obligation of living; upon the poor, the opportunity and obligation of letliving."[114] Positive freedom, a full opportunity to live without fear or want, is not available to the poor.

Croly is much more concerned to discuss the related concept of individualism. We saw that in *The Promise* he had held to a core notion of individualism while attempting to reconcile that concept with nationality and the national democratic ideal. *Progressive Democracy* continues that commitment to individualism, now in the context of a progressive democratic ideal. The work constantly refers to a "better structure of individual and social life" or "the high ideal of individual and collective life implied by progressive democracy" or the "sacred individual and the sacred community."[115] Croly thus stresses an "interdependence" between individual and society, but he assures us that "the two ideals cannot become sufficiently interdependent without retaining a large measure of independence."[116]

I argued previously that Croly's thought exhibits important continuities with classical liberal theory in part because of this very conscious effort to stress individualism even in the context of a strongly social emphasis. This balance can been seen in *Progressive Democracy* in a passage that exhibits signs of both John Dewey's and Josiah Royce's influence:

"The fulfillment of democratic purposes depends upon the existence of relatively authentic knowledge, the authority of which a free man may accept without any compromise of his freedom. . . . All along the line science is going to demand of faithful and enlightened men an amount of self-subordination which would be intolerable and tyrannical in any but a self-governing community."[117] A core emphasis on individual choice ("free man may accept") is evident in this passage, combined with intimations of positive freedom in the sense of fulfillment within a moral community based on truth ("science").

Croly's theory in *Progressive Democracy* thus exhibits a series of balances or reconciliations—between pluralism and the nation, between democracy and rights, and between individualism and a moral community. It seems as if Croly is very conscious of the evolution of his thought from *The Promise* in several important respects. *Progressive Democracy* is more democratic, more pluralist, more accepting of individual rights. But Croly is also unwilling or unable to settle into a new and more fully consistent theoretical formulation. Just as progressivism was exhibiting a range of new, exciting political possibilities, Croly's *Progressive Democracy* shows a range of theoretical directions, all of which are carefully balanced, but none fully selected.

To these balances, we can add another and perhaps even more difficult balance, that between pragmatism and religious conviction. Croly's approach is very consciously and explicitly pragmatic. For example, he writes that "any specific formulations of social law [have] a merely temporary and instrumental value. They have their use for a while and under certain conditions. . . . In this sense democracy is necessarily . . . allied to pragmatism."[118] The "immediate program" of progressive democracy "must be continually reformed and readjusted as a result of the experience gained by its experimental application."[119]

At the same time that Croly advocates an experimental approach, he argues from an explicitly Christian point of view, and relies heavily on the concept of human brotherhood, as he had in *The Promise*. Croly's religious convictions are evident throughout the work, but especially in the concluding chapter. Here Croly argues that "the progressive democratic faith, like the faith of St. Paul, finds its consummation in a love which is . . . at bottom a spiritual expression of the mystical unity of human nature."[120] This progressive faith "cannot be imposed upon reluctant democracies."[121] But if the faith is once accepted, human nature will be transformed. Croly describes this transformation in his last paragraph: humans "will live in an atmosphere of restless and relentless curiosity the object of which will be the knowledge of others and of one's self." The new "social culture . . . might make every woman into something of a novelist and every man into something of a playwright. . . . A society of this kind could put up with almost anything but shirking and shamming. It would be bathed in eager, good-humored and tireless criticism, and the bath would purify as well as cleanse."[122] This is a utopian picture of a progressive heaven on earth.

I think the grounds of Croly's reconciliation between pragmatism and religion are clear in his comment that "The goal is sacred. The program is fluid."[123] Croly's goal in *Progressive Democracy* was "human regeneration" as he so often put it, and this was fixed, if indefinite. The program was progressive democracy, and this was experimental. Thus Croly could now embrace democracy and reject elitism; he could resurrect rights and adopt pluralism. These were important parts of the pragmatic progressive program, but they were ultimately less significant than human brotherhood.

CROLY'S POLICY recommendations are more straightforward, but their relation to his theoretical positions is evident. Many of these recommendations are similar to those in *The Promise*. For example, Croly still emphasizes the need for national action: "Progressive Democracy will need and will value the state governments; but they will be needed and valued . . . as parts of an essentially national system."[124] Government at all levels must be willing to act: "A positive comprehensive social policy implies a strong, efficient and responsible government."[125]

Croly also continues to rely heavily on the bureaucracy. The "large volume of progressive social legislation" inevitably requires bureaucratic support.[126] But this bureaucracy is now experimental—it is actively engaged in pragmatic programs of social improvement. Croly gives us a striking image of a modern bureaucracy as opposed to the more conservative picture of the courts:

In the past, common-law justice has been appropriately symbolized as a statuesque lady with a bandage over her eyes and a scale in her fair hands. The figurative representation of social justice would be a different kind of woman equipped with a different collection of instruments. Instead of having her eyes blindfolded, she would wear perched upon her nose a most searching and forbidding pair of spectacles, one which combined the vision of a microscope, a telescope, and a photographic camera. Instead of holding scales in her hand, she . . . would have a hoe with which to cultivate the social garden, a watering-pot with which to refresh it, a barometer with which to measure the pressure of the social air, and the indispensable typewriter and filing cabinet with which to record the behavior of society; and be assured that our lady would be very much happier. . . . For having within her the heart of a mother and the passion for taking sides, she has disliked the inhuman and mechanical task of holding a balance between verbal weights and measures, the real and full value of which she was not permitted to investigate.[127]

This is the picture of an active, committed government, relying heavily on social scientists to run key parts of the system. Indeed, in what was an infelicitous phrase in 1914, Croly referred to the governmental bureaucracy as a "general staff for a modern progressive democratic state."[128]

Croly is aware that bureaucrats can fail to meet these goals. A bureaucrat can fall into a "routine" and avoid responsibility, or can become "obsessed with his own official importance and [attach] a kind of infallibility to . . . his own judgment. . . . As a matter of fact, many officials succeed both in being the victims of routine and of acting on occasions most arbitrarily."[129] But as he had been in *The Promise*, Croly was (overly) optimistic that in a democratic state, public opinion would prevent administrators from becoming "an agency of oppression."[130]

Croly's reliance on a bureaucracy had been reflected in his earlier desire to establish a national graduate school of public administration. It was also paralleled by a general emphasis on administrative research in the Progressive party. To further its aims, the party had established the Progressive Service at a December 1912 meeting that both Croly and Walter Weyl attended.[131] The service included the National Legislative Reference Bureau in New York to aid Progressives to draw up model legislation, with Walter Weyl, Gifford Pinchot, Jane Addams, and Benjamin Lindsey on the directing committee. These services, which were strongly supported by Roosevelt, were active throughout 1913 and part of 1914. Croly thus had a partial model available of what a progressive bureaucracy could do.

In *Progressive Democracy*, Croly was still skeptical about legislatures: "All American legislative bodies, Congress included, have proved wholly incapable of saving themselves from the enervating and disintegrating effect of excessive indulgence in special [interest] legislation."[132] Croly is also negative about political parties, as he had been in *The Promise*. Parties, he declared, had weakened "administrative independence and efficiency" and "interfered with genuine popular government."[133]

In another emphasis consistent with his former positions, Croly stressed executive leadership as central for progressive reform. "Executive leadership provides popular opinion with an able and indispensable instrument of . . . collective action." As he had been earlier, Croly was convinced that "Progressive democracy needs executive leadership."[134]

The major change in Croly's program between *The Promise* and *Progressive Democracy* concerned direct democracy. Where he had been quite doubtful about, though not totally rejecting of, the initiative, referendum, and recall, Croly now supported these measures much more enthusiastically. This change reflected his new openness to democracy, and it also resulted from his contact with progressive reformers, particularly William U'Ren.

In parts of his analysis, Croly expresses a few lingering doubts.[135] If not instituted with the right intentions, direct democracy may "merely become a source of additional confusion and disorganization." But if done right, it can "bring with it a positive inspiration and genuine social energy."[136] In Croly's system, direct democracy was particularly important as a control on the executive and the bureaucracy. Americans had traditionally relied on the legislature or parties to control the executive, but these were prey to special interests. Even worse was a reliance on the courts, because they usually defended only property. However, the initiative, referendum, and especially recall would allow the coupling of strong government with effective popular control.[137] Croly was optimistic that modern technology and particularly the ease with which people could keep in touch with political events through mass-circulation newspapers ("the active citizenship of the country meets every morning and evening and discusses the affairs of the nation with the newspaper as an impersonal interlocutor") allowed effective popular control. "Public opinion has a thousand methods of seeking information and obtaining definite and effective expression."[138] We could return to ancient Athens or the New England town meeting: "Pure democracy has again become not merely possible, but natural and appropriate."[139]

When Theodore Roosevelt reviewed *Progressive Democracy* (together with Lippmann's *Drift and Mastery,* terming both books "impossible to review save in way of calling attention to their excellence"), he singled out Croly's comments on direct democracy and argued himself that direct democracy offers "not only the best but the only real remedy . . . " for the abuses that progressives were attacking.[140] By 1914, even the eastern progressives had become converts to direct democracy.

Croly's views on direct democracy, executive responsibility, and his pluralism are integrated in the extensive commentary that he provides on William U'Ren's Oregon proposals. Croly had certainly been influenced by meeting with U'Ren, and he presented this plan in an extremely favorable light in an entire chapter, entitled "Visions of a New State."[141] In the

Oregon proposals, the governor would have been greatly strengthened "as chief of the state administration." Most important, "all appropriation bills must be introduced by him. He and his cabinet prepare the state budget and submit it to the legislature very much as does the English ministry."[142] This plan was very similar in principle to Croly's own views on the executive—indeed, one wonders if U'Ren had been somewhat influenced by Croly.

The most radical aspect of U'Ren's plan was a dramatic reorganization of the legislature. No longer would it be organized by parties. Rather a proportional voting system (Croly is inexact on the details) would encourage the direct representation of interest groups: "If the labor unionists could command one-twelfth of the votes, they could elect one-twelfth of the assemblymen; if farmers constituted two-fifths of the population, they could . . . command a corresponding minority in the assembly." Croly thought this form of representation would normally consist of "the fundamental economic and social classes in the community, such as organized labor, business men, the learned professions, and the like," but any group that felt strongly about a cause could seek representation.[143] U'Ren was trying to build Arthur Bentley's groups directly into the legislature, bypassing the existing party system entirely, but the system also has echoes of a Hegelian state, with strong executive leadership and the various social groups integrated into the national whole.

Croly pronounced that U'Ren's system was optimally democratic. The executive would represent the "prevailing majority," while the legislature now would speak for "minor phases of public opinion."[144] The initiative, referendum, and recall then would represent the ultimate popular sovereignty in the system.

Croly did admit that the initiative and referendum could be dangerous when few people voted.[145] He also saw that gaining popular support for such radical changes would not be easy. Indeed, Oregon voters had twice "emphatically repudiated" parts of the U'Ren plan. But Croly's judgment was that U'Ren had shown a "disinterested preoccupation with the welfare of the American democracy," and that the plan was a model for wider consideration.[146]

As we have seen, Croly was skeptical about the courts. He even praised Thomas Jefferson for seeing that John Marshall had usurped power, and he condemned later leaders for assenting to this judicial supremacy.[147] Croly did think that the courts were becoming slightly more hesitant to overrule legislatures, as indeed they were (briefly) after *Muller v. Oregon* (208 U.S. 412; 1908), with its famous "Brandeis Brief." "The police power is being emancipated from the restrictions under which it has until recently been exercised."[148] Croly was hopeful that such judicial self-restraint on property rights would continue. However, he strongly urged that Article V of the Constitution, the process of amendment, be greatly liberalized to "make the Constitution alterable at the demand and according to the dictates of a preponderant prevailing public opinion."[149] The hold of fixed, even obsolete, laws over the political system needed to be loosened. He did not worry that individual rights would thus be endangered: Croly's commitment to democracy over-rode such concerns in this height of progressive optimism.

IT IS IRONIC that Croly does not devote much attention to the issue of government regulation of business in *Progressive Democracy.* The fame of *The Promise* probably rested more on this than any other issue, and in 1912 Croly had been trying to answer Brandeis's arguments for competition. But here Croly really does not deal with the specific topic of regulation at all.

He does write about more general trends in economics, perhaps seeking to place the regulation issue in a more inclusive theory. He argued that business was rapidly changing: "industrial pioneers" were being replaced by a "scientific management" that was very similar to a public bureaucracy. Indeed, "the successful conduct of both public and private business is becoming more and more a matter of expert administration. Both are coming to meet on the same plane of scientific method and social responsibility."[150] Social science would thus serve to rationalize business just as it was rationalizing government. Indeed, Croly's argument presages Franklin D. Roosevelt's comment that "the day of enlightened administration has come."[151]

Croly's was basically an optimistic picture of a socially responsible business community, but he saw that many businessmen would not behave responsibly, and many workers would not take kindly to the increased regimentation of modern methods: "Scientific management is an exacting master. The workers are required to submit to an amount and degree of regimentation not dissimilar to that required of an army."[152] The solution was to marry scientific management to increased worker control in a "self-governing work-shop." Workers should not continue as "dependents," but as they are "made jointly responsible . . . for the success of their work, they may be converted to scientific management."[153] These would be "self-governing communities" whose increased efficiency would, Croly was confident, compare favorably to the old "business autocracies."[154] Industrial democracy would be allied to progressive democracy.

Croly argued that unions were an essential part of this process. Workers could not be left to face employers on their own. Indeed, workers would need to become very conscious of their interests in the pluralist state. However, if they expressed a "class ideal" in the short run, in the longer run everyone must realize that it was only in a "genuinely democratic industrial system" with cooperation among all sectors that true "individual and social fulfillment" could result. "Progressive democrats of all classes" needed to work out this industrial "self-government."[155] Indeed, in words that Jane Croly would have been proud of, Herbert Croly even argued that modern democracy "is proposing not only to emancipate the workers from dependence upon the property owners, but it is proposing to emancipate women from economic dependence on men."[156]

Croly's previous economic theory of *The Promise* has been read with two different emphases. Regulation could mean significant restriction on business; or it could mean a rationalization of the business climate ultimately in business's favor. The same is true of Croly's emphasis on "scientific management" in *Progressive Democracy*. We could emphasize the degree to which business would have to share power and profits with its workers; or we could view Croly's plan as an attempt to bribe workers to accept a corporate efficiency in which they would gain a little but the owners would gain a lot.

I think that the interpretation of *The Promise* that views regulation as pro-business pays too little attention to Croly's long-run proposals. Similarly, in *Progressive Democracy*, it must be clear that Croly had a long-run goal of a gradual equalization of economic position. He was well aware that the current economic system embodied severe inequalities of wealth, and for that reason, Brandeis's rhetoric about believing in private property and yet insisting "upon the rule of special privileges for none" was a "flagrant self-contradiction."[157] Croly was himself not willing to abolish private property, and so these inequalities would continue. However, a progressive democracy must "seek to revise the distribution of privileges in the interest of those classes, if any, which are at present economically disenfranchised."[158] Society had to intervene in favor of the workers and other disadvantaged groups. Croly does not give any further specifics, but the implications of the policy are, I think, more radical than conservative. At the same time, it is clear that Croly is also in favor of increased productive capacity, organized by a technological bureaucracy, and put at the service of the nation. Once again, we see a "balance" in Croly's thought in which very different emphases are held in suspension.

Such was Croly's description of what he now explicitly termed a "new and more liberal progressivism."[159] *Progressive Democracy* was an attempt to reconstruct his political theory and its attendant policy recommendations in light of the advances of the progressive movement. The book was, I think, less strong theoretically than *The Promise*. This historical analysis was less clear, and the logic less incisive. *Progressive Democracy* was originally delivered as lectures, and Croly was writing with the immediate political aim of supporting the progressive movement and particularly the Progressive party. Croly may thus have had less time to think his arguments through.

On the other hand, *Progressive Democracy* shows some very important changes in Croly's thought. The reliance on an elite of the able is now greatly diminished. In its place, Croly has accepted a democratic pluralism and the theory of direct democracy as a control over a strong executive. He has also become much more enthusiastic about individual rights. And he has explicitly endorsed the philosophy of pragmatism as a basis of social policy-making. In his analysis, Croly attempts to integrate these new elements into his previous theoretical assumptions. In the text, this integration is sometimes explicit, but it is sometimes only assumed. In the flush of progressive political optimism, and his own increasing reliance on human "brotherhood," Croly was perhaps hopeful that any theoretical problems could be overcome in practice.

Progressive Democracy was published in October 1914 in the face of two events that immediately cast doubt on Croly's analysis. One event was World War I, which had begun two months previously. After having written at some length on foreign affairs in *The Promise*, Croly had totally ignored the subject in *Progressive Democracy*.[160] The second event that questioned his analysis was the poor showing the following month of the new Progressive party in the 1914 elections. This electoral defeat did not mean the end of the progressive movement as a whole, but it did mean that Croly's optimistic scenario would need revision and that his own partisan commitments would be shaken.

Fortunately, Croly had a vehicle at hand to deal with these developments. For the past year—since the summer of 1913—even as he was finishing *Progressive Democracy*, Croly was preparing a new weekly magazine, a "journal of opinion," to argue the progressive cause. The first issue of the *New Republic* appeared the month after *Progressive Democracy* was published.

6

Domestic Liberalism in a "New Republic"

The *New Republic*'s birth actually took more than two years. It began to take shape off the coast of Asia, in January 1912, when Willard and Dorothy Straight took turns reading *The Promise of American Life* to one another on board the liner *Gouvenor Jaschke*.[1] Willard Straight was a Cornell graduate who had worked for several years in various capacities in China—as a correspondent, a U.S. diplomat, and most important, as the negotiator for a group of American businessmen seeking opportunities in China. He also served as an adviser to J. P. Morgan in Asia.[2] Straight was a self-confessed imperialist[3] and also a devoted supporter of Theodore Roosevelt. Dorothy Whitney Straight was the wealthy daughter of the late William C. Whitney, financier and secretary of the navy under Grover Cleveland. Dorothy had met Willard in 1906 in New York and again on a trip to China in 1909, and they had married in 1911. There was a connection to Theodore Roosevelt through Dorothy also, as she was a close friend of his daughter, Ethel Derby. Dorothy, like her husband, was committed to progressive causes.[4]

As Dorothy later recalled of *The Promise*: "The impact on us was terrific. Croly had bowled us both over. We decided we must get to know the author right away."[5] On their return to the United States some months later, they invited Croly to meet with them to discuss politics generally, and especially to advise Willard on an educational project. Dorothy later recalled that during this discussion, "Herbert Croly told Willard that the real dream of his life was to have a journal of his own to edit. For its subject matter he would like to invite articles by distinguished writers . . . on all the subjects and ideas, political and other, that needed airing."[6] After a number of meetings, Dorothy and Willard agreed to provide the necessary funding. They continued this support jointly until Willard's death in the influenza epidemic of December 1918; then Dorothy alone covered the journal's deficits until Croly's death in 1930, and indeed well after that.[7] Croly later wrote that the organization of the *New Republic*

> implied an unusual act of self-denial on the part of Willard and Dorothy Straight, who furnished the money for its publication. They were to . . . participate in its management only as one member of the group. While they were to be consulted about all important questions . . . they were not, so it was explicitly understood, to possess the power of vetoing the publication of any article which their associates all con-sidered desirable. Of course they could always withdraw their financial support.[8]

Willard and Dorothy apparently respected this agreement, and "the paper" managed to combine financial security with editorial independence.[9]

   With financial backing secure, Croly had to recruit a series of associates to staff the journal. One person he turned to was Walter Weyl, whom he knew from Progressive party meetings. Weyl had published *The New Democracy* in 1912 and was a well-trained economist. As he wrote in his diary: "I received yesterday a letter from Croly. A new paper. Wants me to go on it if it comes out; wants my affiliation at least. I am in entire accord. Meeting to be held with Willard Straight et al—about middle of November."[10]

   Croly also turned to Walter Lippmann, who had graduated from Harvard in 1910 and had just published *A Preface to Politics*. Croly wrote to Learned Hand in December 1913: "I have just been having some long sessions with Lippmann. I have tested him all along the line . . . and he seems always to ring true and sound. I am very happy about him."[11] Two weeks later, Croly further noted that "Lippmann is as you say an interesting mixture of maturity and innocence. The Preface to Politics is an astonishing book for a fellow three years out of College to write; but no matter how he turns out as a political philosopher, he certainly has great possibility as a political journalist."[12]

   Croly, Weyl, and Lippmann wrote the bulk of the political pieces in the early issues, but the *New Republic* was not meant to concentrate only on politics, and Croly asked Philip Littell and Francis Hackett, along with many other contributors, to write on the cultural scene.

   Croly also hoped to lure both Learned Hand and Felix Frankfurter onto the paper. Both refused an editorial connection, but they did provide Croly with many suggestions and with both anonymous and signed articles, as well as often joining the weekly meetings of the editorial board. Both were thus full-fledged "New Republicans" along with the editors and the Straights.[13]

The paper attracted a large number of other important contributors. Randolph Bourne submitted a wide range of articles, and Alvin Johnson and George Soule (both later to become editors) wrote on economics and many other issues. Other contributions came from an enormous number of leading writers, critics, and philosophers, including John Dewey, Amy Lowell, Rebecca West, Paul Rosenfeld, Lee Simonson, George Santayana, Harold J. Laski, Graham Wallas, and Morris R. Cohen. It was indeed a distinguished "paper."

Croly intended that the *New Republic* would be the product of the weekly editorial meetings, rather than his own creature, and indeed he was sometimes outvoted in these meetings.[14] Even so, he clearly played the single most important role. As Lippmann wrote in 1914, "we are a board of six editors, and Mr. Croly is the chief."[15]

Lippmann described the purpose of the journal as follows: "We are trying to produce a thoroughly American critical weekly, dealing with any phase of things about which we can find satisfactory articles. The main thing that we have in mind is the development of a certain critical intellectual temper, rather than the giving of information or the pleading of special causes."[16]

Croly himself had described the purpose of the paper in more political terms to Lippmann. He wrote that

The idea is to start a new weekly paper, modelled on the English Nation and New Statesman. . . . The fundamental object of this paper would be to give a more vigorous, consistent, comprehensive and enlightened expression to the progressive principle than that which it receives from any existing publication. But it would not be the organ of any party, and it would not tie Progressivism down to any fixed or narrow creed. It would conceive Progressivism as fundamentally a human ideal, which under prevailing conditions must receive its expression through the medium of political and economic democracy, but which has its attention fastened on human beings and human values. . . . It would stand . . . for moral freedom, intellectual integrity, social sympathy, and improved technical methods in all the practical and fine arts. Its spirit ought to be aggressive, militant. . . . It would criticize uncompromisingly half-hearted performances, narrow ideas, popular shams, and cheap personalities, and it would try itself to embody a single-minded, whole-hearted and well-balanced liberalism.[17]

The *New Republic* was thus to speak for progressivism in the broad sense, a progressivism that Croly now began to call also by the name of "liberalism." This liberalism had both immediate political but also ultimate moral objectives. As he wrote several years later of the founding of the journal: "Its liberal philosophy would always be focussed in an immediate practical program which sought the amelioration and the increasing revelation of human life, but which would be flexible, realistic and popularly intelligible."[18]

The far-reaching purposes that Croly hoped to achieve were made clear to the Straights from the beginning: "I am trying to do a very difficult thing. I am trying to make a radical social and political policy persuasive to an audience which is far less radical. I succeeded in my first book in doing something of the kind."[19] Croly also stressed the "radical" aspect of the proposed program when writing to invite Randolph Bourne to submit regular contributions: "The idea is in general to start a new journal of political, social, economic, and literary criticism. It will be something like the New Statesman. . . . We shall be radical without being socialistic, and our general tendency will be pragmatic rather than doctrinaire. We are [seeking?] to build up a body of public opinion behind a more thoughtful and radical form of progressivism than that which ordinarily passes under that name."[20]

Croly's description of the program to Learned Hand was somewhat more moderate, especially as concerned the public circular to be sent to potential subscribers: "It does not seem to me wise, in a preliminary announcement, to go too much into detail. If, for instance, I should say that we intended to preach self-government in industry, the nationalization of railroads, a minimum wage, and all the other specific economic and political reforms which will constitute our program, I think we would run the danger of making both illusory friends and unnecessary enemies."[21]

It thus seems clear that Croly expected to use the *New Republic* to further the arguments that he had developed in *The Promise* and *Progressive Democracy*, not only the short-run arguments, but also his conviction that a substantial reform of American political values was necessary. He was convinced that the progressive movement was a salutary force, but also that it had a long way to go in achieving the necessary political, economic, and intellectual transformation of America.

CROLY'S GOALS in 1914 were lofty, but they proved hard to achieve in practice. He seems to have expected that he could develop and explicate a more profound theoretical understanding of progressivism—of a modern liberalism, as he was beginning to call it—while commenting on immediate events, even fitting that commentary within his general theoretical framework. He also clearly expected to concentrate on domestic affairs and to be able to support a growing Progressive party. In practice, of course, American attention was focused more and more on World War I and on the question of possible American participation. In addition, the Progressives were badly beaten in November 1914, and the survival of the Progressive party was at issue as the *New Republic* began publication. Croly thus faced substantial obstacles in achieving the goals he had set for himself and his paper.

Croly may have expected to be able to develop his political theory further in the journal, but for the most part the pressure of commenting on immediate issues overwhelmed his more theoretical concerns. Croly realized this in late 1918 or 1919, when he began to work separately on a new book that could explore issues in greater depth than was possible in the *New Republic*. (I consider this book, *The Breach in Civilization*, in chapter eight.)

Pending the opportunity to return to more leisurely writing, Croly in the *New Republic* continued to argue a political theory very much like that of *Progressive Democracy* in most respects. Of major importance, he remained committed to democracy and did not return to the notions of elite democracy that had tempted him in *The Promise*. This commitment to a popular, progressive democracy is evident in many of Croly's articles and editorials, such as a 1915 appeal for women's suffrage: "Universal suffrage is indispensable to . . . political responsibility in a modern social democracy." Croly goes on to argue for a "really democratic representative system."[22]

Croly also continued, and indeed amplified, the pluralist argument of *Progressive Democracy.* In that work he had argued that humans commit their allegiances to many groups, not just the nation-state that he had concentrated on in *The Promise*. Croly now continued to argue against exclusive state claims on individuals. In perhaps his most theoretical article in the war years, "The Future of the State," Croly wrote that "if democracy were confined to an exclusive choice between an indivisible state and a dismembered society, I would accept the former as the alternative which probably would allow a larger measure of human development." But, happily, we are "not confined to such a choice." Rather, a "coherent national organization must be the reflection not only of independence of character on the part of individual citizens, but of equally genuine independence on the part of those associations which represent its fundamental industrial and social activities."[23] Croly went on to describe the proper situation of such groups in many other articles, arguing, for example, for the legal recognition of trade unions.

The doubts that Croly expressed about the claims of the state in this continued reliance on pluralism were amplified in two areas in which his political theory *can* be said to change in these years: his growing acceptance of the concept of rights and the traditional (negative) understanding of liberty, and his adoption of the term "liberal" to describe his own philosophy.

We saw that in *Progressive Democracy* Croly was somewhat more accepting of the concept of "rights" than in *The Promise*. His writings in the *New Republic* show a further acceptance of rights although still without a full endorsement. Croly was still held back by his conviction that "abstract" rights could not be philosophically justified. For example, when arguing for women's suffrage he refused to ground the argument on rights: "Any graduate student fresh from the political science department of a contemporary university can triumphantly perform the work of demolition. Abstract rights of any kind have ceased to command very much reverence."[24]

On the other hand, the events about which Croly wrote editorials in these years constantly reminded him of the value of individualism and individual rights and liberties. Three issues in particular seem to have been important. First, the *New Republic* was concerned to argue for the importance of academic freedom as a particular manifestation of the large principles of freedom of speech and of the press. Among Croly's frequent contributors were John Dewey and Charles A. Beard, both involved in issues of academic freedom and in the formation of the American Association of University Professors to support that principle. In a number of articles and editorials, the *New Republic* very strongly supported these efforts.[25]

Second, the issue of conscription became important after the United States entered the war. After a slight hesitation, the editors of and contributors to the *New Republic* (with the signal exception of Randolph Bourne) came to support conscription as a necessity and as a democratic way of raising an army. They were even ambivalent about what exceptions could be made for conscientious objectors.[26] These issues continually raised the question of how far individual consciences could be coerced by the state. By early 1919, the *New Republic* had come (retrospectively) to a position of strong support for conscientious objection, on grounds of the sanctity of conscience and individual liberties. "If a man's conscience forbids him to serve in war, or to perform any service that even indirectly bears upon war, we are bound to respect it," the editors wrote. "Our policy in the matter of conscientious objectors was a stupidity; in execution it was a black disgrace. . . . Let us grant amnesty [to those still in prison]. . . . This is not a radical issue, but an issue as old and as respectable as political liberty."[27]

The third issue that brought home the importance of traditional freedoms and the Bill of Rights was the issue of censorship during and immediately after the war. As we shall see in reviewing the position of the *New Republic* on the war,[28] Croly and his associates became increasingly concerned about war hysteria and about various laws, especially the Espionage Act, that allowed government censorship and the denial of mail privileges to "subversive" groups and publications and the prosecution of offenders. This hysteria continued after the war in the "Red Scare" of 1919, and Croly's *New Republic* took a very strong stand against it. Commending this stand, Justice Oliver Wendell Holmes wrote privately to Croly that "it seemed to me that we so long had enjoyed the advantages protected by bills of rights that we had forgotten—it used sometimes to seem to me that the *New Republic* had forgotten—that they had had to be fought for and could not be kept unless we were willing to fight for them."[29] Certainly the need to argue vigorously against censorship made Croly aware of the importance of individual liberties.

These issues thus led Croly and his associates to express increasing doubts about the claims of the nation-state. For example, in late 1917, Croly argued that "the state, by renouncing its absurd claims to impeccability and omnipotence in its relations with its own people" would be more likely to succeed both in negotiating with other states and in providing for human development.[30] Harold J. Laski, who wrote often for the *New Republic*, argued that there was "something of splendor in a defiant challenge" to authority. Laski claimed that German thought had preached submission to the state, and he called on Germany's opponents to oppose this view: "Rather let us follow our state where by its rectitude it demands our sympathy. . . . But we must not fail to register our disapproval where we deem its error crime. Our state, then, is to be but doubtfully sovereign."[31]

This theoretical questioning of the state somewhat parallels Croly's adoption of the term "liberalism." As we have seen, Croly rarely (but occasionally) used this word to describe his own theory in his previous work, but he did begin to use it more often as he developed his plans for the *New Republic*. In the following few years, Croly came to identify himself as explicitly "liberal." For example, in the summer of 1915 he sought to disentangle "the cause of liberalism" from the war objectives of the allied powers.[32] By the next summer, a *New Republic* editorial (unsigned but very similar to Croly's previous language) argued that "American liberalism is seeking a radical transformation of the political and economic structure of the country."[33] By mid-1916, the term "liberal" was in common use in the paper, and Croly clearly now thought of himself as a liberal theorist.

Croly never made it fully clear why he came to use "liberalism" as descriptive of his own theory, after previously having identified the term primarily with classical liberal theory. Perhaps the issues of individual liberty as raised in a war context brought him to change his views enough to think the term now appropriate. Perhaps the defeat of the Progressives suggested the need for a wider theoretical conception than "reform" or "progressivism," his former vocabulary. Or perhaps, as the Laski article suggests, American and British writers set themselves apart from German thought by consciously (or unconsciously) incorporating the traditional English emphasis on liberty into a new political theory. This identification could have been further strengthened in Croly's mind by a series of three articles that George Santayana published in the *New Republic* in the summer of 1915. Santayana's argument was quite complex, but among other points it counterpoised German conceptions of freedom to English "liberal freedom," which Santayana thought stressed individualism and the "liberty of liberalism."[34] Finally, Croly was very admiring of the British liberal party, and he may have begun to adopt the term "liberalism" in part to show a transatlantic solidarity with the Asquith government.[35] Whatever the reason, by 1916 Herbert Croly was writing an explicitly liberal political theory.

In summary, while the format of a weekly journal, and the pressure of commenting on both domestic and war issues, did not encourage a theoretical perspective, Croly did manage to provide some philosophic distance for his arguments. The theory that he advanced was substantially that of *Progressive Democracy,* but by 1919 he had come to emphasize important aspects of the classic theory of "negative liberty" (and even "rights") more fully. Croly particularly focused on the importance of political liberties, clearly giving a priority to free speech issues as a necessary element of a progressive political system. At the same time, he divorced these liberties from the laissez-faire arguments for property rights. Croly now considered himself a "liberal" and his journal a vehicle for liberal opinions.

IT IS CLEARLY BEYOND the scope of this study to examine all of the domestic policy issues on which the *New Republic* took a position in these years. However, we can consider in general terms where Croly's journal stood on political issues, on economic issues, and finally what partisan stands were supported.

The *New Republic*'s positions on domestic policy issues were very similar to Croly's own previous positions. For example, a number of articles argued for the importance of centralized national power and economic planning. The editors also argued that within the national government it fell to the executive to provide the central leadership. For example, in the very first issue the editors called for an enhancement of presidential power over legislation.[36] Six months later, the editors wrote that "the Presidency has in truth become the great representative agency in the national political system, the vehicle through which the prevailing national will gets itself expressed and the dominant public opinion comes to self-consciousness."[37] The journal also argued for the augmentation of the power of state governors, just as Croly had previously.[38] The *New Republic* even went so far as to argue that reformers should support "preparedness" as a means of developing a more efficient domestic administration.[39]

Conversely, the editors were often critical of the "petty personal and partisan games" that the state legislatures and especially Congress played.[40] They also argued that the states by and large were unable to deal with the exigencies of modern society.[41]

Many positions taken by the journal reflected Croly's suspicion in *Progressive Democracy* of political parties and his support of direct democracy and state administrative reorganization. For example, an editorial note in early 1915 claimed that "the American two-party system is intimately associated with fundamental defects in the traditional American political organization" and argued that parties were the "necessary enemy of direct popular political responsibility."[42] A note the previous week also called for easing the process of amending the Constitution, in line with Croly's previous views.[43]

The paper also gave extensive coverage to the results of initiatives, referenda, and recalls. For example, a special insert was prepared by Robert E. Cushman for the March 6, 1915, edition, analyzing the 1914 results (in which California alone had 48 referendum questions). The editorial introduction to this insert was extremely supportive of these progressive principles.[44] Another special supplement, written by Charles A. Beard, reviewed the changes that had been effected in state constitutions and administrative policies during the progressive years. Beard specifically cited Croly's books as important influences on these developments.[45] In short, many of the positions taken by the *New Republic* were drawn quite directly from Croly's previous writings. The best summary example is the conclusion of an article on parties in the second issue: "The American democracy will not continue to need the two-party system to intermediate between the popular will and the governmental machinery. By means of executive leadership, expert administrative independence and direct legislation, it will gradually create a new governmental machinery which will be born with the impulse to destroy the two-party system, and will itself be thoroughly and flexibly representative of the underlying purposes and needs of a more social democracy."[46]

Among the other important issues the journal supported were three important liberal causes: birth control, anti-lynching pressure, and the nomination of Louis Brandeis to the Supreme Court. The *New Republic* argued for birth control as both a "social question of the first magnitude" and a matter of personal privacy.[47] Croly thus expanded his concern for personal liberty beyond strictly political liberties to a wider vision of individual liberty. The journal also argued very strongly against lynching,[48] though less obviously for "negro rights" generally.[49] Perhaps most important, the paper strongly supported Wilson's 1916 nomination of Louis Brandeis. The editors returned to this issue week after week as confirmation was delayed, effectively showing that much of the Boston opposition to Brandeis came from a small group of Brahmins who had been hurt by his many principled stands in previous years.[50] In short, despite the increasing demands of the war, the early years of the *New Republic* evidenced a full domestic agenda and a strong commitment to liberal causes.

MAJOR PARTS of the Wilson administration's most important economic legislation were passed in the hiatus between Croly's writing of *Progressive Democracy* and the first edition of the *New Republic*. In his book, Croly had praised the Underwood tariff, which was passed in October 1913, but Croly hadn't dealt with the three other major laws of Wilson's early years, the Clayton Act, the act establishing the Federal Trade Commission, and the Federal Reserve Act.

The Clayton bill was introduced in the spring of 1914, originally detailing a long list of illegal trade practices. The FTC originated in a bill filed by Rep. James J. Covington that would have created a weak "sunshine commission," which could have conducted investigations of business practices but would have little power. Both bills passed the House of Representatives in June 1914.[51]

At this point, many businessmen objected to the attempt in the Clayton bill to fine various business practices; conversely, the trade commission bill was popular. Wilson was therefore open to suggestions to amend the legislation, and the most important of these came from George Rublee, the former Progressive (and Cornish neighbor) whom Croly had tried to bring onto the *New Republic*. Rublee wrote a new bill that provided for a much stronger trade commission, indeed, one close to Roosevelt's New Nationalism stands of 1912. At first the Democratic House voted this down, but Rublee was able to convince Brandeis to change his long-standing views on this issue and support a strengthening of the FTC bill in a major reversal of policy. Wilson then agreed with Rublee and Brandeis, and provided the political clout to pass the FTC legislation in September 1914. The act provided for a commission of five members with what seemed like reasonable power to regulate corporate behavior.[52]

After the FTC legislation passed, the Clayton bill was further weakened and eventually passed in October 1914. In effect, it did not materially change antitrust policy from the earlier Sherman Act, but the provision of the act exempting organized labor from antitrust prosecution (with some exceptions) was important.[53]

The passage of the Federal Reserve Act was even more complicated. It was clear even before Wilson was inaugurated that changes were necessary in the banking system, but there was considerable disagreement within Wilson's administration and the Democratic Congress as to the degree of national control that was desirable. Nearly a year elapsed before Wilson signed the Federal Reserve Act in December 1913. The act balanced private and public control and regional and national functions, but in total it was a major innovation in the nation's economy and in Arthur Link's view was the "greatest single piece of constructive legislation of the Wilson era."[54]

The reaction to these developments in Croly's new journal was quite positive. In the first issue, Wilson's achievements were praised: "During this [1914] campaign the Democrats made much of their legislative record, of which they could be justifiably proud. . . . Their Federal Reserve Act brought about a desirable centralization of the banking resources of the country. . . . The anti-trust legislation also proved to be better than the preliminary advertisements prophesied. The Trade Commission Act has fastened upon an administrative body an immediate responsibility for preventing unfair competitive methods."[55] However, the editorial went right on to argue that Wilson's allegiance to his party had weakened the progressivism of these measures, and that much more was needed. "The work of a sincerely progressive democracy has only begun. The legislation passed by the Democratic party has not made any impression upon the more serious and difficult social and industrial problems of contemporary America. . . . Nothing of any importance has as yet been accomplished to bestow freedom and peace on the American nation."[56]

Croly strengthened his criticisms two weeks later after Wilson had written a letter to Secretary of the Treasury William G. McAdoo stating that the administration had now righted most of the fundamental problems of the country.[57] Obviously afraid that this meant Wilson would not push for further change, Croly attacked: "President Wilson could not have written his letter unless he had utterly misconceived the meaning and task of American progressivism. . . . Mr. Wilson's sincerity is above suspicion, but he is a dangerous and unsound thinker upon contemporary political and social problems."[58]

However, in early January 1915, the *New Republic* waxed more positive again, particularly praising the FTC and pointing out how much Wilson had changed his position: "The Trade Commission act represents a totally different approach [than the Sherman Act], a spirit strangely contradictory to the campaign theories of the President. . . . In this Trade Commission act is contained the possibility of a radical reversal of many American notions about trusts, legislative power, and legal procedure. It may amount to historic political and constitutional reform."[59]

In the following months, the editors spelled out their own more advanced economic program. They argued for a strengthening of unions beyond the recognition of the Clayton Act and indeed for government discrimination in their favor.[60] They wanted programs created to give work to the unemployed, arguing that not even the meanest laissez-faire theorists could oppose government action in this area.[61] They came out even more strongly for the nationalization of the railroads, as Croly had promised they would: "The nationalizing of the railroads has a chance of converting them into genuine agencies of the national economic interest."[62] And they praised administrative agencies such as the Children's Bureau as "progressively useful agent[s] of a rising civilization."[63]

Wilson's administration did continue to develop its domestic legislative agenda, particularly in the spring and summer of 1916. Among the important acts passed were the Kern-McGillicuddy Act, which provided workmen's compensation for federal employees, and the Keating-Owen Act, prohibiting products of child labor in interstate commerce.[64] These bills were passed by Congress under presidential pressure quite obviously to gain progressive support in Wilson's re-election campaign. Also important was the Adamson Act legislating the eight hour day on the railroads.[65]

These laws were important and certainly controverted Croly's fears that Wilson's party allegiances would hold him back from adopting progressive measures. Even so, Croly was not easily satisfied. Amid a few compliments, the *New Republic* kept up a steady barrage of criticism. The editors found fault with the "quality of Mr. Wilson's thinking,"[66] and particularly criticized him for not raising administrative standards.[67] Still, Wilson's passage of so much legislation that, if not perfect, was nevertheless distinctly progressive brought the editors to a dramatic political choice: the possibility that the *New Republic* might endorse a Democrat in 1916.

THIS DECISION was an agonizing one for Croly. His policies on domestic political and economic issues in the *New Republic* had been remarkably consistent with his previous positions. But his partisan allegiances could not be similarly consistent, as the political world had changed dramatically since 1914.

We should recall that in *Progressive Democracy* Croly had still preferred Roosevelt to Wilson. That preference was shared by most of the other editors and particularly by the Straights, who were personally close to Roosevelt. It was reflected in the positions taken by the paper in its first months. Thus the editors praised Roosevelt's forthrightness on the war in the second issue.[68] In the spring of 1915, they continued public support, declaring that Roosevelt was "the man above all others who has carried new thought into the common consciousness," though they also noted that "he is not as progressive as the best thought of this country. . . ."[69]

However, this public support (even if somewhat qualified) covered an increasing private rift, which had begun in December 1914 with a slight criticism of Roosevelt in the paper. Prior to that the editors had continued to be personally close to T.R. In fact, Croly had been visiting Roosevelt in August when the war had broken out, and Croly and Lippmann had lunched with him at Oyster Bay in November.[70] However, in December Roosevelt had criticized Wilson's Mexican policy in a way the editors thought unfair and prejudiced, and they said so.[71]

Croly had warned Willard Straight of this comment, noting that along with their usual criticism of Wilson, "I may add that in order to make a good balance we have taken a crack at T.R. this week, basing it upon the article . . . in which he seems to hit at Mr. Wilson below the belt."[72] The next week Croly explained further: "The last issue is strong, I think. . . . Lippmann wrote the criticism of T.R., which was disagreeable but necessary. We had to begin sometime."[73]

Roosevelt was quite offended and said to Francis Hackett that the paper had been disloyal.[74] Croly responded directly that he indeed had felt a strong sense of loyalty to Roosevelt and was grateful for past favors; however, the *New Republic's* "whole future success in life depends upon the impression which it makes upon its readers of being able to think disinterestedly and independently."[75] Roosevelt replied coldly that there was no obligation either way in their relationship.[76] After that, there were no more lunches at Oyster Bay, though Roosevelt apparently did try to reconcile briefly with the editors in late 1915.[77]

These private divisions became increasingly public in 1916. In January, Roosevelt made a long speech which, in the editors' view, was meant to update his entire program in anticipation of a possible Republican or Progressive nomination. In a long article called "The Newer Nationalism," they dissected this program, finding it inadequately framed in terms of foreign policy and particularly inadequate in terms of a progressive domestic policy.[78] Roosevelt was proving himself perhaps more Hamiltonian and less democratic than Croly had thought.

In April, the editors went further, praising many aspects of Roosevelt's policies, but commenting that "surround him with defense leagues, and he will go the militarist one better. Great leader that he is, there are few men so easily led." They concluded that "it is the business of the Progressives [at the upcoming convention] to do something more than nominate Theodore Roosevelt. It is their business to fight for the possession of his soul." No doubt thinking of their own ties, they added that "Mr. Roosevelt demands a kind of loyalty which many who admire him will not give."[79]

This editorial was ambiguous, leaving open the possibility that the *New Republic* might support Roosevelt if he ran on the Progressive (or even the Republican) ticket. However, Roosevelt slammed the door on that possibility by refusing the Progressive nomination and urging the remnants of the party to support Hughes, the Republican nominee.[80]

To the editors, the only decent course left was to bury the Progressive party. It had, they wrote, played an important role. "For a while it looked like a serious as well as a gallant political adventure. Unfortunately, like so many other adventurous enterprises, it did not grow up to the necessities and opportunities of its own business." The Progressive platform of 1912 had been a "declaration of middle-class liberalism which sought to accomplish its social program by means of an increase in popular political power and responsibility." However, the party had become overly dependent on Roosevelt: "The soul of the Progressive party was sent to Oyster Bay for safe keeping." And Roosevelt was no longer progressive: his "platform of 1916 as an expression of political and economic radicalism is a joke." The closing sentence of this editorial brought a poignant close to many of Croly's political ideals of the last several years: "The Progressive party is dead, and with it must die the present hope of converting a national party into a faithful agent of progressive political and social ideals."[81]

The death of the Progressive party left many "homeless radicals"—more than a million, the editors estimated. The Socialist party was unsatisfactory, a "new form of [partisan] orthodoxy." Where could they go?

The editors invited the two major parties to bid for progressive support.[82]

As the campaign progressed, Lippmann, Weyl, and most of the other editors gradually endorsed Wilson, while Willard Straight chose Hughes. For Croly the choice was a hard one. There was much that was attractive about Wilson, and in a long editorial in late June, he stated the case for Wilson in very familiar terms:

> In Mr. Wilson's present program there is scarcely a shred left of the fabric of his Jeffersonian revival. With every development of his policy he has been approximating to the spirit and creed of a Hamiltonian nationalist. Our own opinion of Mr. Wilson as a statesman has improved just in proportion as the indiscriminate and irresponsible individualism of his earlier views has yielded to a preference for responsible nationalistic organization. He is a wiser and safer political leader to-day than he was four years ago—one who has a better claim on the support of intelligent liberals.[83]

However, Croly still harbored doubts, and it was not until mid-October, after a series of ambivalent editorials,[84] that Croly finally printed a personal endorsement: "I shall vote for the reelection of President Wilson . . . chiefly because he has succeeded, at least for the time being, in transforming the Democracy into the more promising of the two major party organizations. To be entirely frank, the decision has been reached reluctantly and only after prolonged hesitation."[85] This was hardly a ringing endorsement! Still, after weighing many factors, Croly had decided that "Mr. Wilson and the Democratic party have begun to perform that work of national reconstruction which the Progressive party declared indispensable to the welfare of the commonwealth. They have been adapting the political and economic organization of the country to its more pressing needs and to its better ideals. They have not gone very far, but they have at least started to fasten on the popular consciousness a new and better meaning for the American idea."[86]

The election of 1916 essentially marked the end of progressive reform, as the war became even more dominant an issue when American entry became imminent in early 1917. What, then, was Croly's opinion of what had been accomplished? Just before the election, the *New Republic* emphasized an essential continuity between Roosevelt and Wilson in the cause of progressive reform. Admitting that neither leader would have appreciated the analysis, the editors wrote that Roosevelt's "indefatigable initiative and his exceptional gifts as an agitator were devoted to concentrating public opinion on the all-important task of democratizing the political system of the country and socializing its economic system." After the Taft years, Wilson had again taken up the cause "and did more in four years to incorporate progressive principles into the national economic system than his predecessors had accomplished in twelve. . . . His work in this respect is clearly a continuation, if not a consummation, of that begun by Mr. Roosevelt. . . . Mr. Wilson wrote into law the connection between a progressive policy and national unity."[87] These phrases evoke the arguments of both of Croly's books, and we may conclude that Croly thought that many of his political values had been realized by 1916.

That would be to misunderstand Croly's thought. The Roosevelt-Wilson achievements were important, but they were only a start toward a really substantive reform program, as he often argued. Wilson may have achieved some of Croly's short-term proposals for regulating the economy, but the long-run transformations remained unattempted. In a speech that Croly gave at a meeting of the American Academy of Political and Social Science earlier in the year, he had remarked that "the most conspicuous aspect of the progressive movement during the past fifteen years has been the contrast between the enormous effort and the meagre results."[88] For Croly the idealist, much more was needed.

Of course, Croly could have applied much the same criticism to his own "paper." Croly had managed to articulate a program consistent with his previous theoretical writings, but he hadn't been able to advance that theory very much. The increased concern for individual liberty was an important point, further affirming Croly's intellectual descent from classical liberty theory. But beyond that point, it had proven very difficult to pick a fully coherent route through the maze of political issues that demanded the editors' attention. Still, Croly was hopeful that liberalism could be further clarified in theory and further embodied in public policy in a second Wilson administration. Unfortunately, as in later reform eras, the specter of war intervened, and when the war was over, America had become a very different society, much less receptive to liberal political theory.

7

Liberalism and War

In domestic affairs, Croly could draw heavily upon his previous thinking and writing in developing positions for the *New Republic*. The same was not true of foreign affairs. He had devoted modest attention to foreign policy in *The Promise of American Life*, developing only the outlines of an internationalist outlook. Croly had even expressed mild concern about the militaristic competition he saw developing in Europe. But domestic policy was clearly much more important to him. *Progressive Democracy* had focused exclusively on domestic reform, and the initial planning for the *New Republic* also had been almost exclusively domestic in focus. As Walter Lippmann later wrote: "We never dreamed that there would be a World War before our first issue was printed."[1] Still, Croly tried to be optimistic: "The war will also, I hope, prove in the end an active help to the 'New Republic.' It will tend to dislocate conventional ways of looking at things and stimulate public opinion to think about the greater international problems. . . . It will create, that is, a state of mind in which a journal [of] political and social agitation will find its words more influential."[2]

Croly's associates were as unprepared in foreign policy as he. As Ronald Steel remarks, "until August 1914 Lippmann had hardly given a thought to foreign affairs."[3] Walter Weyl had written primarily on domestic economic issues. Thus all the New Republicans had to learn fast about foreign policy; they had to develop categories and concepts of analysis as well as individual positions on each issue. But of course the same was true of progressivism and indeed of the country as a whole. World War I came as a shock to the American political system, and it took a while to adjust.

Croly acknowledged this national unpreparedness in the first issue: "The American people were as ill-prepared to meet the spiritual challenge of the war as they were to protect themselves against its distressing economic effects. Their sense of international isolation has bred in them a combination of crude colonialism with crude nationalism." Croly drew on his previous arguments to prove that laissez-faire had given rise to isolationism: "Independence in the sense of isolation has proved to be a delusion. It was born of the same conditions and the same misunderstandings as our traditional optimistic fatalism; and it must be thrown into the same accumulating scrapheap of patriotic misconceptions." Instead, the United States would need to become better organized and take charge of its destiny internationally as well as domestically.[4]

This was a clear but not distinctive position—blaming laissez-faire, calling for national organization, and most important, renouncing isolation. But Croly did go further: it was also clear that the United States in renouncing isolation had to develop a positive policy of its own. In this first article on the war, he argued for "the positive and necessary policy of making American influence in Europe count in favor of international peace." This emphasis on peace was to become a consistent theme, though Croly did not yet propose any specific steps that the United States should take.

The editors held to these basic points for the next several months, while largely responding to the unfolding military action. They were clear that the United States could not remain isolated from the war; that would not be realistic for a modern economic and political power. At the same time, we should not get directly involved. Rather, the proper course in international as in domestic affairs was the middle way: the United States should work for peace, should seek to conciliate the parties, and should also support its own and other nations' neutral rights to trade with all belligerents. In addition, the country should modestly build up its own forces to be able to support these positions. Thus, in late December, the editors argued that America should remain pacifist, but that was not the same as "passivism." Remaining passive "repeats in the larger region of international politics the error which the advocates of *laissez-faire* used to make in domestic policies." At the same time, the editors argued from the early days of the war that the United States probably could not commit to remaining outside the conflict forever. "A nation does not commit the great sin when it fights. It commits the great sin when it fights for a bad cause or when it is afraid to fight for a good cause."[5] The "pacifism" of the editors was thus very definitely not a principled opposition to war. Rather, it was a pragmatic judgment that the United States was not (yet) appropriately involved in this conflict. In the meanwhile, it was wise to anticipate trouble, and in the winter and spring of 1915, the editors amplified their arguments for a moderate U.S. "preparedness."[6]

Another theme of their policy early in the war was the need for multilateral action. The paper issued a very ambiguous initial verdict on the idea of a "League to Enforce Peace" as a way to prevent future wars, praising the idea but adding that "the fatal objection to any alliance of this kind is that it does not really meet the difficulty that no state will abandon its sovereignty." The editors went on to provide a "realistic" view of a League in international politics: "The vice of all such schemes is that they are based too one-sidedly on the idea of preventing wars. They take a static view of the world. . . . They ignore the fact that life is change. . . . We must deal with causes, must provide some means alternative to war by which large grievances can be redressed."[7] However, the league was at least a positive proposal, and in the next several months the editors began to warm to the idea. As Croly wrote to Lippmann in June 1915: "We ought to adopt a fundamentally sympathetic attitude toward the League of Peace. Of course we can be critical as well as sympathetic and point out its limitations and dangers, but . . . it [the League] seems to me [to be], the most promising concrete proposal that has been made since the war began."[8] This support would shortly become considerably more enthusiastic.

In terms of the actual course of the war, the editors also protested (but relatively mildly) against the British policy of preventing trade with Germany. This virtual blockade violated the accepted rights of neutrals. However, they were determined to be realistic: there was nothing that could be done about it at the moment, "but the day will come when neutrals, instead of begging belligerents for a few crumbs of legal observance, will insist upon a set of rules the advantage of which lies with people who keep rather than people who break the peace."[9]

While protesting British behavior, the editors had remarked that the Germans would do the same thing, but didn't have the means. "The German threat to innocent neutral commerce with England was wanton, but it was incidental."[10] This judgment was proven dramatically wrong in the first major incident of submarine warfare, the sinking of the *Lusitania*, in May 1915. This disaster, in which over 100 American citizens were killed (as well as many more British subjects), in the editors' opinion nearly led to war between the United States and Germany. In addition, it showed them that this country was very closely tied to Great Britain, demonstrating that British shipping was necessary for American commerce, which was consequently jeopardized by the German determination now to attack all kinds of British shipping.[11]

One lesson was that the United States had to build up its own resources. Another and even more important lesson, in the editors' view, was that the United States was correct in now leaning toward the Allied side in the war. Germany's violation of the rights of neutrals to travel on passenger liners (even those of belligerent nations) confirmed and compounded its violation of the rights of neutral nations such as Belgium. Of course, Britain was also violating neutral rights in blockading Germany, but in a less "barbarous" fashion. "We have a fair chance of living amicably with the fellow countrymen of the majority of the Lusitania victims, but we cannot live amicably with the nation who so deliberately and remorselessly condemned them to death."[12]

From then on, the *New Republic* clearly favored Great Britain in the war. This leaning toward Britain was strengthened by the many British contributors to the paper, contributors often from the British Left but still sympathetic to the Allied cause.[13] Indeed, a year later, Lippmann wrote to Graham Wallas that the *New Republic* had been committed to England from the *Lusitania* incident on, but that American public opinion was such that this position needed to be carefully constructed and partially concealed: "We decided just about a year ago, precisely at the time the Lusitania was sunk, to devote the paper to the creation of an Anglo-American understanding. We felt then that the traditional hostility to England in this country could not be overcome by a paper which didn't take what might be called a strongly American view of the situation."[14] When he wrote, Lippmann was trying to overcome Wallas's concern that the journal was not sufficiently supportive of the Allied cause, and he may have exaggerated the commitment. Still, the editors usually did come down against Germany from early 1915 on.

FROM THE *LUSITANIA* sinking through much of the rest of 1915, the *New Republic* thus sought to maintain American neutrality, while leaning toward and usually arguing for the Allies. As a lead article noted in June 1915: "The cause for which the Allies began fighting . . . was on the whole a good cause. Germany was the immediate aggressor." The United States could not stand apart entirely. She would have to enter the war if forced by Germany. The editors even went so far as to argue that if the Allies "were in danger of being overwhelmed, a sufficient reason may have existed for American participation in the war, provided a sufficient pretext was presented. But the Allies are now in no danger of being overwhelmed." Therefore, "it would be well for the world to keep one great Power disinterested. The United States ought to be that Power."[15]

Croly's signed articles in this period show his own personal ambiguity on the war, displaying a skepticism about Allied war propaganda, but also an ultimate support of the Allied cause. "If we cannot acquiesce in the formulas which seem to consecrate the war, neither can we acquiesce in unqualified condemnation of it." He resisted pressure to join the Allies (perhaps more than Lippmann did) and instead called for an "attitude of judicious skepticism." It was clear that Croly would *never* support Germany. But the Allies were not perfect either, and liberalism could not be too closely identified with their aims in the war: "The cause of liberalism would be perverted and impoverished by being subordinated to the necessities of the anti-German combination." Croly therefore concluded that "if we are forced into the war we ought not to lose sight of our special work. . . . Our participation should be made on some basis of limited liability [for the Allied policies]. . . . If we remain neutral our work . . . should consist in making neutrality articulate and discriminate. If we become a belligerent we should adapt our belligerency to the attainment of our own special purposes."[16]

The *New Republic* did support Wilson's plans for increased "preparedness"—for an increase in American forces. The editors noted that this was both necessary and good politics, otherwise militant nationalists would be appropriating the issue. Wilson's "policy has the enormous merit of being one on which good citizens who are neither alarmists nor non-resistant pacifists can unite."[17] Of course, the editors also criticized the president for not making his policy more clear.[18]

True to Croly's original emphasis on peace, the editors wrote with enthusiasm about a possible end to the war in November 1915. A few "timid voices" had recently been raised on both sides wondering whether "the time is ripe, if not for an official statement by the belligerents of the terms of an acceptable treaty of peace, at least for the partially . . . public discussion of those terms." For their part, the editors expressed the hope that these voices would grow into a "voluminous chorus," and they judged that "an inconclusive ending to the war and a treaty of compromise and adjustment has a much better chance of contributing to the ultimate peace of Europe than has the ruthless subjugation of Germany."[19] For these thoughts, the *New Republic* was sometimes called pro-German, a charge they naturally rejected. They were, they argued, simply trying to hold to the requirements of a neutral position.[20]

In early 1916, the editors were encouraged by Wilson's success in extracting concessions from Germany on submarine warfare (the "Sussex Pledge"), and they were optimistic that American neutrality could be maintained, though they were increasingly explicit that it was a neutrality tilting toward the Allies.[21] Indeed, they were quite explicit about their preference for the Allies. "The *New Republic* has supported the policy of emasculating the submarine and of confining American protests against the British embargo within the bounds of ineffectuality."[22] They thought Wilson's policy was similar: a neutrality clearly slanted toward the Allied side.

The editors still saw their (and Wilson's) policy as a middle way: "Aggressive pacifism is the third alternative which will rescue the United States from the fatal choice between sheer belligerence and neutral isolation."[23] This optimism survived several submarine attacks, one of which, in April 1916, brought Wilson close to a break with Germany. The editors would have supported a break, but questioned whether it was yet appropriate.[24] However, Germany backed off, and the situation continued relatively stable through the election.

The major event in the spring and summer of 1916 was Wilson's endorsement of the idea of a league, which came in a speech of May 27 to a meeting of supporters of the League to Enforce Peace. Wilson did not endorse all aspects of that group's program, but he did argue eloquently that the war showed that a new kind of diplomacy was needed in the future. In a full statement of his own values, Wilson emphasized the principles of national self-determination, for small as well as for large nations, and he argued that aggression was unacceptable as a means of settling disagreements. Most important, he asserted: "I am sure that I speak the mind and wish of the people of America when I say that the United States is willing to become a partner in any feasible association of nations formed in order to realize these objects."[25]

In an article by Lippmann, the journal reacted enthusiastically, indeed with almost indiscriminate enthusiasm. Wilson's declaration, Lippmann guessed, "may well mark a decisive point in the history of the modern world. No utterance since the war began compares with it in overwhelming significance to the future of mankind. For us in America it literally marks the opening of a new period of history and the ending of our deepest tradition [of isolationism]."[26] Lippmann judged (erroneously, as it turned out) that "the whole preparedness agitation, which has been running wild of late by piling jingoism on hysteria, is given a new turn. It becomes our contribution to the world's peace." Indeed, Lippmann hoped that "our offer to join in a guaranty of the world's peace opens up the possibility of a quick and moderate peace. It gives to the liberals of Europe a practical thing to work with."[27] In the result, Wilson's speech unfortunately did not have the effect of ending the war, jingoism did not subside, and European liberals did not revive. But Wilson's support of a league and of a push for peace did help to tie the *New Republic* to his cause, and it was for reasons of foreign as well as domestic policy that Lippmann, and eventually Croly too, supported Wilson's re-election.[28]

WILSON'S SPEECH and the *New Republic*'s support brought the editors, especially Lippmann but also Croly, into increasingly close touch with the administration—with Wilson directly and especially with Colonel Edward M. House, his informal adviser, who lived in New York. The editors seem to have met with House first in March 1916, at which time Croly wrote to Willard Straight: "We were not able to find out just what the object of the interview was unless . . . Col. House wished to look us over." Croly noted that House "seems to be reading The New Republic regularly" and he judged that "it will be a useful thing to have established a means of communication with him so that in the future we can get at the President through him, or get information from him when we critically need it."[29] No doubt House and Wilson also thought the connection would be useful in securing progressive support!

Lippmann met with Wilson later in March[30] and again in August, when he wrote to Graham Wallas that after talking with Wilson he had no doubt about the president's firm commitment to the idea of a league. He predicted that Wilson would go "so far even to accept the doctrine The New Republic has been preaching that in the future the United States cannot be neutral in a world war."[31] In December, Lippmann even rode the train to Washington with Colonel House for dinner at the White House.[32]

The editors were thus optimistic in early 1917, optimistic that the administration was pushing for a peace based on the idea of a League and optimistic that their own views were once again directly influential on a major political figure.

Croly summed up his current thinking about the war, and especially about the idea of a league and the goal of peace, in a long January 1917 editorial.[33] He reviewed his own previous commitment to the ideal of nationalism and asked whether this conflicted with the internationalism of a league. His very interesting answer was that it did not. Rather, "the peculiar merit of the plan of a League to Enforce Peace, as compared to other plans of pacifist organization, consists in the promise of its proposed method. . . . It establishes international order on the foundation of national responsibility. It seeks to create a community of living nations rather than a community of superseded nations of denationalized peoples." The former nationalist thus convinced himself that it was not illogical now to support internationalism as well. Indeed, while terming the international arena an inferior "medium in which liberal democratic nations have been obliged to live," Croly now discovered a fact about nationalism that he had overlooked in 1909: "The spirit of nationalism has always needed for its fruition the organization of an international community."[34]

This article, Croly's last major piece before the United States entered the war, reveals his continued hope that the step would not be necessary, and indeed that the war could be ended by agreement rather than force of arms. He argued that a peace treaty at present, by itself, would simply constitute "an invitation to future wars." However, by adding the force of a league, particularly with "the new stabilizer formed by the accession of existing neutrals to a league of nations," a more effective continued balance of power might be restored.[35] The plans for the league were still rudimentary, but Croly was hopeful. His former moralism was now projected on an international level: "Those nations who had formerly conceived their highest duty to be that of neutrality in a world of conflicting national ambitions would all acknowledge the higher duty of being aggressive and even belligerent on behalf of the common security. For the first time in the history of Europe it might be less important for any one nation to be powerful than to be right."[36]

Croly's and Lippmann's arguments for peace and the League reinforced Wilson's "peace offensive" in this period, and he in turn signaled appreciation of their efforts. For instance, the *New Republic* had just sent Charles Merz to open a new Washington bureau when Wilson pulled him aside after a press conference and said: "I wish you would write Mr. Croly and Mr. Lippmann and tell them that I appreciate the work they are doing and *that I am in entire agreement with their articles on peace.*"[37]

A high point of this interaction came on January 22, when Wilson made his famous "Peace without Victory" address to the Senate. The president had written on December 18 to all of the warring governments, asking them to state the terms on which they would make peace. He now came, he said, to report to the Senate on the replies, which were sufficiently forthcoming for him to propose U.S. participation in encouraging a general peace settlement.[38]

A central part of Wilson's proposal was that this must be a "peace without victory," that is, that there could be no clear victors and no clear vanquished. The rights of all nations must be recognized, as must the rights of neutrals. Wilson didn't specifically endorse the idea of a league in this speech, but he certainly implied it when he said that the "people and Government of the United States will join the other civilized nations of the world in guaranteeing the permanence of peace."[39] Perhaps most appealing to the liberal journalists at the *New Republic* was the president's comment toward his closing: "May I not add that I hope and believe that I am in effect speaking for liberals and friends of humanity in every nation and of every programme of liberty? I would fain believe that I am speaking for the silent mass of mankind everywhere."[40]

The editors were ecstatic. Wilson had in fact used one of their titles for his speech,[41] and even if that article hadn't really provided the basis of

Wilson's argument, his speech *was* in very close agreement with their general line of argument and included an eloquent appeal to liberals to support an internationalist foreign policy. Colonel House reported to Wilson (perhaps exaggerating, as he often did)[42] about the reaction to the speech: "Lippman[n], Croly, Bainbridge Colby etc. etc. all characterize it in unmeasured terms of praise. Croly told me that he felt that it was the greatest event in his own life."[43] The next day, Croly wrote (if less deliriously): "Dear Mr. President: I should like to add one small word of congratulation to the many letters which you must be receiving. . . . It seems to me that . . . you marshall with great lucidity and eloquence every important fact . . . and every important principle. . . . It is, I am sure, a document which will leave a permanent mark on the moral consciousness of, and I hope in the actual institution, of the American people, and which will reverberate throughout history."[44]

In a passage eerily suggestive of the events of two years later when they would be on different sides, Croly also asked: "May I make one suggestion? There seems to be a tendency among Republicans all over the country, but particularly in Congress, definitely to oppose the participation of the United States in a League of Nations under any conditions. . . . Of course they are making a great mistake in doing this. . . . Would it not be well after Congress adjourns to make a certain number of speeches throughout the country appealing directly to the people?"[45]

Wilson's reply must have provided a most gratifying sense of influence: "My dear Mr. Croly: Your letter of January twenty-third has given me the deepest gratification. I was interested and encouraged when preparing my recent address to the Senate to find an editorial in the New Republic which was not only written along the same lines but which served to clarify and strengthen my thought not a little. In that, as in many other matters, I am your debtor."[46]

Croly was thus once again influential with a major political figure, and he must have been optimistic that his ideas would have real, positive influence. The *New Republic* also benefited from public perception of the editors' influence, and its circulation, which had begun in late 1914 with 875 subscribers and had reached only 17,000 by August 1916,[47] suddenly went over 20,000 and then over 30,000, even reaching as high as 45,000 for some issues in the next few years.[48] The *New Republic* was an influential journal, a leading voice for American liberalism.

Years later, Walter Lippmann downplayed the imputed connection to the Wilson administration:

Our relations with Wilson were never personal. I don't think Croly ever saw Wilson when he was President; in the winter of 1916 I had two or three interviews, such as any journalist has with the President. Croly and I did begin to see something of Colonel House. It was a curious relationship.... He never told us what the President was going to do. We never knew anything that hadn't appeared in the newspapers.... Partly by coincidence, partly by a certain parallelism of reasoning, certainly by no direct inspiration either from the President or Colonel House, The New Republic often advocated policies which Wilson pursued. The legend grew that The New Republic was Wilson's organ, and once to our intense surprise the stock market reacted when an issue of The New Republic appeared on the news stands. The paper was never the organ of the Wilson administration. We never knew any secrets, we never had a request to publish or not to publish anything, and we were not in a confidential relationship. Colonel House made it his business to see all kinds of people, and we were among the people he saw. Occasionally the President and Colonel House took an idea from The New Republic as they took it from many other sources.[49]

These comments may be strictly true, but Lippmann and Croly would probably have phrased them quite differently in early 1917.

THE OPTIMISM of January 1917 was dashed when Germany began unrestricted submarine warfare at the end of the month, breaking the "Sussex Pledge" of the previous year.

The editors, in a special postscript, called for an immediate break in diplomatic relations, for the seizure of German ships, and for plans to aid the Allies economically and militarily. They did not call specifically for a declaration of war, but suggested that was likely: "With all clearness possible the terms and conditions of our entrance into the war should be discussed and announced." Americans must unite: "Partisanship within the country must disappear, and every bit of effort and mind [be] concentrated on clarifying American purpose and making it effective."[50]

Wilson's policies were similar: he broke relations and began mobilization, but waited for two months to take the final step of asking Congress to declare war. In this period of waiting, the editors argued various justifications for American entry if it came, especially the defense of neutral rights.[51] Probably the most significant argument was Lippmann's defense of an "Atlantic community": "What we must fight for is the common interest of the western world, for the integrity of the Atlantic Powers. We must recognize that we are in fact one great community.... Our entrance into it would weight it immeasurably in favor of liberalism, and make the organization of a league for peace an immediately practical object of statesmanship."[52] For all the editors, Germany was a barbarous "rebel nation." Once several American ships were sunk in the new submarine offensive, they hesitated no longer: war was inevitable. "The United States will never have a better justification for declaring that as a consequence of German violence a state of war exists between the two countries."[53] However, the editors made it immediately clear that in their view war could and should not be carried through to the "utter humiliation of Germany. . . . So far as the United States is concerned, it will not be a party to schemes of conquest and subjugation."[54] Croly, Lippmann, and Dewey were willing to justify war, but it must be war with a limited and moral objective.

When Wilson did ask Congress to declare war, the editors supported the decision and pledged their support: "Mr. Wilson is to-day the most liberal statesman in high office. . . . He represents the best hope in the whole world. He can go ahead exultingly with the blessings of men and women upon him."[55]

In private, Croly was pleased with the *New Republic's* role in thinking through these issues and also extremely optimistic about the changes that war might make possible in American society. Writing in response to letters from Willard Straight praising the editors,[56] he replied: "We have, I think, in spite of all our errors been more nearly right than any other paper in the country; and we have exerted a little actual influence. . . . But what a rare opportunity is now opened up, my dear Willard! During the next few years, under the stimulus of the war and its consequences there will be a chance to focus the thought and will of the country on high and fruitful purposes, such as occurs only once in every hundred years. We must all try . . . to make good use of it."[57] Croly was probably never to be so optimistic about politics again.

AMERICAN ENTRY into the war put increased burdens on Croly. Lippmann left the paper in June to become a special assistant to Secretary of War Newton D. Baker. In October, he returned to New York but to participate in "The Inquiry," the research team assembled by Colonel House (and directed by House's brother-in-law, Sidney Mezes) to gather data on all issues likely to be discussed at a peace conference. (Wilson based his "Fourteen Points" speech of January 8, 1918, on work from this group.) In June 1918, Lippmann then left the inquiry team and went to Europe to do propaganda work for the War Department, continuing on as staff support during the Paris Peace Conference.[58] He only returned to the *New Republic* in March 1919, at the close of the conference. Walter Weyl was also often away from the journal, partly because of increasing illness. The result was that Croly carried a large bulk of the political commentary in the war period, often to the point where Willard and Dorothy Straight were concerned about his own health.

Croly always expected that the Allies would win the war, even after Russia's withdrawal.[59] He also remained supportive of Wilson's statement of war objectives. However, as the war progressed, there were a number of points that troubled him deeply. As early as June 1917 he was concerned that the Allies were not as clear in stating their war aims as Wilson had been. Croly rejected the idea that the war should be won before postwar aims were discussed: "This is to reckon without democracy and its insistence upon sufficient reason to justify the sacrifices involved in defeating Germany."[60] Croly particularly wanted a firm Allied commitment to the concept of a league. He became even more concerned about Allied intentions in the fall of 1917, after the Bolshevik government published the "secret treaties" that Russia had signed with her allies in 1914.[61]

At home, Croly supported conscription for the army. Liberals, he argued, must learn to depend on force. "The world cannot afford thus to have liberalism a noncombatant attitude. It must find its roots deep amongst our soldiers."[62] He thus firmly rejected pacifist arguments. However, he became increasingly concerned that America was forgetting Wilson's original aims, which Croly very much saw as insisting upon a limited victory. He wrote that public opinion and "an important section of the American press" were displaying a "blinding bitterness of temper which, if it increases, can only end by making wise decisions concerning [the war] impossible."[63] Croly was finding that the American public did not hold to the middle way of liberalism very consistently. His previous assumptions about the rationality of public opinion were increasingly called into question.

By December 1917 Croly had come to a more radical position, one that very much reflected the moralism of his earlier writings. In a long, signed article, he continued to support the war as based on a "clear violation of right by one of the combatants," but he deplored those who were "fighting jubilantly or thoughtlessly or with absolutely righteous self-satisfaction." To Croly, the heroes were those who fought, "but who have never ceased to regard the performance of that obligation with abhorrence." Croly expressed the depth of his increasing frustration with the war by suggesting a turning away from politics altogether: "If wars are to be prevented, the agency of prevention will not be leagues of peace and political democracy, but a chastening of the human spirit, a profound conviction of the inability of government, even when infused with good will and enlightened by science, to heal the spiritual distempers of mankind."[64]

Croly's positions alarmed some of his associates. Lippmann, now committed to the war effort, noted in his diary a conversation with Croly: "I told him, he couldn't afford to . . . simply express his vexation every week because the war is a brutal and unreasonable thing." Lippmann thought the *New Republic* now "sounded as if it were bored with the war and was ready to snatch at any straw, no matter how thin, which pointed toward peace."[65] But the point was that Croly *did* desire peace—so long as it was a "peace of justice" based on the original war aims that Wilson had stated, and Croly had made that clear from the beginning of the war.

The approach of the end of the war found Croly caught between optimism and pessimism. His optimism depended heavily on Wilson and his continued eloquent defense of a nonpunitive peace, and particularly on what was now called the League of Nations. Wilson restated his positions in a speech at the Metropolitan Opera House on September 27, 1918, which the journal judged "luminous" and "triumphant." Wilson had "infused into his reiterated programme a fresher, larger and more definite meaning. . . . His speech is both an appeal to the peoples of the world for support in building his programme into the structure of an international society and a warning to the statesmen both in friendly and in enemy countries not to stand in the way." Wilson "must insist on impartial justice for a beaten Germany," a policy which would "bring about revolutionary changes in the traditional relationship among nations."[66]

But Wilson's task was not easy. Even at home, other leaders had other views. For example, Senator Henry Cabot Lodge had recently issued a statement that in Croly's view "did not propose to be just. . . . On the contrary, he planned to use victory for the purpose of writing into the treaty of peace discrimination against Germany. He confuses justice with punishment."[67] Croly also wrote to Hand about his forebodings about the Allies: "The indications are increasing day by day that our friends abroad have not the slightest intention of writing anything but a punitive peace, and they will do this with Mr. Wilson's consent if possible, or against it if necessary. In that case, any League of Nations formed as a result of the war would merely be an organization for force."[68] A lot would depend on Woodrow Wilson.

BEFORE EXAMINING the results of the Versailles Conference and Croly's break with Wilson, we need to consider his views on two policies at home during the war, government regulation of the economy and the increased censorship practiced by the Wilson administration, and on a major international development, the Russian revolution. All of these were important in defining Croly's liberalism during the war and the postwar period.

For Croly, as for many progressives,[69] the war was an important opportunity to advance many previous policies. From the beginning, the editors emphasized the need for government control over the economy. As they often reiterated: "The war has thrust upon us the necessity of extending the power of government over our economic life."[70] An important part of this policy was government ownership of the railroads. This was the perfect opportunity to put into practice what Croly had long favored— complete government control of this vital industry.[71] The editors also favored government recognition and organization of labor and welcomed the "loyal co-operation of the workers" in the war effort.[72] They also called for financing the war through higher income and inheritance taxes, as opposed to a heavy reliance on borrowing.[73] The claims of social justice required that the wealthy should carry a major part of the war's costs.

Many of these themes are summarized in a January 1918 article (clearly written by Croly). Government nationalization of the railroads and of ocean shipping and greatly increased control of the coal mines and of food supplies are all praised as working well. Also praised are the "official attempt to recognize organized labor and to secure its loyal cooperation . . . [and the] schedule of taxation for large incomes and excess profits, which a few years ago would have been considered sheer confiscation." These changes in the American economy reflected many of Croly's previous goals. But they were not necessarily permanent: "Those who look with favor on the increasing nationalization of the business and labor organization of the country have no right to demand that innovations . . . during the war be retained." However, "they are entitled to demand that automatic restoration of the status quo ante should not be promised or expected."[74] The war thus might usher in a new economic system. Croly couldn't resist adding that "every one of these emergency measures was adopted to meet evils in the old system to which its critics had long called attention in vain and which the war had rendered intolerable."[75] In this respect, the war was a progressive force for liberalism.

The issue of censorship was a totally different story. Croly and the other editors had been somewhat worried from the beginning about the effects of war propaganda.[76] By October 1917 they were extremely concerned: "How is it possible to pretend that a war conducted in such a spirit can make for enduring peace?" they asked. In the editors' view, "the government cannot escape some measure of responsibility for the ugly and sinister mask which is being fastened on the face of American patriotism. . . . It was not prepared to resist a militarist agitation which was dangerous to its work on behalf of enduring peace, and it could think of no answer to an agitation in favor of immediate peace except violent suppression."[77]

Among the policies they protested were the suppression under the Espionage Act of the Industrial Workers of the World (I.W.W.) in the summer of 1917 and the denial of mailing privileges to socialist papers in the fall of that year. As John Dewey wrote in all-too-prophetic words: "It behooves liberals who believe in the war to be more aggressive than they have been in their opposition to those reactionaries who also believe in war. . . . Let the liberal who for expediency's sake would passively tolerate invasions of free speech and action, take counsel lest he be also preparing the way for a later victory of domestic Toryism."[78]

Croly also wrote directly to Wilson: "The censorship over public opinion which is now being exercised through the Post Office Department is, I think, really hurting the standing of the war in relation to American public opinion." Croly went on to protest the suppression of socialist papers and suggested instead that the government "negotiate with the Socialist press and persuade them to keep their agitation within certain limits without at the same time forcing them to abandon . . . their convictions."[79] Croly noted that the New Republic had even come in for criticism and therefore found it difficult to state the moderate position that he was sure Wilson shared: "We are constantly being crowded between two extremes. When we try to draw attention to the pacific and constructive purposes which underlie American participation in the war we are accused of being half-hearted, and even of being pro-German, and we necessarily do look half-hearted as compared to the war propagandists."[80]

Croly clearly had written a careful letter, framed as coming from a supporter with common objectives. Wilson's cold, formal reply to the effect that Postmaster General Albert S. Burleson had been "misunderstood" and that he was "inclined to be most conservative in the exercise of these great and dangerous powers,"[81] coupled with Wilson's sponsorship of the Espionage Act in the first place, must have been very worrisome to Croly.[82]

As the war drew to a close, patriotic fervor built, and the incidents of repression increased. The New Republic was quite explicit in response. For example, in June 1918 the editors remarked that America was winning the war, but "might still be losing her democratic soul. Intolerance of minority opinion, blind hatred for . . . enemy peoples might be steadily undermining our morale as a free people."[83] In this period, the Nation was denied mailing privileges at least once, and Croly was afraid the New Republic would be also. He wrote to Dorothy Straight: "I received from an indirect but authoritative source a threat that the N.R. was in danger of suppression, because we published the advertisement signed by John Dewey and others, asking for the means to secure to the I.W.W. a fair trial. . . . What do you think of that?"[84]

Croly could sometimes make light of the situation, as in writing to H. L. Mencken that "so far from wishing to burleson it, we have decided to publish your article immediately."[85] But he knew the seriousness of the principle and drew on his friendships with Frankfurter and Hand to persuade Zechariah Chafee of Harvard to do a careful analysis of the legal basis of the Espionage Act, the law under which Burleson was acting. Chafee's research was published in several long articles in the *New Republic* and led to his later extended and important work on free speech.[86]

After the war, the censorship issue continued and in fact grew during the "Red Scare" of 1919 and 1920. The *New Republic* stood strongly against the tide, attacking mobs that broke up socialist meetings and the establishment acquiescence in and even encouragement of such behavior: "The really dangerous revolutionists in America at the present moment are those conservatives who are wantonly and frivolously overthrowing the moral supports of the American democracy."[87] The editors opposed the deportation of aliens, continually hammered at the free speech issue, and called for the release of Eugene V. Debs from prison.[88]

Perhaps the intellectual culmination of the *New Republic*'s stand against the Red Scare came in Croly's strong support of Justice Holmes's dissent (Brandeis concurring) in *Abrams v. United States* (250 U.S. 616; 1919), in which the conviction of Jacob Abrams for distributing circulars critical of Wilson's policy of sending troops into Russia was upheld by a majority of the Court under the Espionage Act.

In this famous dissent, Holmes challenged the developing series of cases in which the Supreme Court had upheld restrictions on free speech in wartime. Holmes had stated his famous "clear and present danger" standard in *Schenck v. United States* (249 U.S. 47; 1919), where he wrote for the Court in upholding Schenck's conviction for distributing leaflets to draftees opposing conscription. Holmes had reiterated this standard in again upholding the government in *Debs v. United States* (249 U.S. 211; 1919). However, he had subsequently been influenced to reconsider his views by discussions with Learned Hand, Chafee, and Harold Laski (all New Republicans), by articles in the *New Republic* by Chafee and Ernst Freund, and by his own dismay at the developing hysteria. The result was what Holmes's most recent biographer has called one of the "most-quoted justifications for freedom of expression in the English-speaking world."[89] Holmes argued in *Abrams* that "the best test of truth is the power of the thought to get itself accepted in the competition of the market. . . . I think we should be eternally vigilant against attempts to check the expressions of opinions that we loathe."[90]

Croly's response to the *Abrams* dissent was enthusiastic. He praised Holmes's "clear and imminent danger" standard as a reasonable balance between the need for order and individual rights and argued that Abrams's behavior did not exceed this standard. Croly also affirmed Holmes's pragmatic reasoning: the Constitution "is an experiment associated with certain convictions about government and property and human liberty which cannot be more than tentatively true at any one time, but which, if the American Republic is to remain a free democracy, American public opinion must constantly re-adjust in the light of its collective experience." At the same time, Croly sought to reaffirm the "traditional American ideal of toleration of opinion" and the "constitutional safeguards on freedom of speech."[91]

Croly's stand against the Espionage Act and the "many outrageous cases" under that act,[92] and against the Red Scare in general, was a major contribution to American liberalism. As Walter Lippmann later recalled:

> The most exhilarating experience we had, as I look back now, was the resistance of The New Republic in 1919 and 1920 to the Red hysteria. It is difficult today to remember the idiotic intolerance which descended upon the country in those days. . . . It was the most disgraceful exhibition of general cowardice and panic which any of us is likely to experience. The New Republic stood firm and took its punishment, and the credit is Herbert Croly's. He had the cold courage of a man who does not enjoy martyrdom. He was as brave and as imperturbable as any editor can hope to be. I have no pleasanter memory than of those days with Herbert Croly.[93]

Major factors in the Red Scare were, of course, the Russian revolution of 1917 and the postwar fear in the West that bolshevism would spread to central Europe and even to some of the Allied countries themselves.

The editors' initial response to the February–March revolution overthrowing the czar was most positive. It came as a "great victory" in the dark period of the war, for "the most corrupt government, the most detestable despotism, which has survived among the nations of the modern world" was ended. As long as the czarist regime survived, "true liberalism, wherever it existed . . . could count on one ultimate and uncompromising enemy."[94] In succeeding months, however, the editors were disturbed at the provisional government's seeming willingness to make what they viewed as a too easy peace with Germany.[95] However, the *New Republic* opposed early "White" reactions and supported the Provisional Government and Alexander Kerensky as a promising democratic alternative.[96]

The journal's reaction to the Bolshevik November revolution was muted, in part because information was scarce and the editors were not sure how permanent the regime was. However, they continued to deplore (out of American self-interest, they admitted) the willingness to make a separate peace. They continued to hope that the Constituent Assembly in Russia, which they termed the "last symbol of progressive nationalism," could stand against the Bolsheviks.[97] But they also supported Wilson's abortive attempt to establish ties to the "Moscow Soviet" as an appropriate contact between democracies. "The American democracy has no reason to fear the revolutionary ferment, has, indeed, every reason to encourage the people of Russia in their efforts at emancipation."[98]

Holding to liberalism's "middle way," the editors made it clear that they did not support the Bolsheviks: "The New Republic holds no brief for the present leadership of the Russian Revolution. . . . We consider the social and political programmes of the Bolsheviki wholly unsound, and wherever a general or sustained attempt is made to put them into practice the result would in our opinion be calamitous." Or as they later remarked, "the ideal of Lenin, if realized, does not appear to us a beautiful ideal."[99]

But they strongly opposed United States military intervention in Russia in a series of editorials over the several years when that policy was discussed and implemented.[100] Indeed, at the height of the Red Scare, the *New Republic* published a long article comparing its own beliefs to communism. The editors rejected communism but also rejected American fears of it, appealing to "our governments and ruling class press" to "abandon the incredibly stupid, arbitrary, timid policy of treating the Russian Bolshevik organization as an ideal so seductive as to draw to itself everybody who is permitted to know anything about it." It was, the editors urged, "not our business to go crusading for our particular conception of social and political organization."[101]

George F. Kennan later wrote that the *New Republic* had "no monopoly on the expression of American liberal thought in the years 1917–1920. . . . But there was certainly no more powerful and lucid voice within this camp than that of the remarkable circle of men grouped around Herbert Croly in the editorial rooms of the *New Republic*." In Kennan's view, "their vision had its imperfections," but he concludes that "had the views of the *New Republic* on the Russian problem in the final stages and aftermath of World War I been heeded, the Western governments could have saved themselves some grievous mistakes. . . . What more could the editors of a weekly journal hope to have said of their labors from a distance of forty years?"[102]

THE CRISIS in the *New Republic*'s foreign policy came with the publication of the Versailles Conference peace treaty and the editors' very difficult and painful decision to oppose ratification. The journal had argued that the war was being fought for a better world, and they had consistently supported Wilson's framing of the issues, which they took to insist that the treaty not embody the conservative, nationalistic aims they saw as so prevalent in both Europe and America. If it did express these aims, it would fail to lay the basis for a just and lasting peace. Indeed, the editors were prescient in predicting that a policy forcing a punitive peace on the Central Powers would encourage their peoples both to seek revenge and to embrace bolshevism.

Croly and his associates were fearful in late 1918 that their ideals would not be realized.[103] They admitted that Wilson had weakened his own political position at home by failing to include the Senate in the negotiation process: "He never sufficiently shared his responsibility with those of his fellow countrymen who were entitled to share it. . . . He is left dangerously isolated."[104]

However, on the eve of the peace conference, Croly still defended the possibility of a moderate peace combined with a league of nations. In response to charges that he was trying to throw away "the legitimate fruit of victory," Croly recalled Wilson's "Peace without Victory" speech. Abandonment of the ideals that Wilson had articulated then would simply yield a "Victory without Peace"—it would only set the stage for a new war. Croly wrote that "the immediate outlook, be it admitted, is not cheerful. The victorious statesmen who are about to assemble in Paris have not learned what should be for them the ultimate lesson of the war. . . . They betray little or no disposition to repent and reform." Invoking an increasingly heavy religious imagery, Croly continued: "They have failed to divine that unless their work begins in contrition, renunciation and prayer they will betray the millions of young men who have expiated with their lives the past sins of European statesmen." For Croly, the "issue is being clearly drawn between the friends and the enemies of international socialization." He concluded by appealing that "that the law of retaliation may be renounced and men will look candidly and trustingly into one another's eyes."[105]

Several months of international and domestic skirmishing ensued, with the New Republic essentially defending the administration position,[106] while urging Wilson to hold firm to his principles.[107]

In late April, just before the treaty was to be made public, Croly again summed up his thought in a long article that both contains increasingly radical political positions and illustrates his increasing reliance on religion. It was, he wrote, "chiefly capitalism which is on trial at the Peace Conference." If the Allies continued to try to extract too high reparations and other punishments from Germany, "they condemn the German nation to revolutionary socialism." Croly proposed that political power must be shared with the workers in all the advanced democracies. If power and economic resources were thus shared, "the social democratic common-wealth will for the first time have a fair chance." Claiming that his pre-scription was "precisely the opposite of Marxian socialism," and that the conferees by their stubbornness were really aiding bolshevism, Croly suggested in his conclusion that a middle way between "unredeemed capitalism and revolutionary socialism" should come from the Christian religion. The conferees "must reach towards the peremptory gospel of human brotherhood."[108]

In early May, the feared event occurred: the treaty was made public, and it was clear to Croly that the peace was punitive. To make matters worse, President Wilson argued that his original statement of war aims was embodied in this peace. Croly led his editorial board to the decision that the treaty violated everything they had stood for over the last two years, and that they must oppose its ratification. As Lippmann later re-called:

> The decision to oppose ratification was Croly's. I followed him, though I was not then, and am not now, convinced that it was the wise thing to do. That the Treaty was a deplorable breach of faith was clear; the question was whether the Covenant of the League was an instrument for perpetuating or for correcting the evils of the Treaty. We decided that it would perpetuate them if America ratified, where-as if America abstained, revision was inevitable. . . . A strong case can be made for and against this view. If I had to do it all over again I would take the other side; we supplied the Battalion of Death with too much ammunition.[109]

Croly's own thoughts were summarized in "Peace at any Price." He was both unbending and consistent in his arguments: "If liberals and humane American democrats who seek by social experiment and educa-tion to render their country more worthy of its still unredeemed national promise" were to "connive at this treaty," they would "be delivering themselves into the hands of their enemies, the reactionaries and the revolutionists." Croly returned to an old theme: "The future of liberal Americanism depends upon a moral union between democracy and na-tionalism." But he explained it in more radical ways: "Such a union is compromised so long as nationalism remains competitive in policy, exclu-sive in spirit and complacently capitalist in organization."[110]

The betrayal of Wilson's original war aims thus pushed Croly to a more radical position. America's allies had proven themselves unrecon-structed nationalists, unmoved by morality or even long-range considerations of self-interest. Perhaps even worse, America's liberal leader, Woodrow Wilson, had concluded and then endorsed this peace; Croly's national executive had betrayed his own principles. Finally, public opinion, on which Croly had previously depended to check governmental power, had shown itself dangerously receptive to the most primitive kind of nationalist hysteria. Very substantial elements of Croly's political theory were thus severely challenged.

Croly admitted that "the Treaty of Versailles subjects all liberalism and particularly that kind of liberalism which breathes the Christian spirit to a decisive test. Its very life depends upon the ability of the modern national state to avoid . . . irreconcilable class conflict to which, as the Socialists claim, capitalism condemns the future of society. In the event of such a conflict, liberalism is ground, as it is being ground in Russia, between the upper and lower millstones of reaction and revolution." He concluded that "it is essential that the ratification should not take place with the connivance of the sincerely liberal and Christian forces in public opinion. . . . Liberal democrats cannot honestly consent to peace on the proposed terms." Not even the League of Nations, which Croly supported, could save this punitive peace.[111]

The discussion of the treaty persisted for many months. The *New Republic* hoped at times that a compromise might be reached in the ratification process, but the intransigence of Wilson on the one side and Senator Lodge and the even more extreme senators in the "Battalion of Death" on the other allowed the tragedy to continue. The editors were particularly concerned to show that Wilson's speeches after the treaty were not at all consistent with his previous positions, and that he had thus failed as a negotiator, however understandable that failure was. Wilson's suffering a stroke on the very kind of cross-country campaign that Croly had suggested two years earlier put an end to any hope that he might be willing and able to reverse things.[112]

The Republican Senate soon completed the rout. As the editors wrote, the European authors of the treaty had seemed to argue "that the old-fashioned diplomacy of the secret treaties was valid for Europe while the newer ideal of the League was valid for America." By its insistence on reservations, even then failing to ratify, "the Senate liquidated the inconsistency." The final verdict was clear: "There is no permanence in any of it."[113] The end of the tragedy (or perhaps the beginning of the next act) came with the election of Warren G. Harding in November 1920.

Developments in foreign policy—a field that Croly had come close to ignoring before 1914—had thus forced many changes in his theory and ultimately brought him to question a number of fundamental assumptions. The war had initially led him to move further from his nationalist positions of 1909. Indeed, Croly and his associates were instrumental in influencing American liberalism to adopt an internationalist perspective, emphasizing the importance of international institutions as a limit to national self-interest. This identification of liberalism with an internationalism that provided a middle road between isolationism and imperialism was certainly important for later American liberalism. However, the failure of Wilson's policy and in particular the popular hysteria during the Red Scare forced Croly to reexamine his rather optimistic assumptions that a national executive, restrained by democratic public opinion, could bring liberal progressivism to fruition. Instead, the experiences of the war taught that personal liberties needed stronger support against public opinion, as the classical liberals had argued. They also taught that liberalism's basic assumptions needed to be rethought.

8

Liberalism in
an "Age of Normalcy"

By the beginning of 1920, Croly was a chastened and discouraged man. He had supported American participation in the war but was appalled at its cost in lives and at the disastrous peace treaty that marked its conclusion. He had trusted in the liberalism of Woodrow Wilson, only to find that liberalism betrayed in the repression of the Espionage Act and in the war hysteria and Red Scare of American public opinion. Croly's editorials from mid-1918 on had shown a growing radicalism in politics and an increased emphasis on religion, and the end of the war further emphasized these points. Clearly events were forcing a rethinking of some of Croly's most fundamental assumptions about politics and about human nature. His liberalism needed to be restated in response to the war and its attendant results.

Croly used a series of *New Republic* editorials to develop his reevaluation, but he also felt the need to return to the more extended and flexible format of a book. Sometime in late 1918 or early 1919, Croly began work on a new book, *The Breach in Civilization*. This work was in fact written and even typeset. It was scheduled for publication in March 1920,[1] but Croly was dissatisfied with the argument, and publication was first postponed to the fall and eventually the book was withdrawn. As Croly wrote to Learned Hand: "The trouble was I had written it in the same state of mind as if I was dealing with the matter in a long editorial."[2] Whatever the reason for withdrawing *The Breach*, we have portions of the manuscript,[3] and Croly's views are evident in this manuscript and in his editorials.

Croly's indictment of the failures of liberalism was severe. "In 1914," he wrote, no doubt thinking of his own *Progressive Democracy,* "there was much excuse for the inability of liberals to understand how far liberalism had failed and why. . . . A liberal could still plausibly cherish the illusion that modern industrialism was flexible, tolerant, realistic and both able and willing, if not to prevent war, at least to limit and localize its destructive effects."[4] Croly blamed "property owners" for much of the reaction, but government was not exempt. In 1914, a liberal "could still maintain with some show of reason that the democratic state, even though it did and must insist on immediate obedience, did not make its own safety depend upon persecuting and exterminating people who had honest moral scruples against the righteousness of its behavior."[5] As he wrote in an autobiographical passage a few years later: "I among others imputed to the thoroughly democratic commonwealth the power to contribute enormously and speedily to human welfare. It was a mistake."[6]

After the war and the resulting popular hysteria, "candid liberals no longer possess any sufficient excuse for the cherishing of these illusions." The extent of Croly's own disillusionment was shown in one of the most bitter sentences he ever wrote: "The calamity of the past five years constitutes a naked and ultimate exposure of the moral wilderness which irresponsible industrialism, democracy, stateism, newspaper propaganda and applied science can make of human behavior."[7] This remarkable list, which included some of Croly's own former cherished beliefs, illustrates the depth of his anguish in these immediate postwar years.

CROLY NARROWED the issues somewhat in twin editorials published in the fall of 1920, one concentrating on domestic issues and one reflecting on the war. His points were further influenced by his disgust at the presidential election of 1920, which was a further disaster for liberals: "The chief distinguishing aspect of the Presidential campaign of 1920 is the eclipse of liberalism or progressivism as an effective force in American politics."[8]

Croly's prescription for domestic politics was that liberals must perceive "the need of adopting a more radical and realistic view of the nature and object of a liberal agitation under the conditions of the American democracy." Most important, they must recognize class divisions in society more fully than previously. Croly noted that the "propertied class" was strongly advantaged by existing political and economic institutions, and the state "has done nothing to prevent" this imbalance and the resulting class cleavages. Liberalism had failed to focus on this issue: "Liberalism has always believed that popular self-government can ultimately overcome such a partial appropriation of the state by one class."[9] In practice, however, public opinion had been too easily won over to illiberal ends, which often supported the dominant economic class.

Croly's analysis was thus becoming more class-oriented, and even tending toward a Marxist view that the state was simply the creature of the dominant class. However, he resisted that ultimate conclusion. Of the former liberal assumptions that a democratic government could overcome class divisions, he wrote: "I would be the last to suggest the abandonment of this article in the liberal creed." However, at least temporarily, stronger measures were necessary. "Just at present popular self-government is sick . . . it lacks the recuperative power to come to the assistance of a divided society. Class cleavage born of one-class domination itself poisons the democratic government." The answer was that "political democracy must call to its assistance social and industrial democracy in order to regain its health."[10] The power of business must be fought in the economic as well as the political arena.

Croly went on to argue that liberals needed to ally with "the one group whose interests, whose numbers and whose existing social disenfranchisement qualify it to redress the balance . . . the workers." He called for a "redistribution of power among classes" to set the stage for "an ultimate class concert. For labor and liberalism alike, class rule, disguised by protective coloration to look like traditional democracy, is the common enemy. They need to make common cause against it."[11]

In calling for an alliance with "the workers," Croly was moving slightly away from his previous assumptions, yet it is clear even in this immediate postwar period that Croly continued to hold to a view of liberalism as a "middle way," and that he continued to support the ultimate (if not the immediate) goal of progress for the society as a whole rather than of any one group or class. American democracy must "[credit] to the organized workers a salutary social purpose which transcends class interests but which under the circumstances they cannot attain without class organization and consciousness."[12]

Croly thought that this bargain had already been struck in England: "A large fraction of the English liberals have already assumed this attitude towards the labor movement. They have joined the Labor party and so created a fighting organization."[13] Croly endorsed the Farmer-Labor candidate in the 1920 election as the American equivalent of the "Lib-Lab" collaboration in England.

LIBERALISM DID NOT need simply a domestic reformulation. In a parallel article, Croly attempted to summarize his thoughts on the war and on the larger issue of the relation of war and liberalism.

Croly was stung by immediate criticism from the *Nation* commenting on his previous editorial. The *Nation* had charged that "the temporary [death] knell of American liberalism was sounded the minute its false leader [Wilson] put it into the war. This fact naturally does not appeal to the *New Republic*, because its editors have boasted that they helped to put the country into the struggle."[14]

The *Nation* may have been the immediate critic, but Croly must also have been thinking of the charges that his former associate on the *New Republic*, Randolph Bourne, had levied in 1917 against the journal, and especially against John Dewey, who had written several pieces supporting the war and the possibilities it offered for reorganization of the country. Bourne had charged that Dewey's (and Croly's) rational pragmatism did not provide an effective philosophy for analyzing a fundamental moral issue such as war, one in which irrational forces would be loosed. Bourne had asked: "Is not war perhaps the one social absolute, the one situation where the [instrumental] choice of ends ceases to function?"[15] He had gone on to argue that since "war is the health of the State," pacifism was the only proper answer.[16]

Croly hadn't answered these arguments at all directly during the war, but now he responded to the *Nation*'s charges by admitting some points in the indictment but holding firm on the central issue. He reviewed his own position on the war at some length, arguing as he had previously that America necessarily had an effect on the outcome of the war whether she joined or stayed out. The realities of international politics required that a great power play some role in a world war. Croly wrote that he had eventually supported American intervention, "but intervention conditioned on the acceptance by the Allies of a program of international conciliation." Wilson in fact did seek entry with the same object, Croly asserted.[17]

What, then, went wrong? Croly wrote that he had expected the Allied governments to push for a punitive peace, as they did. However, "the miscalculation in my own case consisted chiefly in false anticipation of what the psychology of the American people would be. . . . I assumed that they would preserve even during so terrible a war a somewhat disinterested American point of view. . . . These suppositions proved to be wrong. Although the President continued to wave his program of pacification as a justification . . . , the American nation as a whole thought only of victory and little of its supposed political objects." Wilson had therefore sailed for France to do battle with the Allies "severely handicapped by the opposition and misunderstanding of his fellow-countrymen. The insecurity of his position betrayed him into the fatal error of consenting to a vindictive Treaty."[18]

This analysis explained what had happened in 1917–1919, but what did it prove about the larger issues? Here Croly again held firm: "The endorsement of any war does not sound the `knell' of any and all liberalism." Many, perhaps most, wars *are* illiberal. Yet, "wars sometimes occur without creating or implying militarism or at least without implying the kind and amount of militarism which is dangerous to our traditional anaemic liberalism. Wars have even occurred whose purposes and effects are inimical to militarism and helpful in the long run to what is known as liberalism."[19] Some wars were therefore justified.

Croly went on to reargue a position not very different from his previous internationalism, or from Wilson's "making the world safe for democracy": "The positive and permanent justification of American intervention from the liberal point of view consists in the extent to which it committed America to initiating and participating in the coming experiments in pacific international organization. Non-intervention would have confirmed an unreal isolation."[20] He thus continued to support what we might call a "realist" interpretation of America's necessary international position, as well as to argue that some wars were morally acceptable. Croly therefore disagreed with the *Nation*'s analysis in several respects. It was true that the World War was awful.[21] However, Croly continued to argue that *some* wars could be fought for justifiable ends, and he argued that pacifism was impractical in international politics, as well as morally unconvincing.

While Croly thus held to the essentials of his 1917 position in international politics, he was set back by the inherent dynamics of war and also by the ways in which he, Lippmann, Dewey, and Wilson had miscalculated American public opinion. Liberals had been overly optimistic about these matters, and the most fundamental lesson for Croly was not that war was wrong, but that liberals needed to reexamine their liberalism. A more thoughtful, better grounded liberalism might head off some wars, and it would offer firmer guidance and play a stronger influence on public opinion when one was necessary. Croly urged his fellow liberals to turn to this task of rethinking liberal assumptions.

CROLY'S OWN SEARCH for a firmer foundation for liberalism in *The Breach in Civilization* led him through a lengthy (and somewhat confused) historical examination, such as he had undertaken in his previous books—only now it was not American history he studied but European. Focusing particularly on the Protestant Reformation, Croly argued that Western thought had "erected in the sanctuary of modern civilization an altar to ignorant and irresponsible individualism."[22] Liberalism had been born out of, and partly in reaction to, the Reformation, inheriting the same individualism but relying on "science" instead of religion. "Complete reliance on natural science distinguishes what came to be known as liberalism from other doctrines of salvation."[23]

Croly's historical analysis purported to show that political liberalism had gone astray when it adopted the "hedonistic psychology" of utilitarianism. He thought hedonism an insufficient picture of human nature, "for man is not merely a pleasure-seeking pain-avoiding animal."[24] In recent years, the individualism of utilitarianism had been properly superseded, but its psychology still prevailed. Thus Croly argued that liberals hadn't thought through fully enough what the psychological and philosophical basis of a "reformist liberalism" could be.[25]

This rethinking was particularly important because Croly assumed that liberalism now relied on state intervention in social and economic issues. Laissez-faire was a doctrine of the past, and liberals were for positive government: "The great majority of what are called liberals at the present time are, indeed, occupied in calling upon the government to safeguard society against the abuses of capitalism. They have abandoned their former distrust of collective interference and their former faith in unregulated individualism. They are conceiving the state . . . as the positive and indispensable agency of social democracy." But this dependence on the state, when "proposed by liberals, demands a modification of the formative principles of the older liberalism more profound than its advocates seem to realize."[26] The "new school of liberals" (presumably including Herbert Croly in his earlier writings) "did not pause to discuss" these issues. They were content to "fall back uncritically on the state as the conscious agency of individual and social liberation." In so doing, they played into the hands of their enemies, the "property owning class," who used the state rather as an instrument of class aggression than of class concert.[27]

Croly asked: "Assuming the government must interfere, what authoritative ideal of human behavior can it call to its assistance?"[28] In other words, what principles *were* available to guide the needed state action? The central part of Croly's proposed reformulation of liberalism consisted of his attempt to answer this question, and his answer comprised a combination of what to him was a more modern psychology than utilitarianism, a psychology emphasizing the role of self-consciousness, with a sort of socialized Christianity.

Croly struggled to make this combination clear in the many articles and manuscripts he wrote in the last decade of his life, but he was never fully satisfied with its expression. We will focus on the topics of religion and psychology separately but a few passages may make clear Croly's attempt to tie these points to liberalism. Thus in 1921, he wrote: "If liberals and radicals are ever to infuse into public opinion the . . . knowledge which the carrying out of any thoroughgoing program of social reconstruction demands, they will have to abandon . . . problems of power. They will have to substitute . . . a search for an increasing knowledge of human behavior. . . . And this substitution will be equivalent [to getting] . . . human beings to believe in the reality and the necessity of human salvation."[29] Or in words familiar from *The Promise*, a 1922 article claimed that "the fulfillment of their [Americans'] national promise will . . . become an exploration of the undeveloped possibilities of human nature—an exploration which . . . will demand physiological and psychological inquiry, social experiment, literary and artistic expression, and in the end something in the nature of religious regeneration."[30] Or as another article put it: "Liberals have no alternative but to seek human regeneration by the introduction of some effective method into their own personal conscious effort to lead a good life. They must somehow derive from their consciousness of the actual processes of living a liberating knowledge. . . . They can furnish the world with the example of a man who by self-acquired knowledge of himself and the world has achieved the captaincy of his soul."[31]

At times, Croly's search wandered fairly far from politics. He was, he wrote in 1923, "sick of politics": "The chief function of the wise liberal during the next generation is to investigate the ability of individuals and groups to bring about an improved quality of human relation by other than political means."[32] This knowledge, in turn, could lead to a more sure knowledge of human behavior and eventually to a more effective political strategy.

Croly's rejection of politics—at least in the short run—is particularly clear immediately after the 1924 election, in which the poor showing of Robert M. LaFollette's Progressive Party was a further discouragement.[33] Calling himself both a liberal and a progressive in these years, Croly sought to distinguish these terms. The *New Republic* should "dissociate its own use of the word [liberal] from any necessary alliance with practical politics and to identify it with a philosophy and method of individual and social conduct."[34] A *New Republic* associate, George Soule, later wrote of Croly's "conclusion that liberalism must be distinguished from political progressivism. Liberalism was really a mental attitude. . . . In his later years, Herbert Croly was careful not to apply the word liberal to any political movement. And he valued the content which he gave it above any specific political aims."[35]

A partial exception to this point is a quite interesting series of articles that Croly wrote on liberalism in the fall of 1927.[36] Here Croly partially reasserted his political theory of liberalism and also displayed a more hopeful outlook than he had in 1920 or 1924. He argued once more for a

middle way between the dogmatic extremes of a "class conscious capitalist" and a "militant socialist." Liberals refused to believe in an inevitable
class struggle, and their toleration and avoidance of "dogmatic prophecy"
was needed to head off the class division increasingly evident both in
fascism in Italy and communism in Russia.

Croly asserted that America was particularly liberal: "The United
States was born liberal. It was the first national state whose founders set
up an operating balance in the law and government between liberty and
authority and so sought to prevent class struggles from becoming irreconcilable."[37] Liberals needed to reassert this heritage in these troubled times.

Two weeks later, Croly again focused on class issues, attacking capitalism for not allowing workers to lead a more full life (again suggesting
but not developing a theory of "positive freedom"). But liberals should
not depend on a class analysis: "What a wholesome society needs is not
the domination of any one class but an adjustable balance among the
classes."[38]

In response to letters from readers, Croly took up the issue again in a
third article. After again asserting that America had been founded in the
spirit of liberalism, Croly argued that "what liberals need is not a new
concrete political or social program. They need a new evaluation of all
programs . . . a new method of giving reality to them." Liberals haven't yet
been "asked to revolutionize and reform the inside of their own minds."
This lack of intellectual insight meant that most liberals were inevitably
superficial in their views, however worthy their immediate programs:
"Even those people who labor for the social welfare or agitate for disinterested causes rarely rise above moral and intellectual mediocrity."[39]

Croly asserted the importance of his own search: "What liberals need
to practice, then, is some activity of the mind which will increase the ad-
equacy and self-possession of their personal lives while, at the same
time, throwing light upon the adjustment of the individual to other individuals and to the world." Liberalism was failing because liberals hadn't
thought through the foundations of their theory: "The doubts and defeats
from which liberalism is now suffering are traceable to the neglect by
liberals of this truth. . . . Opinions about social affairs and projects of social
welfare are, and will remain, rationalization of economic interests or some
other mechanism of human behavior unless individuals can neutralize the
controlling effects which unconscious motives now exert on their conduct and thinking."[40] A conscious exploration of our own mind, then,
aided by religion might provide a firmer long-term foundation for political liberalism.

These articles show the direction of Croly's search in his last years. He
was trying to formulate his ideas clearly enough to write another book,[41]

but he was not able to do so. The formulations in the articles of the fall of 1927 are thus Croly's final published attempt to describe his vision of liberalism, for a year later he had a paralyzing stroke, and eighteen months after that he was dead.

RELIGION WAS an important part of Croly's search in his last years. He wrote of his own belief in 1920: "When I was a young man I possessed for a few months a vision of religious truth . . . which subsequently . . . became dim and almost expired. It is only recently that I really began to believe again."[42] Leonard Elmhirst, Dorothy Straight's second husband, who knew Croly well in these years, later wrote that the "essential Croly" was "his belief in the regeneration of mankind and his certainty that the powers of evil can have only temporary victories."[43]

Many of Croly's long-time associates were distressed by his search for religious truth. Learned Hand, for example, wrote to Graham Wallas in 1921 that the *New Republic* was "getting a bit over evangelical."[44] Harold J. Laski reported to Justice Holmes that "Croly has the religious bug very badly."[45] Later he wrote that "Croly is really a big fellow, patient, curious, sincere, and penetrating." But he also noted again: "I must say he seems to me heavy and immovable; and there is about him a queer streak of religiosity I don't understand."[46]

In part, Croly's interest in religion in these years was expressed in his participation in a number of Christian conferences, many of them focusing at least in part on the social mission of the church. Croly occasionally reported on these conferences in the *New Republic*. For example, in 1924 he published a long article on a conference on the "Christian Way of Life." "The major object of the conference . . . ," he wrote, "was to arouse professing Christians to the need of associating the salvation of the individual soul with some measure of social amelioration and to inquire what Christians should do in order to give reality to their religion in social conduct."[47] Croly also carried on an active correspondence with the leaders of this conference and participated in a commission on international relations that reported to the conference.[48]

Croly sought to work out his own personal beliefs in a series of manuscripts in these years, many of them exploring the relation of Christianity and liberalism. For example, in a forty-page manuscript entitled "Religion in Life," he argued for the inadequacy of either alone: "Liberalism and Christianity are, consequently, fighting a losing battle with a secularism which is indifferent both to the humanitarianism of the liberals and the personal salvationism of the traditional Christianity."[49] In this manuscript, Croly again advocates a psychology of self-study: "The experiment, consequently, which is to my mind clearly indicated . . . is an experiment in systematic self-observation as an essential and continuous part of the very process of living." He noted that "those who search for self-knowledge and self-development through self-observation must assume the indefinite elasticity of consciousness."[50]

Some of Croly's interest in self-observation also arose from less traditional religious ties. He was attracted for a while, along with Dorothy Straight, Amos Pinchot, Mabel Dodge Luhan, and many others, to the teachings of the Russian mystic Gurdjieff and his disciple A. R. Orage, a London editor who traveled often to New York.[51] Gurdjieff claimed to have a "method" for penetrating and expanding one's own consciousness. Orage held meetings that Croly attended to explore this method. According to T. S. Matthews, a *New Republic* associate who also attended, Gurdjieff's method was "self-observation with non-identification," meaning that one tried to become entirely aware of one's own body and mind, but in a completely objective fashion. Once over this hurdle, one's mental powers increased. According to Matthews, it remained a constant question among the devotees whether anyone actually was ever "able to do it."[52] Croly apparently tried and seems to have thought the experience useful.[53] He even published a few of Orage's essays in the *New Republic*.[54]

CROLY'S SEARCH for self-awareness was partly religious, but also an exploration in psychology. He was very much interested in trying to understand the nature of consciousness and how it could be expanded. Croly wrote to Felix Frankfurter in 1927 that it was "important to remind people constantly that attaching consciousness to life is a double-faced process--both analytic and synthetic at the same time. All this is very abstract as I see it, and at best it is extremely hard to express . . . but I am spending a large part of my time puzzling how to express it."[55] However he expressed it, Croly was convinced in these years that "all human life is not accessible by consciousness, but a very much larger part is accessible than that which our minds are at present capable of attaining."[56]

In part, Croly's interest in psychology in the twenties revolved around his friendship with Eduard C. Lindeman, who wrote fairly often for the *New Republic*. Lindeman published a book entitled *Social Discovery* in 1924, to which Croly contributed a long introduction.[57] This work, an exploration both of the methodology of the social sciences and an attempt to spell out the major assumptions of psychology, expanded some of Croly's own thought on the centrality of the process of self-awareness.

Croly also participated in a group in the early 1920s that met to discuss "psychological questions"; other members included Dorothy

Straight, the Hands, Alvin Johnson, Stark Young, Sherwood Anderson, Lindeman, and Heywood Broun, with Harry Overstreet leading the discussions.[58] Croly's interests in religion and an introspective psychology would, I think, have appalled his positivist father. He had strayed very far from his early teachings.

THE EXTENT OF Croly's retreat from politics in the 1920s should not be overstated. Bruce Bliven, who joined the *New Republic*'s editorial staff in 1923 and who succeeded Croly as editor in chief, recollected of Croly's influence in these years that "although in theory the editorial board acted as a group, he dominated all political discussions, and the paper never took any editorial position with which he was not in agreement."[59] The editorial positions of the journal thus testify to Croly's interests and to the application of his philosophy to the many varied issues of the "age of normalcy." We obviously can't review them all here, but a few of the major emphases should be mentioned.

In domestic affairs, the editors expressed strong support for labor unions, and especially so in the period immediately after the war when there was considerable labor turmoil. They argued strongly for "worker partnership with the property owner in the control of the economic power and resources of the community."[60] The journal even suspended publication for several weeks in 1919 rather than print in a nonunion shop. They also argued (futilely) for the preservation of government control over the railroads and other industries that had developed during the war. In the area of social policy, they strongly attacked the decisions of the Supreme Court resurrecting substantive due process on child labor in *Adkins v. Children's Hospital* (261 U.S. 525; 1923) and in other labor cases. The Taft decision in *Truax v. Corrigan* (257 U.S. 312; 1921), which upheld a conviction of union organizers picketing a restaurant as a violation of due process rights of the owner, they termed "intolerable authoritarian rule by five men in contested fields of social policy."[61]

A number of editorials continued Croly's oft-expressed negative views on the role of political parties. For example, in 1924 the journal editorialized ironically that "the American party system is the most effective instrument which has ever been worked out to distract and fatigue subversive economic discontent and agitation. The Republican and Democratic parties have between them . . . absorbed and neutralized a huge amount of economic and sectional discontent. . . . They have enabled the people who have profited most from the prevailing economic [situation] . . . to weather the hostile political attacks."[62]

Perhaps the leading liberal cause of the 1920s was the Sacco-Vanzetti case. The *New Republic* argued in a large number of editorials and articles that, whatever the truth of the charges, the two men had clearly not been given a fair trial. Felix Frankfurter, who was very involved in the defense, wrote some of these editorials.[63] Croly's own views are evident in a letter written the month following the two men's executions, inviting Lippmann to a dinner. The purpose of the dinner was to honor those involved in defending Sacco and Vanzetti, but "second to see what further steps are possible in connection with the case, and third to discuss the situation in American life which it has revealed, which seems to us the most serious challenge to liberalism in many years."[64]

The *New Republic* also devoted a certain attention to issues of racial justice, as in printing an article by Walter F. White, then the assistant secretary of the National Association for the Advancement of Colored People (NAACP), arguing for the improvement of "negro conditions" in the South.[65] However, this issue was not as central to liberalism as it would later become.

In foreign policy, the *New Republic* continued to argue that the peace terms that had been imposed on Germany were draconian and could not succeed in establishing a lasting peace, and they also attacked gunboat diplomacy in Central America.[66]

Croly's view of the Soviet Union became more skeptical during the 1920s, and he was sure that Soviet policies would ultimately fail. He wrote to Leonard Elmhirst in 1927: "I have never been able to understand how Communism could possibly develop a technique either in industry or in agriculture which had any chance of being really adequate to carry out its purposes." The Soviet system, he argued, rests "on highly centralized political tyranny. . . . They are, of course, obliged to do everything by giving orders and they cannot wait for the gradual creation of cooperative processes under scientific direction, which is indispensable to any socially creative work. I am quite sure that their extremely centralized organization could not be successfully applied to agriculture."[67] The paper also took strong stands against Soviet violations of human rights. In Croly's view, communism was "an ominous apparition, born of the sins of a capitalism which will remain to haunt the banquet of modern society until the banqueters repent."[68] The extremism of the right called forth the extremism of the left. Neither would provide a permanent answer for modern man.

Perhaps the most interesting question about foreign policy in the twenties concerns Croly's view of the rise of Italian fascism. John P. Diggins, in his study of the American reaction to fascism, has charged that the

New Republic printed several apologies for fascism, and that Croly's own views, in particular, can be called "pro-Fascism."[69] I think Diggins significantly overstates this case.

The controversy began in January 1927, when the *New Republic* published a letter from Horace M. Kallen, a liberal philosopher who had just returned from Italy, and who praised some aspects of the regime while criticizing others.[70] The paper, in an article almost certainly written by Croly, then commented on the Kallen letter. Croly's argument was balanced, and Diggins is correct in citing some approving comments. For example, Croly evoked echoes of his previous reliance on a national promise and nationalism when he wrote: "Whatever the dangers of Fascism, it has at any rate substituted movement for stagnation, purposive behavior for drifting." He also argued that an "outside watcher" needed to be somewhat skeptical in imposing his own values on the Italians and should "beware of outlawing a political experiment which arouses in a whole nation an increased moral energy and dignifies its activities by subordinating them to a deeply felt common purpose."[71]

However, Croly's article is also substantially critical. He is careful to set the journal apart from Kallen's comments ("in his opinion," "there is something to be said," etc.). More important, Croly makes clear, I think, that he does not favor fascism. It is too repressive of human liberties: "No doubt the dangers are serious.... Before they are through with Fascism, they [the Italians] will probably pay dearly for the sacrifice of liberty with which they have purchased their national revival." Liberty thus should not be exchanged even for a formative national purpose. Croly went on to analyze the fascist system and to argue that its "pretensions are nine-tenths moonshine," and he called it a "sincere, a virile and a somewhat pathetic attempt" to overcome Italy's weaknesses. Croly's judgment was that "the experiment can hardly fail to end in a bloody reaction."[72]

The controversy continued when the sociologist Robert M. MacIver wrote to say that the *New Republic* was not sufficiently liberal on this issue and that it didn't recognize the dangers of fascism.[73] Croly responded by attempting to restate his views. He argued that Italian liberals, who had to take a political position, should certainly find more to oppose than to support in the fascist regime: "A liberal [in Italy] who would have to act only for or against it would have to act against it." But outside observers needed to take a more disinterested view. There were some advantages to a regime that had managed to "invigorate" the country. Even so, it was again clear that Croly's own opinion was predominantly negative. He wrote that "it is not, in our opinion, a 'good thing' [as MacIver had charged] for a nation to seek a more intense national consciousness . . . by the violent suppression of opposition." Admitting that events sometimes drove regimes to extreme positions, Croly issued a very conditional judgment on whether Italy had in fact been in that position. He went on to express his hope and expectation that the fascist regime would be supplanted by a more liberal system. It would, he guessed, soon "dig its own grave," at which point the Italian people "will know enough to create a liberal republic."[74]

In answering MacIver, Croly again expressed his insistence that liberalism needed a better grounding in psychology and religion. "The difference between Mr. MacIver and ourselves is traceable to a difference in the meanings we attach to the word liberalism. . . . If there are any abstract liberal principles, we do not know how to formulate them. . . . Liberalism, as we understand it, is an activity. It is the effort to emancipate human life by means of the discovery and the realization of truth. But the truth only emerges as a function of individual and corporate life, and it needs for its vindication the subordination of principles to method."[75]

Diggins argues that Croly's writing represents the "pragmatic strain of progressivism" and "social engineering," and he sees what he takes to be Croly's admiration for fascism as both typical of many pragmatists and a continuation of his earlier nationalism. I think this is a misreading of Croly's arguments. In fact, Croly was no longer a nationalist; his disillusionment after 1919 had robbed him of any lingering illusions about trusting to a nation-state. I also think that Croly's response to MacIver, while it does read like a pragmatic, instrumentalist argument, is more correctly read in terms of his own psychological and religious search in these years, a search that did emphasize a personal experimentalism, but that was fundamentally religious in inspiration. The "method" that Croly mentions is no longer primarily pragmatic but religious. It is also true that he probably would have later regretted being as tolerant of fascism as he was in these articles. But it seems to me quite wrong to call him "pro-Fascist" in any sense. Fascism was as extreme to him in its way as communism; a good political system would take the middle path.[76]

CROLY'S PARTISAN positions in these years were consistent with his more theoretical arguments. In 1920 Croly supported Parley P. Christensen, the Farmer-Labor candidate for president. Croly's concern to strengthen American labor as a counterweight to business, and his deep disgust at the campaign waged by the Democrat, James Cox, and particularly the Republican, Warren G. Harding, led him to this admittedly futile cause. Croly had earlier hoped that Herbert Hoover, whom he viewed in 1920 as a progressive and also an excellent administrator, would run on a third-party ticket, but Hoover's refusal left Croly no choice but to support Christensen.[77]

The election of 1924 was more hopeful, and the *New Republic* publicly supported Robert M. LaFollette's candidacy on the Progressive Farmer-Labor ticket. The editors had hoped as early as 1922 that progressivism was making a comeback,[78] and by July 1924 Croly guessed that "the fight is between Coolidge and LaFollette." He thought the Democrat, Davis, was appropriately forgotten.[79] Croly endorsed LaFollette just before the election.[80]

In private, however, Croly was not enthusiastic about LaFollette's campaign, misgivings he made public a year later on the senator's death. LaFollette, he complained, had relied in 1924 on views and tastes "not essentially different from those which he could have used ... in 1912." LaFollette had "sacrificed the opportunity" of updating progressivism and of crafting a new appeal to all classes. Instead, he had relied on tired slogans and outdated class appeals.[81]

The 1928 campaign was of greater interest to Croly. The *New Republic* had supported Al Smith as a strong and reasonably progressive candidate from early in the year,[82] and Croly had written an analytic but favorable piece as well.[83] By mid-summer, Croly was discouraged by the vicious attacks on Smith's Catholicism; indeed he hoped to "collect some of these stories and by publishing them expose their absurdity."[84] The result was that Smith was on the defensive, and he and Hoover "are merely maneovring [*sic*] at arms length and are saying and doing as little as they can."[85] Croly had also found Hoover a plausible candidate, a "conservative and a believer in government subordinated to business, but ... not a stand-patter."[86] The election was thus a pleasant choice.

Croly analyzed the election as an interesting one for progressives--and very different from 1924. The Socialist candidate, Norman Thomas, was an able man "who belongs to the reformist rather than to the revolutionary wing of the party," and who might reasonably attract progressive support. "On the other hand, the candidates of the Republican and Democratic parties are not as completely disqualified for the consideration of progressives as the corresponding candidates were in 1920 and 1924." Croly's advice to his readers was to wait and see which candidate emerged as more progressive.[87]

By late August, Croly was working actively for Smith. He wrote to Dorothy Elmhirst on August 23 that part of Smith's speech that evening was "based on memoranda which were written by editors of The New Republic." Croly praised the speech and told Dorothy that "we shall actively support him hereafter."[88] Accordingly, the *New Republic* came out strongly for Smith in early September, arguing that he had been explicitly progressive on issues like prohibition, Latin America, public power, and "labor and social problems in general."[89] The editors also argued a week later that while the Socialist platform "expresses a much closer approximation to a progressive national policy than that which the Democratic party, under Smith's leadership, can in the near future possibly accept," a vote for Norman Thomas would be wasted.[90]

The election of 1928 had reawakened Croly's interest in partisan politics. His editorials in this period are among his most incisive political commentaries. Once again he had found a leader he could support, and it is likely that he would have personally endorsed Smith later in October. However, Croly's stroke in early October 1928 cut short this commitment.

AN ACCOUNT OF Croly's thought in the 1920s would not be complete without a consideration of his commitment to two educational and cultural institutions, the New School for Social Research and the *New Republic* itself.

The idea for the New School was generated in October 1917, when Charles A. Beard and James Harvey Robinson resigned from Columbia University over the firing of two professors who had opposed American entry into the war. Their actions touched off an extensive debate over academic freedom, in which the *New Republic* participated extensively. Both men had written for the paper previously, and Croly both supported their action and provided them with an intellectual base.[91] Beard and Robinson had earlier discussed with Croly the idea of setting up an institute for adult students and for the support of social science research.[92] This idea was certainly in Croly's mind as early as his 1910 proposal for a national graduate school of political science,[93] and he now worked with Beard and Robinson in assembling a planning group. Many of Croly's friends and associates were involved, including Felix Frankfurter, Learned Hand, Lippmann, and Alvin Johnson, in addition to John Dewey, Horace Kallen, John P. Mitchell, the former mayor, and many others. Dorothy Straight also was centrally involved and provided essential financial support.[94]

As planning proceeded, Croly provided advanced publicity for the school, describing it as the American equivalent of France's Ecole Libre des Sciences Politiques. It would, Croly wrote in very familiar words, "contribute to the social education of the American people and to the better realization of the social ideal, implicit in American democracy."[95]

The New School opened in February 1919 in a row of houses quite near the *New Republic* offices. The experiment ran smoothly for a few

years, and popular support for the classes was high. However, the founding group began to splinter. Croly had always emphasized the research
side of the project and wished to expand in that direction, particularly
emphasizing the Labor Research Bureau that would provide research assistance to labor unions.[96] Robinson, on the other hand, wanted to emphasize adult education. The result was a reorganization of the school in April
1922, in which Alvin Johnson of the *New Republic* staff assumed direction
of the school. Robinson, Beard, and Croly all dropped their connections
with the school after this reorganization.[97]

Croly never fully explained his break with the school. He had been
centrally involved in its operation for several years but may have thought
that he could not give it sufficient attention with his other projects. Or
perhaps he was unable to win enough support for his ideas and left in
anger. In any case, the disintegration of this ideal would certainly have
added to his disillusionment in the early 1920s.

The central focus of the last fifteen years of Croly's life was the *New
Republic* itself, and his central friendship was with Dorothy Straight who
provided to him the financial but also intellectual and moral support to
allow the paper to continue. Croly depended on her, but he and his wife,
Louise, also grew to love Dorothy, and the very extensive personal correspondence that exists in the Dorothy Straight Elmhirst Papers (she remar-
ried in 1925) is the single best source of insight into Herbert Croly's shy
personality.

This friendship with Dorothy Straight had many advantages for
Croly, and many costs as well. At her request, he agreed to write the
biography of Willard Straight after his death in late 1918. This was an
enormous project that absorbed a lot of Croly's energy for several years,
the result being a 569-page work that detailed Straight's life with enormous and loving care.[98]

The work is heavily based on Straight's own diaries and is a careful
but not a critical work. Dorothy Straight was fully involved in the process
of composition, and Croly was quite open about her part in the composition and about his own personal tie to his subject. As he wrote to Dorothy
in September 1922:

> Now that we have practically finished the writing of Willard's life,
> there is something I very much wish to say to you about it all–about
> your part in it, and mine and Willard's. I shall always look back upon
> my poor share in it as something which I have had more happiness
> in doing . . . than any of the major jobs of my working life. . . . In writ-
> ing his life I found myself in the rare and wonderful situation . . . of
> admiring and believing in Willard the more just in proportion as I

knew him better. . . . It was a precious experience also to have shared the work with you.[99]

After reading many of his letters, I am convinced that these are sincere sentiments. However, I can't help but think that *The Breach in Civilization* might have been a better work if Croly had not also been writing this extensive biography in these years.

The *New Republic* also prevented Croly from writing the book that he longed to write in these last years, as he often complained.[100] But he remained committed to his "paper," leaving only for short trips and brief vacations.

The other personnel on the paper changed completely in these years. Walter Weyl had died in 1919, and while Lippmann returned that year, he was often absent and left completely at the end of 1921. Lippmann wrote to Felix Frankfurter that he had "decided to quit the *N.R.* and go onto the [New York] World January first next. . . . Herbert and I no longer learn from each other, and for two years our intellectual relationship has been a good natured accommodation rather than an inspiring adventure."[101]

Croly was often lonely at this loss of past associates. As he wrote to Dorothy Straight in 1924, "it is depressing to see so many of one's friends drifting away intellectually and spiritually. Of the original New Republic group there is no one left but Felix, Louise, you and I. . . . It makes one feel lonely."[102]

However, while he might grow depressed, Croly's commitment to the importance of the *New Republic* never faltered. He managed to rebuild his staff, adding political writers such as Bruce Bliven and George Soule and a brilliant staff of literary and cultural critics, including Stark Young, Malcolm Cowley, and Edmund Wilson.[103] The staff of the paper at Croly's death in 1930 was probably the equal of its staff at its creation in 1914. This was an enormous achievement, and it is Croly who deserves the credit.[104]

9

Conclusions

By all accounts, Herbert Croly was an extremely shy man.[1] Indeed, his personal reserve probably kept him from being as actively involved in politics as he might have been if he had been more comfortable personally in situations of conflict. He was also a hesitant writer who labored over his prose with less success than most of his colleagues, who were all too well aware of his inability to express himself as clearly or concisely as he or they would have liked. For example, in early 1919 Harold Laski urged Walter Lippmann to return to the *New Republic* because he was so good in "bringing to maturity the ideas and hopes which struggle for expression in Herbert's mind."[2]

Yet these same associates testified to Croly's intellectual influence and to many admirable personal characteristics that held their loyalty. Felix Frankfurter called *The Promise of American Life* a "notable, seminal book" and claimed that "Croly planted not a few of the seeds" of the changes in American society engendered by the progressive movement. To Frankfurter, his friend Croly was "a noble creature.... He was noble, in the sense that to a rare degree he had a sense of justice. He was one of the most just-minded men I ever knew on or off the Supreme Court of the United States."[3] Edmund Wilson, a younger man of very different temperament, who knew Croly only in his later years, also admired him: "It seems to me that Croly was one of the most admirable men I have ever known.... [H]e was never dogmatic and never incoherent, always modest about his own limitations...."[4] A significant influence on such very different people, Croly clearly was a serious writer who tried over many years to express a consistent picture of politics and the possibility of reform. But did he succeed? What was Croly's achievement?

I HAVE ARGUED in this work that Croly was important in developing a conception of modern American liberalism. As I noted in the Introduction, there is no one synthetic political theorist who delineates American liberalism in a complete and systematic political theory.[5] Indeed, this absence of a single, full theoretical statement may explain some of the problems that liberals have had in articulating a consistent vision in the face of a radical opposition from the "New Left" in the 1960s and 1970s and a resurgent American conservatism in the 1970s and 1980s. I think Herbert Croly's writings come close to stating the fundamental founding assumptions of modern liberalism, closer than any other writer with whom I am familiar. The weaknesses or failures of his theory may also indicate some of the deeper problems in modern American liberalism. Let me explain how.

Most obviously, Croly and many other progressives elaborated modern liberalism's emphasis on the responsibility of government, and especially the national executive, to improve social and economic conditions in the United States. This reliance is clear in the entire range of Croly's work, from the early rejection of laissez-faire theory in *The Promise* to the strong support for Woodrow Wilson's domestic politics in 1916 to the issues of the 1920s when, even as he became disillusioned to a degree with politics, Croly still called for government intervention in many areas of the economy. Croly's emphasis on the importance of the national government to solve the nation's ills and his emphasis on the expanded role of the executive at all levels of government are staple beliefs of modern liberalism. His stress on the important role of government regulation—of the economy in particular—and on the central position of a government bureaucracy in this regulatory process (recall the image of the bureaucrat tending the "social garden" in *Progressive Democracy*) are central elements in liberal politics from Roosevelt's New Deal through Johnson's Great Society.

Of course, Croly didn't initiate these ideas by himself. He was responding, in part, to the example of an activist president, Theodore Roosevelt, when he wrote of the importance of the executive, and he was allied with many progressives in working for an active government. But Croly succeeded in embedding these arguments in a broader perspective on politics, and thus "planting seeds" in his readers' minds, as Frankfurter argued. He made an expanded role for government part of a larger picture of what a good society should be, and his argument that government should actively seek the realization of the national "promise" was of enormous influence.

Croly's theory was also representative of liberalism in his belief in the possibilities of a "middle way" between laissez-faire and socialism, between capitalism and communism. He came to think of liberalism as a conscious attempt to create a centrist politics that would be reformist but that would at the same time appeal to a broad spectrum of groups and individuals. Croly consistently rejected a class analysis of politics, even in his period of severe disillusionment in the early 1920s. Rather, he argued in 1909 that America's promise was open to everyone and again in the late 1920s that America had always been "liberal" in the sense that the class-based politics of Europe were inappropriate here. His religious conviction always bore witness to a regeneration of society as a whole. This support of a "middle way" is typical of modern liberal thought.

But did Croly appropriately call his theory "liberal"? As we have seen, he rarely (though occasionally) used this term prior to 1915. Rather, he originally described his theory as "progressive," or as simply "reform." Was his appropriation of the liberal heritage justified?

I have argued that Croly's political theory shared significant continuities with the classic theory that he originally thought of as "liberal." Classic liberalism emphasized individualism and individual rights and liberties as the central values of politics. As we have seen, Croly was committed to the importance of individualism even in *The Promise*, and he never deviated from that conviction. The individual could not be isolated; Croly always emphasized a "social will." At times, the ties of society were strong indeed in his theory. The national organization and its general will, public opinion, were to be very significant influences on any individual. But we need to be clear that, for Croly, society never swallowed up the individual.

Croly was admittedly reluctant initially to endorse the concept of "rights," and particularly any theory of "natural rights," because of the close identification of that concept with conservative theories emphasizing property rights. However, as we have seen, he came to accept notions of rights as early as *Progressive Democracy* in 1914, and he particularly used the concept more fully in reaction to the war and the repression of individual liberties in the Red Scare of 1919–1920.

Freedom was also important to Croly. In *The Promise*, he began to suggest that this concept, so central to classic liberalism, could be understood in several ways. He did not originally emphasize the traditional notion of "negative freedom" or "freedom from" government control, but even in 1909 he accepted this understanding of freedom as a political good. Later, he appreciated more fully the contemporary importance of this conception of liberty, as in his defense of freedom of speech during the Red Scare. Certainly, contemporary liberalism has continued the classic liberal emphasis on the importance of personal freedoms such as the freedom of speech or of religion or the rights to privacy.

But Croly didn't write of "negative freedom" only. Rather, his analysis in *The Promise* began to explicate the new understanding of a "positive freedom" or "freedom to" develop one's abilities free of what Franklin Roosevelt described as the "fear" and "want" of severe economic coercions. Indeed, Croly is one of the first American writers to describe this understanding of freedom. It is unfortunate that he did not elaborate this theory more fully in his later writings.

Croly thus drew on classic liberal theory in significant ways, but he changed it into a new and different liberalism, a "reformist liberalism" as he specifically argued in some of his last writings.[6] One adaptation was of course his reliance on the role of government, especially the executive and the bureaucracy, as opposed to the classic liberal fear of government. Another adaptation was his suggestion of "positive freedom" as a supplement to "negative freedom." A third was the separation of personal freedoms from a strong emphasis on property rights.

Perhaps Croly's most important adaptation of liberalism was to tie it to democratic theory. In his (I believe correct) reading, classic liberals such as Alexis de Tocqueville or John Stuart Mill had been afraid of democracy, consistently emphasizing individual rights—minority rights, if you will—over democratic majority rule. Croly was not temperamentally a democrat,[7] as can be seen in his hesitation to endorse the concept of equality in *The Promise*. But he understood that democracy was necessarily a central tenet of any American theory of politics, and he consequently argued a form of democratic theory from the beginning. His commitment to the progressive cause in the years 1910-1916 brought him to a much more wholehearted democratic position, to which he held for the rest of his life, even when disillusioned with American public opinion during and after the war. Croly's disillusionment never resulted in an anti-democratic reaction. Rather, he argued that liberals needed to rethink how better to ground their liberal theory to make it convincing in a democratic society. For Croly, then, modern liberalism had to be democratic, while preserving the traditional emphasis on individualism and individual liberty.

Croly also helped develop the notion of pluralism, of a central emphasis on the role of interest groups, that is often seen as an identifying feature of modern liberal theory.[8] Croly did not originate this argument and indeed may emphasize the centrality of interest groups less than many other liberal theorists, especially given his stress on a strong executive. However, his writings, particularly *Progressive Democracy*, do show that he relied on a pluralist perspective.

Croly's new understanding of liberalism thus combined the classic emphasis on individualism and freedom with democracy, pluralism, and the centrality of government. When we remember that his political program also emphasized a pragmatic approach to social experimentation, we are approaching a description of modern liberalism. Thus Otis L. Graham, who has written of the ties between progressivism and the New Deal, argues that "the redefinition of freedom, the critique of laissez-faire, the intellectual preparation of a creed for a popular interventionist state— these were provided by turn-of-the-century thinkers such as Dewey, Ward, Beard, and Croly. . . . Liberalism performed a transvaluation of means in the pursuit of the ancient ends. It is a triumphant historical record, culminating in the 1930's with the creation of that long-desired welfare state of liberal predisposition."[9]

Graham may understate some differences in emphasis between Croly's liberalism and the New Deal. For example, Croly's policy of regulation never included such extensive government responsibility for the unemployed and the disadvantaged as Franklin Roosevelt developed in response to the Great Depression.

It is even more evident that Croly never emphasized certain elements of what we take as "liberal" in the last years of the century. Most obviously, he was never very concerned with "civil rights," meaning the rights of minorities. Croly's somewhat conditional endorsement of equality did not extend to a concern for racial equality and certainly not to such policies as affirmative action. Indeed, we would consider some of his views as racist. In these areas, his theory is not at all representative of contemporary liberalism. However, we should recall that Franklin D. Roosevelt's New Deal was not very concerned with "civil rights" either. This is a comparatively recent element of the liberal creed.

Croly was also not an advocate of gender equality. He was not even a strong supporter of women's suffrage, which is particularly surprising considering his mother's stand on that issue. In this respect, again, Croly does not speak to contemporary liberalism. On the other hand, his *New Republic* did provide strong support for personal rights such as birth control that are important to contemporary liberals.

In summary, Herbert Croly's political theory is not identical to the liberalism of the late twentieth century or even to the liberalism of the New Deal. But many of the major emphases of modern liberalism can be seen in the work of this seminal theorist.

UNFORTUNATELY, Croly never brought his theory together as a whole. He never wrote the book that could have expressed his political thought in a systematic way. Indeed, *The Promise of American Life* is probably his most systematic work; yet he changed major parts of his theory in later years, while never returning fully to the fundamental arguments or perhaps to the philosophic rigor of the early work. Croly realized that he had changed many of his views. He said often to friends that he wanted to publish another book that would integrate his arguments. But he never did.

There seem to be several reasons why Croly didn't succeed in putting his thoughts together late in his life. The need to get out an issue of the *New Republic* fifty-two weeks a year was an enormous intellectual and even physical challenge. Croly was also committed by bonds of friendship to write Willard Straight's biography in the very years in which he was best equipped to integrate his early theory with the experiences of the war and the Red Scare.

Of course, Croly *did* try to produce a book in this period, and it was perhaps his greatest intellectual failure that this work, *The Breach in Civilization*, was not a better book. The reasons for this failure are again several, including the pressures on his time just mentioned. The fact that Croly chose to turn, in part, from politics to religion in these years seems crucial in attempting to understand both his search and perhaps also his failure. It is clear that his ability to write a systematic work in political theory was greatly affected by his search for religious truth after 1919.

Croly wrote that he had begun to "believe again" after the experience of the war. However, it is evident from reading his earlier works that a religious concern was never absent. He may not always have focused on personal belief, but Croly always did believe in human salvation, in the possible "regeneration" (to use a word he constantly employed) of human beings. This concern, which we can see as a generalized religious belief, or certainly as a "moralism" with strongly religious overtones, is evident in many arguments in *The Promise*. It is particularly clear in the near-utopian final pages of *Progressive Democracy*, and it runs through many of Croly's articles.

What thus seems to have happened after the war is not that Croly turned from politics to religion, but that his religious concerns, which were always present and indeed integrated into many parts of his political theory (as in the stress on "brotherhood" in *The Promise*), became more dominant in his thought. Edmund Wilson, who knew Croly only in the 1920s, wrote that "it is not at all difficult to imagine him becoming, in some other period, not a writer on politics, but, say, the founder of a religious order."[10] Wilson overstates the case; certainly Croly continued to write extensively and acutely on politics until his stroke. But his religious concerns *were* central in the 1920s.

What, then, was the role of religion in Croly's thought, particularly in the 1920s? A focus on religion in politics is often a nonliberal emphasis. It can often signal a reliance on tradition and on the claims of an authoritative belief system and hierarchy, rather than on individual choice and equality. However, Croly's "religion" was not at all orthodox. Rather, quite in consonance with his liberalism, it emphasized a pragmatic individual search for truth, often in the realm of one's own consciousness. Croly's Christianity in the twenties was heavily laced with psychological and mystical elements. In contrast to a later liberal, Reinhold Niebuhr, who also emphasized a religious base for his theory,[11] Croly's Christianity lacks a sense of sin, of *necessary* human failure. His religion is "easier," more optimistic, than Niebuhr's.

But what was Croly seeking, and how did it relate to his politics? Answers here are necessarily speculative. Like many of his friends and associates, I don't understand fully the arguments he was attempting to make about religion and psychology in his last years. But before dismissing these arguments, we should remember that Croly thought that liberalism needed a more firm philosophical grounding than had yet been provided. The conclusion he drew from the war was not only that individual rights needed to be reemphasized in liberalism and integrated with a progressive democratic theory, but also that the whole basis of liberalism needed to be reviewed.

Croly's search for a philosophy of liberalism had earlier involved a rejection of laissez-faire and the emphasis on the concept of "natural rights" as convincing bases on which to build. In *The Breach in Civilization*, he shifted his attack to the inadequacy of utilitarianism, which he thought was an oversimplified theory of human psychology and politics. He was searching for a conception of religion and of human psychology that could more adequately undergird the political liberalism he espoused with its emphasis on public opinion, positive freedom, and government responsibility. Unfortunately, Croly never was able to state this relation to his own (and especially not to his associates') satisfaction.

We may be more sympathetic with Croly's diagnosis of the ills of liberalism, if not with his inexact prescription, if we believe that American liberalism hasn't developed a satisfactory substitute for the utilitarian philosophic basis on which Croly thought liberals were still relying. For instance, John Rawls, in a work generally taken to be the most important statement of contemporary liberal theory, has written that "my aim is to work out a theory of justice which represents an alternative to utilitarian thought generally."[12] Other critics of contemporary liberalism take a slightly different line, emphasizing "communitarian" values and arguing that liberals still rely too fully on an isolated, self-interested individualism.[13] Indeed, Croly's emphasis on fraternity, or brotherhood, as a necessary element in any good polity may even speak to some of the concerns that communitarians express about a self-interested liberalism.

Croly's concern for religion and for a psychology of self-consciousness was thus an attempt to deal with what he took to be the inadequacies of liberalism. His particular prescription for these ills has not been influential. At the same time, it is unfortunately the case that contemporary liberalism probably hasn't succeeded any better than Croly did in integrating a specifically political picture of government power and social responsibility with the philosophical and psychological arguments necessary to support a wholly coherent and convincing political theory. It is our loss as well as his that he was unable to complete his arguments satisfactorily in *The Breach in Civilization*.

CROLY WAS BEST known by many of his readers for his writings on specific political and economic policy issues, and we also need to consider his achievements in these areas.

No doubt, Croly's writings on economic reorganization and on the regulation of the trusts were his best-known domestic policy recommendations. As we have seen, Croly's "short-run" program in *The Promise* was influenced very substantially by Theodore Roosevelt's previous policies. Yet Croly in turn provided Roosevelt with a wider picture and a more systematic theory within which to position his policies. I think he certainly had some influence on Roosevelt, but the influence *from* Roosevelt was more important.

At the same time, we should remember that it was Croly's short-run recommendations that Roosevelt inspired. Croly's long-term prescriptions, emphasizing the nationalization of industries and significant tax changes to render the distribution of wealth more equal, were significantly more radical than Roosevelt (or any politician) could accept, and he moved to even stronger positions in the early 1920s. It seems to me that some commentators have failed to see that Croly's economic theories were often quite radical in their implications. I find arguments that he was essentially conservative or pro-business or a "corporate liberal" unpersuasive.[14]

It is interesting that while Croly provided T.R. with a general rationale for a regulated economy, it was Charles Van Hise's *Concentration and Control* that provided the specific economic arguments to counter Louis Brandeis's detailed arguments for competition. Croly was not an economist, and his contributions to the theory of regulation were thus not technical. Indeed, he wrote about most policy issues as a generalist rather than as a specialist, and it is clear that his particular interests lay not in policy-making but in the larger project of reforming society as a whole. Croly was a reformer and a theorist, not a policy analyst.

One partial exception to this judgment might be the issue of state political reorganization on which he did develop a specialized interest in the period 1910 to 1916. This interest was strongly evident in *The Promise* and became more specifically focused on state executives and on issues of direct democracy in Croly's paper at the American Political Science Association in 1911 and in *Progressive Democracy*. It seems likely that Croly would have continued to develop this interest if progressivism had continued after 1916 rather than being cut off by the war.

I think an ambivalent judgment is appropriate regarding Croly's discussion of the war. I'm not sure he ever worked out a fully consistent understanding of the reasons for American participation. He argued a "realist" position: that the United States was now a great power and would be involved whether she consciously chose to be or not. But Croly the moralist could not rest in this realist argument, and he also justified American intervention on varied moral grounds: to seek an ultimate peace, to advance Western democracy, to defend Anglo-American liberalism against German authoritarianism. These arguments were not unconvincing, but I don't think Croly ever anchored them very fully to his more fundamental theory, and he never tied his moral arguments and his realism together in any sustained way. In this sense, Randolph Bourne was at least partially correct: Croly's liberalism did not provide full moral guidance for such a fundamental issue as war. Of course, this was one reason why Croly sought to reformulate his liberalism, but it is not clear that his reformulations would have been any more useful in thinking through this issue.

Certainly later liberal leaders facing World War II, the Korean War, and the Vietnam War have responded much as Croly, Lippmann, Dewey, and Wilson did to the First World War. Indeed, the combination of liberalism's active government with an internationalist perspective and a willingness to use force in achieving "moral" international objectives has been a central feature of later liberal politics. However, it is unclear that these later leaders have thought through the basic philosophical arguments any more successfully than Croly and Woodrow Wilson did.

CROLY'S ENDURING achievements were his two major books and the *New Republic*.

The Promise of American Life was an extraordinary work. It is, I think, one of the most theoretically important books in American political thought. The historical treatment was incisive, the proposed combination of nationalism and democracy was carefully argued, and Croly's discussion of the relation between democracy, equality, liberty, and fraternity was theoretically quite subtle. In addition, the relations between the theory and the policy recommendations in the book were nicely elaborated, and the policy recommendations themselves were persuasive.

Progressive Democracy seems to me a less successful book. Croly's historical analysis is more rushed and less insightful. He is also less interested in engaging in theoretical explorations; too many points are assumed rather than argued. The book's attractions are its strong argument for democracy, its new pluralist approach, and particularly its detailed commentary on specific progressive reforms. *Progressive Democracy* clearly demonstrates how Croly had responded to the progressive movement and how he in turn was trying to guide the movement.

The *New Republic* was perhaps Croly's most important achievement. Under his editorship, it was a distinguished "journal of opinion" that provided its readers with superb commentary on a wide range of political and cultural issues. I doubt that any American journal since has matched the intellectual level of the *New Republic* under Herbert Croly.

On Croly's death in May 1930, one of his frequent English contributors, N. H. Brailsford, wrote to Louise Croly:

I suppose he must often have asked himself, as all journalists are forced to do, what would be left of this seemingly impermanent work. In his case I have no doubt about the answer. He gave us what is, I think, the most inspiring spectacle that a man can give his fellows—the spectacle of a mind of unusual power and still rarer integrity, struggling to apply its high standards and ideals to the daily world. That remains, and the memory of it will not soon fade. . . . I am sure that apart altogether from its good work in forming opinion, and spreading knowledge, The New Republic as he shaped it, and led it, must have become a great builder of character, an intellectual architect, for many thousands of its readers.[15]

Herbert Croly, the lifelong student of both politics and architecture, would have appreciated this deserved praise.

Notes

PREFACE

1. Eric F. Goldman, *Rendezvous with Destiny: A History of Modern American Reform* (New York: Alfred A. Knopf, 1952).
2. Charles Forcey, *The Crossroads of Liberalism: Croly, Weyl, Lippmann and the Progressive Era, 1900–1925* (New York: Oxford University Press, 1961).
3. David W. Levy, *Herbert Croly of the New Republic: The Life and Thought of an American Progressive* (Princeton, N.J.: Princeton University Press, 1985).

CHAPTER ONE. INTRODUCTION

1. An excellent summary of liberal theory is provided by Stephen Holmes, "The Liberal Idea," *American Prospect* 7 (Fall 1991): 81–96.
2. It is interesting to note that as early as 1884, Herbert Spencer was criticizing the British liberal ministries of Lord John Russell and William Gladstone for "greatly increasing the compulsions and restraints exercised over citizens." See Herbert Spencer, *Man versus the State* (1884; rev. ed., London: Penguin Books, 1969), 81. See chapter 1 in particular.
3. Benjamin DeWitt, *The Progressive Movement* (1915; reprint, Seattle: University of Washington Press, 1968), part 1.
4. R. Jeffrey Lustig, *Corporate Liberalism: The Origins of Modern American Political Theory, 1890–1920* (Berkeley: University of California Press, 1982), 4.
5. "The New Books," *Outlook* 93 (December 4, 1909): 788–89.
6. Walter Lippmann argued that the term "liberalism" was "introduced into the jargon of American politics by that group who were Progressives in 1912 and Wilson Democrats from 1916 to 1918." "Liberalism in America," *New Republic* (*NR*) 21 (December 31, 1919): 150.
7. See, for example, Herbert Croly to Eduard C. Lindeman, May 28, 1925,

Lindeman Papers, in which Croly discusses a major project for the "exposition of the status of liberalism in the modern world."

CHAPTER TWO. YEARS OF PREPARATION

1. One sibling died in infancy and another as a young adult. Two sisters survived with Herbert.
2. The best source on Jane Croly is a volume edited by a friend and club associate, Caroline Morse, *Memories of Jane Cunningham Croly, "Jenny June"* (New York: G. P. Putnam's Sons, 1904); see particularly an article by her brother, John Cunningham, "A Brother's Memories," 3–12. See also a manuscript by her daughter, Vida Croly Sidney, "Jennie June Croly," Sorosis Files, Sophia Smith Collection, Smith College. See also Muriel Shaver, "Jane Cunningham Croly," *Dictionary of American Biography* (New York: Charles Scribner's Sons, 1929), 2: 560–61. Jane Croly's own remarks on her early years in journalism can be found in "Thirty Years in Journalism," *Demorest's Monthly Magazine* (September 1886): 1756–60. Secondary works include Elizabeth B. Schlesinger, "The Nineteenth Century Woman's Dilemma and Jennie June," *New York History* 42 (October 1961): 365–79; Karen J. Blair, *The Clubwoman as Feminist: True Womanhood Redefined, 1868–1914* (New York: Holmes and Meier, 1980). Jane's pseudonym was sometimes spelled "Jenny June" and sometimes "Jennie June." I have omitted the pseudonym in all citations.
3. Jane C. Croly, *Jennie June's American Cookery Book* (New York: American News Company, 1866). Further editions were published in 1870, 1874, and 1878.
4. Jane C. Croly, *Jennie Juneiana: Talks on Women's Topics* (Boston: Lee and Shepard, 1864).
5. In the view of Herbert Croly's biographer, David W. Levy, Jane Croly was an inconsistent thinker in general and an opponent of women's suffrage in particular. David W. Levy, *Herbert Croly of the New Republic: The Life and Thought of an American Progressive* (Princeton, N.J.: Princeton University Press, 1985), 4–11, 18–29. "She opposed women's suffrage in the most violent and uncompromising terms" (10). These judgments seem to me quite wrong, and because I differ with this interpretation I have quoted at some length from Jane Croly's work.
6. Jane C. Croly, "Talks with Women: Woman's Rights," *Demorest's Monthly Magazine* (August 1866): 203. As regards tactics, Jane recommended reasoned argument, which she (mistakenly) thought was likely to produce the suffrage for women in Britain shortly: "Sensible women know what they want, and ask for it quietly and rationally. When a majority of the American women do this, they will get it easily enough; as Englishwomen appear likely to now" (204).
7. Ibid., 204.
8. Jane C. Croly, "Women in Politics," *Demorest's Monthly Magazine* (March 1875): 97.
9. Ibid., 98. On suffrage, see also an 1869 *New York World* column quoted by Blair, *Clubwoman*, 40. Jane Croly recommended that women use the tongue and the pen to advance their interests while waiting for the vote.
10. Jane C. Croly, *For Better or Worse* (Boston: Lee and Shepard, 1875), 191. Croly's arguments are similar to John Stuart Mill's famous arguments for democracy in the third chapter of *Considerations on Representative Government*.
11. Jane C. Croly, "A New Question in Politics," *Demorest's Monthly Magazine* (November 1884): 40–41. Jane supported the Prohibition party in this election.

12. Jane C. Croly, "The Industrial Problem, and How It Was Solved in the Maison Le Claire," *Demorest's Monthly Magazine* (April 1886): 390–92.

13. Ibid., 392. Emphasis in the original.

14. Jane C. Croly, "Women Abroad," *Demorest's Monthly Magazine* (December 1885): 100–103, quotation from 103, emphasis in the original.

15. Jane C. Croly, *Thrown on Her Own Resources; Or, What Girls Can Do* (New York: Crowell and Company, 1891), 25.

16. Ibid., 62, 143–44.

17. Letter of Mildred Ahlgren, consultant to the General Federation of Women's Clubs, to the author, August 4, 1980. Blair judges Jane Croly to be "the single most important figure in the woman's club movement" (*Clubwoman*, 15).

18. See the Sorosis Files in the Sophia Smith Collection, Smith College. Members included former abolitionists, utopian community activists (including Mrs. Robert Owen), suffragists, and many professional women. See Blair, *Clubwoman*, 22.

19. Morse, *Memories*, 45.

20. Jane C. Croly, *The History of the Woman's Club Movement in America* (New York: Henry G. Allen, 1898).

21. Jane Croly, "Letter to Sorosis," May 1899; reprinted in Morse, *Memories*, 149–50. This stress on unity sometimes caused Croly to de-emphasize divisive issues within the club, including the topics of the suffrage and religion. Blair, *Clubwoman*, 23. She also opposed racial integration, at least in the short run: "I am very, very sorry the color question has been raised again. It almost made a split six years ago. It was, at the least, premature" (Jane C. Croly, letter of October 3, 1900; reprinted in Morse, *Memories*, 158).

22. Jane C. Croly, "Letter to the Society of American Women in London," November, 1901; reprinted in Morse, *Memories*, 151–52.

23. Jane C. Croly, address on "The Advantages of a General Federation of Women's Clubs," New York, 1890; reprinted in Morse, *Memories*, 117–23; quotation from 121–22. The organization of the General Federation fulfilled an earlier dream of Croly's—to create a national women's organization. In 1869 she had encouraged Sorosis to convene a "Woman's Parliament" to "represent women upon all subjects of vital interest to themselves and their children" (quoted in Blair, *Clubwoman*, 39).

24. Blair, *Clubwoman*, 98. The full history of the relation between late nineteenth-century feminism and progressivism has yet to be written, but see Robyn Muncy, *Creating a Female Dominion in American Reform, 1890–1935* (New York: Oxford University Press, 1991). Clearly women were increasingly involved in various aspects of progressivism, including educational reforms, child-welfare legislation, temperance issues, and pure food and drug legislation. Jane Croly proposed the establishment of a "State Industrial School for Girls" to deal with delinquency and moral reformation. See Morse, *Memories*, 188.

25. Louise Croly to Felix Frankfurter, April 2 (1931?), Frankfurter Papers, Library of Congress. Various commentators have followed this judgment. See Levy, *Herbert Croly*, 26; Forcey, *Crossroads of Liberalism*, 13. One of the few commentators who emphasizes Jane Croly's influence is Henry Ladd Smith, who writes: "Croly's mother may have been an even greater influence in his life [than his father]." "Editing for 'The Superior Few,' " *NR* 131 (November 22, 1954): 24.

26. Vida Croly Sidney, "Jennie June Croly," Sorosis Files, Sophia Smith Collection, Smith College. See also an undated letter in the Schlesinger Library file on Jane Croly, in which she asks for a job for Herbert on the Washington *Sunday*

Capitol as a condition for accepting an editorial position herself. Jane Croly to (?), n.d., Schlesinger Library, Harvard University.

27. Levy's treatment of David Goodman Croly is very thorough. See especially 11–19, 22–42. See also Shaver, "David Goodman Croly," *Dictionary of American Biography*, 560; John Cunningham, "A Brother's Memories," in Morse, *Memories*.

28. Levy, *Herbert Croly*, 14, 17. Blair writes that David Croly was ill with Bright's disease (chronic nephritis) from 1879 to 1889, and that Jane had to assume increasing support for the family. *Clubwoman*, 16.

29. David G. Croly, *Miscegenation* (New York: H. Dexter, Hamilton and Co., 1864), 1.

30. See Sidney Kaplan, "The Miscegenation Issue in the Election of 1864," *Journal of Negro History* 34 (July 1949): 274–343. Croly wrote another book to support the Democratic ticket in 1868: David G. Croly, *Seymour and Blair, Their Lives and Services* (New York: Richardson and Company, 1868).

31. David G. Croly, *The Truth about Love* (New York: David Wesley and Co., 1872). See Levy, *Herbert Croly*, 15.

32. David G. Croly, *Glimpses of the Future* (New York: G. Putnam's Sons, 1888), title page. Compare Edward Bellamy, *Looking Backward, 2000–1887*, also published in 1888.

33. Shaver, "David Goodman Croly," *Dictionary of American Biography*.

34. Jane C. Croly, "The Positivist Episode," in Morse, *Memories*, 73.

35. H.C. to Royal Cortissoz, October 7, 1916, Houghton Library, Harvard University.

36. See Croly, autobiographical "fragment," Felix Frankfurter Papers, Library of Congress. See also Edmund Wilson, "H.C.," *NR* 63 (July 16, 1930): 268.

37. On Jane Croly and positivism, see the section in Morse, *Memories*, "The Positivist Episode," 51–76. I agree with Levy that positivism otherwise does not seem a major interest of Jane Croly's. Levy, *Herbert Croly*, 23–24.

38. David G. Croly, *A Positivist Primer: Being a Series of Familiar Conversations on the Religion of Humanity* (New York: David Wesley and Co., 1871), 13, 18.

39. Ibid., 29, 45.

40. Ibid., 85.

41. Ibid., 31.

42. Ibid., 57, 64.

43. H.C. "From a Testimonial by Herbert D. Croly," in Morse, *Memories*, 61–62. Croly noted that there were many Christian influences on him that his father hoped to oppose, presumably influences from Jane Croly and her family, among others.

44. Levy, *Herbert Croly*, 43–45.

45. Ibid., 57. See Bruce Kuklick, *The Rise of American Philosophy: Cambridge, Massachusetts, 1860–1930* (New Haven, Conn.: Yale University Press, 1977), an excellent treatment of the Harvard Department of Philosophy and of the entire university in this period. See chapter 12 on Palmer and chapters 9, 10, and 14–17 on James.

46. H.C. to Louise Emory, June 1, 1891, Houghton Library, Harvard University.

47. David G. Croly to H.C., October 4, 1886; October 10, 1886; October 28, 1886, Houghton Library, Harvard University.

48. David G. Croly to H.C., October 31, 1886; reprinted in Morse, *Memories*, 64.

49. John Stuart Mill, *Auguste Comte and Positivism* (1873; reprint, Ann Arbor: University of Michigan Press, 1961). Mill had introduced Comte to English readers but soon had come to question major parts of the philosophy. An excellent modern edition of Comte's writings is Gertrude Lenzer, ed., *Auguste Comte and Positivism: The Essential Writings* (New York: Harper Torchbooks, 1975).

50. Ibid., 127.

51. H.C., "Testimonial," in Morse, *Memories*, 62–63.

52. David G. Croly to H.C., November 6, 1886, and March 20, 1887, Houghton Library, Harvard University.

53. David G. Croly to H.C., May 11, 1887, Houghton Library, Harvard University.

54. David G. Croly to H.C., May 18, 1887, Houghton Library, Harvard University.

55. David G. Croly to H.C., April 28, 1887, Houghton Library, Harvard University.

56. David G. Croly to H.C., March 10, 1887, Houghton Library, Harvard University.

57. David G. Croly to H.C., March 4, 1887, Houghton Library, Harvard University.

58. Levy, *Herbert Croly*, 61–62.

59. Ibid., 62.

60. J. Laurence Laughlin, *The Study of Political Economy: Hints to Students and Teachers* (New York: D. Appleton and Company, 1885). See pp. 9–12 for readings.

61. Ibid., 46–47, 150.

62. Ibid., 49.

63. Jacob Viner, "Introduction," to Jacob Viner et al., *Explorations in Economics: Notes and Essays Contributed in Honor of F. W. Taussig* (New York: McGraw-Hill Book Company, 1936), 5.

64. Joseph Schumpeter, "Professor Taussig on Wages and Capital," in Viner et al., *Explorations in Economics*, 218.

65. Talcott Parsons, "Introduction: On Certain Sociological Elements in Professor Taussig's Thought," in Viner et al., *Explorations in Economics*, 362, 364.

66. Ibid., 366. An early article of Taussig's in which he commented on the Homestead strike may give some indication of his views close to the time that Croly would have been his student. In this dispassionate review of that bloody strike, Taussig finds both capital and labor to blame, as well as the state authorities. His concluding point is that "the responsibilities of wealth and power were in some degree disregarded." F. W. Taussig, "The Homestead Strike," *Economic Journal* 3 (1893): 318.

67. I think Levy, *Herbert Croly*, follows David Croly much too closely in concluding that Herbert's economics at Harvard were "typical Manchester School laissez-faire theory" (62). See also 67. Taussig might reasonably be called "neo-classical" but not "Manchester School."

68. David G. Croly to H.C., October 22, 1887, Houghton Library, Harvard University.

69. Levy, *Herbert Croly*, 63.

70. David G. Croly to H.C., January 8, 1888, Houghton Library, Harvard University. See also letter of December 14, 1887.

71. Kuklick, *Rise of American Philosophy*.

72. Ibid., 219, 225.

73. Ibid., 46–54, 159–86.

74. Ibid., 184.

75. This openness was noticed by one of Croly's contemporaries: Norman Hapgood, *The Changing Years: Reminiscences of Norman Hapgood* (New York: Farrar and Rinehart, 1930), 60.

76. See Kuklick, *Rise of American Philosophy*, chapter 14. An accessible collection of Royce's writings can be found in John K. Roth, ed., *The Philosophy of Josiah Royce* (Indianapolis: Hackett Publishing Company, 1982).

77. Commentators on Croly disagree on the influence of Royce's thought. Forcey downplays the influence; Charles Forcey, *Crossroads of Liberalism*, 18. David Noble, *The Paradox of Progressive Thought* (Minneapolis: University of Minnesota Press, 1958), chapter 3, sees a greater influence, as does Levy, *Herbert Croly*, 65–67.

78. On Fiske, see Kuklick, *Rise of American Philosophy*, 80–91.

79. H.C. to Royal Cortissoz, October 7, 1916, Houghton Library, Harvard University.

80. See Levy, *Herbert Croly*, 41–42.

81. Levy, *Herbert Croly*, 73.

82. Column of August 30, 1890, quoted in Levy, *Herbert Croly*, 75. Levy also points out that Croly reviewed a number of works by contemporary economists such as Simon Patten, E. R. A. Seligman, and Richard T. Ely. I think this shows that Croly's economics training at Harvard had left him open to an interest in modern economic theory.

83. H.C., "Art and Life," *Architectural Record* 1 (October-December, 1891): 219–227; quotation at 227.

84. Biographical summary of Herbert Croly enclosed with letters from David G. Croly, Houghton Library, Harvard University. There is a chance this summary was written by Felix Frankfurter; it is unsigned.

85. Levy, *Herbert Croly*, 77.

86. Edward Cummings, "Action Under the Labor Arbitration Acts," *Quarterly Journal of Economics* 1 (July 1887): 487–97.

87. Edward Cummings, "Industrial Arbitration in the United States," *Quarterly Journal of Economics* 9 (July 1895): 353–71.

88. Edward Cummings, "The English Trades-Unions," *Quarterly Journal of Economics* 3 (July 1889): 403–35.

89. Edward Cummings, "Co-operative Production in France and England," *Quarterly Journal of Economics* 4 (July 1890): 357–86; for Maison Leclair, see especially 386. For American cooperatives, see Edward Cummings, "Co-operative Stores in the United States," *Quarterly Journal of Economics* 11 (April 1897): 266–79.

90. Ibid., 386.

91. Edward Cummings, "A Collectivist Philosophy of Trade Unionism," *Quarterly Journal of Economics* 13 (January 1899): 151–86; quotation at 183.

92. Ibid., 186.

93. Levy, *Herbert Croly*, 77–78.

94. Kuklick, *Rise of American Philosophy*, 351–57.

95. See Ronald Steel, *Walter Lippmann and the American Century* (Boston: Little, Brown, 1980), 19–22 for a discussion of Santayana as a teacher.

96. Kuklick, *Rise of American Philosophy*, 358.

97. Levy, *Herbert Croly*, 78.

98. Ibid., 79.

99. Ibid., 79–80.

100. Ibid., 80–82.

101. See H.C. to Learned Hand, n.d. (1910), Hand Papers, Harvard Law School Library, indicating that Hand was involved in the awarding of the degree.

102. Levy, *Herbert Croly,* 81.

103. Quoted in Kuklick, *Rise of American Philosophy,* 265. On James's pragmatism, see 179, 264–74.

104. Kuklick, *Rise of American Philosophy,* 275.

105. Josiah Royce, *The World and the Individual* (New York: Macmillan, 1900), 1: preface.

106. Ibid., 15.

107. Ibid., 470.

108. Levy, *Herbert Croly,* 81. Levy emphasizes the course with Norton, which was primarily a consideration of the (sad) state of American culture.

109. Ibid., 82.

110. H.C. to Felix Frankfurter, July 14, 1913, Frankfurter Papers, Library of Congress.

111. H.C., Autobiographical fragment, Felix Frankfurter Papers.

112. Kuklick, *Rise of American Philosophy,* xxii–xxiii.

113. Ibid., 248–56.

114. Harry W. Desmond and Herbert Croly, *Stately Homes in America* (New York: D. Appleton and Co., 1903); William Herbert [Herbert Croly], *Houses for Town and Country* (New York: Duffield and Company, 1907).

115. Robert Grant, *Unleavened Bread* (New York: Charles Scribner's Sons, 1900).

116. H.C., "Why I Wrote My Latest Book: My Aim in 'The Promise of American Life,' " *World's Work* 20 (June 1910): 13086.

117. H.C. to Robert Grant, December 3, 1914, Houghton Library, Harvard University. It is interesting to note that Theodore Roosevelt was also quite taken by the novel but saw it primarily as the moralistic tale of a woman who neglected the duties of motherhood in favor of social advance, suffering in the end her just punishment. John M. Blum, *The Republican Roosevelt* (New York: Atheneum, 1962), 30.

118. H.C., "The Architect in Recent Fiction," *Architectural Record* 17 (February 1905): 139.

119. H.C., "New York as the American Metropolis," *Architectural Record* 13 (March 1903): 200.

120. See Desmond and Croly, *Stately Homes,* 279.

121. H.C., "Henry James and His Countrymen," *Lamp* 28 (February 1905): 52.

122. H.C., "American Artists and Their Public," *Architectural Record* 10 (January 1901): 257.

123. Ibid., 260.

124. See H.C., "Art and Life," 227.

125. H.C., "American Artists," 260–61.

126. H.C., "New York as the American Metropolis," 197.

127. H.C., "Henry James and His Countrymen," 48.

128. H.C., "The New World and the New Art," *Architectural Record* 12 (June 1902): 153. By 1907 Croly saw the beneficial effects of the nationalizing process affecting even architecture. See William Herbert [Herbert Croly], *Houses for Town and Country,* 4.

129. Hans Kohn notes that there were 1.1 million immigrants in the single

year 1906. Hans Kohn, *American Nationalism: An Interpretive Essay* (New York: Collier Books, 1961), 160.

130. Richard Hofstadter, *The Age of Reform: From Bryan to F.D.R.* (1955; reprint, New York: Vintage Books, 1960), 134–37.

131. See, for example, George Mowry, *The Era of Theodore Roosevelt and the Birth of Modern America* (1958; reprint, New York: Harper Torchbooks, 1962), 86; John A. Gable, *The Bull Moose Years: Theodore Roosevelt and the Progressive Party* (Port Washington, N.Y.: Kennikat Press, 1978), 44; John A. Thompson, *Reformers and War: American Progressive Publicists and the First World War* (New York: Cambridge University Press, 1987), 27.

132. Croly had reviewed an earlier Wharton novel. He presumably was familiar with *The House of Mirth*.

133. Grant, *Unleavened Bread*, 15, 115. See also 146.

134. Ibid., 347, 363, 374, 382, 388, 391. Grant also asks, in effect, whether larger industries are more efficient, a central question in Croly's later economic theory. See 389. Earlier commentators on Croly have entirely overlooked the importance of the third section of the novel for his thought. See, for example, Charles Forcey, *Crossroads of Liberalism*, 22–24, or David Levy, *Herbert Croly*, 92, 118, 123–25. Levy goes out of his way to de-emphasize Croly's own references to Grant so as to elevate the Comtean heritage of David Croly.

135. Richard L. McCormick, *From Realignment to Reform: Political Change in New York State, 1893–1910* (Ithaca, N.Y.: Cornell University Press, 1981), 195, 202; quotation from 205. See also 256, where McCormick points out that state regulation increased dramatically in the 1905–1906 period.

136. Grant, *Unleavened Bread*, 273.

137. Mowry, *The Era of Theodore Roosevelt*, 209.

CHAPTER THREE. POLITICAL THEORY
AND "THE PROMISE OF AMERICAN LIFE"

1. H.C., "Why I Wrote My Latest Book," *World's Work* 20 (June 1910): 13086.

2. Walter Lippmann, "Notes for a Biography," *NR* 63 (July 16, 1930): 250.

3. H. G. Wells, *The Future in America: A Search after Realities* (New York: Harper and Brothers, 1904). Wells wrote the series of essays about his impressions of a trip to America. Croly would have appreciated a number of points, including the following attack on Spencer's laissez-faire theory, written after experiencing the "stink . . . brutal economic conflict and squalid filthiness" of "packing-town": "I wish I could catch the soul of Herbert Spencer and tether it in Chicago for awhile to gather fresh evidence upon the superiority of unfettered individualistic enterprises to things managed by the state" (61). Croly also quotes in the beginning of *The Promise of American Life* (New York: Macmillan, 1909; reprint, Hamden, Conn.: Archon Books, 1963) from Hugo Munsterberg's *The Americans* (New York: McClure, Phillips and Company, 1904). Munsterberg was a philosophy professor at Harvard, and though Croly apparently never took a course with him he would have been familiar with his views. On Munsterberg, see Kuklick, *Rise of American Philosophy*, 196–214.

4. H.C., *The Promise*, 2–5.

5. Ibid., 6.

6. Ibid.

7. Ibid., 23.

8. Ibid.

9. Ibid., 426.

10. Ibid., 20.

11. Ibid., 21.

12. Ibid., 278.

13. Ibid., 170.

14. Ibid., 315. Croly's mother's writings, or Taussig's economics, may also have influenced Croly in this area. On the search of Social Democrats and Progressives for a middle way, see James T. Kloppenberg, *Uncertain Victory: Social Democracy and Progressivism in European and American Thought, 1870–1920* (New York: Oxford University Press, 1986), 145–60 and passim.

15. This is a complicated issue. The basic point for classical liberal theory is that an emphasis on individual liberties implied a rejection (at least in theory) of groups and classes and called for certain forms of equality such as equality of rights. The classic statements are John Locke's argument "to have one Rule for Riche and Poor, for the Favourite at Court, and the Country Man at Plough." John Locke, *The Second Treatise of Government*, paragraph 142; or Thomas Jefferson's reprise: "That all men are created equal, that they are endowed by their Creator with certain unalienable Rights." Of course, the political effect of this theory, as in Locke's, may be a critique of both a hereditary aristocracy and a property-less poorer class and the elevation of middle-class values. For the views of modern liberals, note the emphasis in the work of Leonard Hobhouse, an English contemporary of Croly's, on the "welfare of the whole community" and the "ultimate good of society as a whole." Leonard Hobhouse, *Liberalism* (1911; reprint, New York: Oxford University Press, 1964), 41. Or note Lyndon Johnson's comment that he wished to be "President of *all* the people." I return to a more extended discussion of Croly's liberalism below.

16. Richard L. McCormick, *From Realignment to Reform*, 264.

17. Josiah Royce, *The Philosophy of Loyalty* (New York: Macmillan, 1908), 309–10. Croly uses "loyalty" extensively in *The Promise*.

18. H.C., *The Promise*, 28.

19. Ibid., 268.

20. Ibid., 27. Croly noted that "as a matter of fact, the ideal itself has been sensibly modified during the course of this attempt to give it an historical application" (27).

21. Ibid., 6.

22. I will argue below that Croly stated the ideal more narrowly than he actually reasoned. His treatment of democracy inevitably caused him to think about equality as well. Even more important, the centrality of freedom in American thought was not acknowledged in Croly's "national democracy," but his full analysis of the American condition very much took account of the concept of freedom.

23. H.C., *The Promise*, 2.

24. Ibid., 29.

25. Ibid., 40.

26. H.C. to Walter Lippmann, March 30, 1921, Series I, Box 7, Folder 303, Lippmann Papers, Yale University Library.

27. Merrill D. Peterson, *The Jefferson Image in the American Mind* (New York: Oxford University Press, 1962), 339.

28. H.C. *The Promise*, 51. Croly's frequent use of "sterile" versus "fruitful" is a most suggestive turn of phrase. It runs all through his writings.

29. Ibid., 169. In his historical analysis, Croly credited the "Western pioneers" or "Western Democrats" (such as Andrew Jackson) with first effecting the combination of nationality and democracy. But they didn't follow out the implications of this combination in practice. *The Promise*, 61.

30. Ibid., 250.

31. Ibid., 251–52.

32. Ibid., 254–55.

33. Ibid., 284.

34. Ibid.

35. Ibid., 42.

36. Ibid., 43.

37. Ibid., 29. Surprisingly, Croly referred to Jefferson's "intellectual superficiality and insincerity" (29). He also wrote of Jefferson's "triumphant intellectual dishonesty, and of the sacrifice of theory to practice" (419).

38. Ibid., 45.

39. Ibid., 43.

40. Ibid., 43, 44. This and a number of other passages in *The Promise* suggest the influence of Alexis de Tocqueville. Croly does not cite Tocqueville, but he does mention other French liberals and it seems likely he had read *Democracy in America*.

41. Ibid., 176.

42. Ibid., 177, 178. I return to Croly's view of "constitutional liberals" and "genuine liberty" in my discussion of freedom in a following section of this chapter.

43. Ibid., 178, 179.

44. Ibid., 179–80. Croly specifically identified this view with a "square deal," suggesting the point that he makes explicitly elsewhere: that T.R.'s views needed to be "reconstructed" as well.

45. Ibid., 180.

46. Ibid.

47. Ibid., 181.

48. Ibid., 182.

49. Ibid., 184, 185.

50. Ibid., 188.

51. "I agree with you that there is a natural aristocracy among men. The grounds of this are virtue and talents. . . . May we not even say, that that form of government is the best, which provides the most effectually for a pure selection of these natural aristoi into the offices of government?" Thomas Jefferson to John Adams, October 8, 1813, in Adrienne Koch and William Peden, eds., *The Life and Selected Writings of Thomas Jefferson* (New York: Modern Library, 1944), 632–33.

52. H.C., *The Promise*, 189.

53. Ibid., 193.

54. Ibid., 194.

55. Ibid., 198.

56. Ibid., 199.

57. Ibid., 180. My emphasis.

58. Ibid., 195, 196.

59. Ibid., 196.

60. Ibid., 214.

61. Ibid., 207.

62. The literature on democratic theory is vast. See, for instance, Henry B. Mayo, *An Introduction to Democratic Theory* (New York: Oxford University Press, 1960). An interesting discussion of the relation of equality to democratic theory is Charles R. Beitz, *Political Equality: An Essay in Democratic Theory* (Princeton, N.J.: Princeton University Press, 1989).

63. I think that this discussion is related to Croly's argument for a steep inheritance tax. See chapter 4.

64. H.C., *The Promise*, 89.

65. Ibid., 90–91.

66. Ibid., 98. Compare to Hegel's theory of "World-historical individuals" who assist the realization of the world-spirit.

67. Ibid., 170.

68. Compare James Kloppenberg's discussion of Sidney and Beatrice Webb's views. James T. Kloppenberg, *Uncertain Victory*, 205.

69. H.C., *The Promise*, 399.

70. Ibid.

71. Ibid., 400, 454.

72. On John Stuart Mill's use of "regeneration," see Stephan Collini, "Introduction," to Mill, *On Liberty and Other Writings* (New York: Cambridge University Press, 1989), xxi–xxii.

73. H.C., *The Promise*, 281.

74. Ibid., 281–82.

75. Ibid., 282.

76. Ibid., 208. Croly clearly contrasts "brotherhood" to the materialism of laissez-faire theory. It is interesting that his emphasis on brotherhood does not translate into an emphasis on the moral *equality* of individuals. The community is very important to him, but it is a structured not an equalitarian community.

77. Ibid., 79.

78. Ibid., 271.

79. See Kloppenberg, *Uncertain Victory*, 234.

80. H.C., *The Promise*, 35.

81. Ibid.

82. Ibid. Croly's point is inexact. It could be read simply as an endorsement of the amending process of the U.S. Constitution. However, I think Croly's "necessarily prolonged deliberation" and "decisive majority" are meant to be less restrictive.

83. Ibid., 36.

84. Ibid., 200.

85. See Thompson, *Reformers and War*, 72–73.

86. H.C., *The Promise*, 81. It is not wholly clear whether Croly is arguing an innate or a cultural equality, or whether he means for the comment to be specific to the period of slavery.

87. Isaiah Berlin, *Four Essays on Liberty* (New York: Oxford University Press, 1969). See particularly chapter 3 and the introduction.

88. Ibid., 122–31.

89. H.C., *The Promise*, 233, 238–39. By terming the idea English, Croly is suggesting both its importance for American thought and its insufficiency to be the American "formative idea," for which he has proposed "national democracy."

90. Ibid., 235.

91. Ibid., 237. Kloppenberg writes that for European social democrats at the end of the nineteenth century, "the negative concept of liberty had become a pretense shielding privilege" (278). This is precisely Croly's point, but I think he rejected somewhat less of the original (noneconomic) conception of liberty. Lustig (*Corporate Liberalism*, 3) argues that liberalism is inevitably tied to capitalism. I disagree.

92. Berlin, *Four Essays*, 133; see 131–34 for positive freedom.

93. Ibid., 133–54. Berlin's own criticisms of this concept are evident.

94. There *are* elements of Berlin's sense of positive freedom in Royce. See, for example, Josiah Royce, *The World and the Individual: Second Series: Nature, Man and the Moral Order* (New York: Macmillan, 1901), 265, 348. But see also: "Every finite life . . . must be itself unique" (352).

95. Franklin D. Roosevelt, "The Annual Message to the Congress," January 6, 1941, in Franklin D. Roosevelt, *The Public Papers and Addresses of Franklin D. Roosevelt*, ed. Samuel I. Rosenman (New York: Macmillan, 1941), 9: 152. For an excellent brief discussion of positive freedom, see Amartya Sen, "Individual Freedom as a Social Commitment," *New York Review of Books* 37 (June 14, 1990): 49–54.

96. T. H. Green, "Liberal Legislation and Freedom of Contract," in R. L. Nettleship, ed., *Works of Thomas Hill Green* (London: Longmans, Green and Co., 1888), 3: 371.

97. Ibid., 372. Berlin (*Four Essays*, xlix) argues that this passage indicates the first (moral) sense of positive freedom. It *is* related, but I think the passage is not Hegelian but rather emphasizes economic security. See Kloppenberg, *Uncertain Victory*, 396, for other passages in which Green describes positive freedom in this sense. I agree with Kloppenberg's emphasis on the differences between Hegel and Green.

98. Hobhouse, *Liberalism*, 71.

99. Ibid., 78. Hobhouse emphasizes state compulsion as countering economic restrictions on the individual.

100. H.C., *The Promise*, 205.

101. Ibid., 409.

102. Ibid., 416.

103. Ibid., 196.

104. Ibid., 414.

105. Ibid.

106. David G. Croly, *A Positivist Primer*, 85.

107. H.C., *The Promise*, 453. This emphasis on brotherhood could echo Comte's "religion of humanity," but it seems to me a more general religious inspiration that runs through Croly's life and thought. Much of his religious terminology is specifically Christian rather than Comtean and seems to derive more from Jane Croly's influence (her brother was a minister) and particularly from Herbert's extensive study of Christianity at Harvard. I disagree with Levy's very strong emphasis on the Comtean influence. See, for example, Levy, *Herbert Croly*, 131.

108. Santayana, quoted by Croly, ibid., 454.

109. Ibid.

110. Hobhouse, *Liberalism*, 70.

111. Ibid., 118.

112. John Rawls, *A Theory of Justice* (Cambridge, Mass.: Harvard University Press, 1971). "The Idea of Social Union" is the title of section 79. Rawls resists the

label of "liberal," but most commentators have viewed the book as the best statement of contemporary liberal political theory.

CHAPTER FOUR. "THE PROMISE"
AND REFORM POLITICS

1. Historians have diverse interpretations of the progressive movement. See Richard L. McCormick, *The Party Period and Public Policy: American Politics from the Age of Jackson to the Progressive Era* (New York: Oxford University Press, 1986), especially chapters 7 and 9, for an overview of historical interpretation of the period.
2. H.C., *The Promise*, 274.
3. Richard Franklin Bensel, *Yankee Leviathan: The Origins of Central State Authority in America, 1859–1877* (Cambridge, Mass.: Cambridge University Press, 1990) provides an interesting argument that a nationalized American state eventually emerged from the Civil War.
4. H.C., *The Promise*, 275.
5. Ibid., 276.
6. Ibid., 278.
7. McCormick, *The Party Period and Public Policy*, 272.
8. H.C., *The Promise*, 69.
9. Quoted in Mowry, *Era of Theodore Roosevelt*, 227. Emphasis in the original.
10. H.C., *The Promise*, 330.
11. Ibid., 329.
12. Ibid., 333.
13. Ibid., 339.
14. See McCormick, *Realignment to Reform*, chapters 7 and 8; McCormick, *The Party Period and Public Policy*, chapters 8 and 9.
15. H.C., *The Promise*, 340, 341.
16. Robert H. Wiebe, *The Search for Order, 1877–1920* (New York: Hill and Wang, 1967), 181. Wiebe argues that corporations were also instrumental in developing this new administrative emphasis.
17. Ibid., 160. Wiebe includes Croly as one of the major originators of this view, 159. See also Samuel Haber, *Efficiency and Uplift: Scientific Management in the Progressive Era, 1890–1920* (Chicago: University of Chicago Press, 1964), especially pages 83–89.
18. McCormick, *The Party Period and Public Policy*, 305.
19. On the growth of bureaucracy in the American system, see William E. Nelson, *The Roots of American Bureaucracy, 1830–1900* (Cambridge, Mass.: Harvard University Press, 1982); Stephen Skowronek, *Building a New American State: The Expansion of National Administrative Capacities, 1877–1920* (Cambridge, Mass.: Cambridge University Press, 1982).
20. H.C., *The Promise*, 343.
21. For a discussion of the elite theory of democracy, see Mostafa Rejai, "The Metamorphosis of Democratic Theory," *Ethics* 77 (April 1967): 202–8. See also E. E. Schattschneider, *The Semisovereign People: A Realist's View of Democracy in America* (New York: Holt, Rinehart and Winston, 1960).
22. H.C., "A Great School of Political Science," *World's Work* 20 (May 1910): 12887–88, at 12888. The article also comments favorably on the establishment of the Rockefeller Foundation.

23. McCormick, *The Party Period and Public Policy*, 271.

24. H.C., *The Promise*, 69, 320–27.

25. Ibid., 133.

26. Ibid.

27. Ibid.

28. Ibid., 136.

29. William Allen White, *The Old Order Changeth* (New York: Macmillan, 1910), 57.

30. H.C., *The Promise*, 320.

31. Ibid.

32. Ibid., 327.

33. Ibid., 328.

34. Ibid. For a contemporary account of the Oregon system, see James Barnett, *The Operation of the Initiative, Referendum, and Recall in Oregon* (New York: Macmillan, 1915).

35. H. L. Mencken, "Roosevelt: An Autopsy," in *Prejudices: Second Series* (London: Jonathan Cope, 1921), 123.

36. See McCormick, *The Party Period and Public Policy*, chapter 4, especially 176–80. See also chapter 2 in which McCormick reviews works by historians and political scientists on the theory of critical elections or crucial realignments in the party system. It is normally assumed that 1896 was the crucial election dominating the party system of the progressive period, but it is not clear that this theory explains much about progressivism.

37. McCormick, *From Realignment to Reform*, 227.

38. Ibid., 244. The Hughes bill continued to give party organizations a greater role than many more radical progressives desired.

39. H.C., *The Promise*, 342.

40. On the commission and its founder and chief force, Charles Francis Adams, see Thomas K. McGraw, *Prophets of Regulation* (Cambridge, Mass.: Harvard University Press, 1984), chapters 1 and 2.

41. Ibid., 62.

42. Ibid. See also Lewis L. Gould, *The Presidency of Theodore Roosevelt* (Lawrence: University Press of Kansas, 1991), for a full study of Roosevelt's administration.

43. On the FDA and Roosevelt's involvement, see Robert M. Crunden, *Ministers of Reform: The Progressives' Achievements in American Civilization, 1889–1920* (New York: Basic Books, 1982), chapter 6. Crunden's evaluation of the effectiveness of this legislation is primarily negative; see 196–97. See also James Harvey Young, *Pure Food: Securing the Federal Food and Drugs Act of 1906* (Princeton, N.J.: Princeton University Press, 1989).

44. David Vogel, "The 'New' Social Regulation in Historical and Comparative Perspective," in Thomas K. McGraw, ed., *Regulation in Perspective* (Cambridge, Mass.: Harvard University Press, 1981), 166.

45. Ibid. Vogel's point raises the large question of the relation of business to progressive regulation. Lustig, *Corporate Liberalism*, emphasizes the benefit that many businessmen derived from regulation. No doubt this was true in many cases. However, my own sense is that Richard McCormick better captures the political dynamic when he writes that "commonly, the affected interests opposed state regulation until its passage became inevitable, at which point they entered the contest in order to influence the details of the law" (McCormick, *The Party Period and Public Policy*, 354n).

46. Theodore Roosevelt, Annual Message to Congress, 1906, in William Harbaugh, ed., *The Writings of Theodore Roosevelt* (Indianapolis: Bobbs-Merrill Company, 1967), 96. See Gould, *The Presidency of Theodore Roosevelt*, 212–15, for Roosevelt's theory of regulation.

47. Ibid., 94.

48. Ibid., 95.

49. Mowry, *Era of Theodore Roosevelt*, 221–22.

50. H.C., *The Promise*, 355.

51. Ibid., 351–52, 360. Croly clearly hoped that the Court would take the step that it finally did take in 1937 and refuse to intervene in most questions of regulating the economy. Many of Croly's points in his economic analysis could have been influenced by arguments in a work he cited early in the book: Hugo Munsterberg, *The Americans*, trans. Edwin B. Holt (New York: McClure, Phillips and Co., 1904), especially 301–18. Munsterberg's comparisons to Germany make an interesting contrast. German social legislation was certainly one influence on Croly.

52. H.C., *Marcus Alonzo Hanna: His Life and Work* (New York: Macmillan, 1912; reprint, Hamden, Conn.: Archon Books, 1965).

53. See, for example, Gabriel Kolko, *The Triumph of Conservatism* (New York: Free Press, 1963; reprint, Chicago: Quadrangle Books, 1967), 216.

54. H.C., *Marcus Alonzo Hanna*, 467–71.

55. Ibid.; see also *The Promise*, 24.

56. H.C. to Learned Hand, "Tuesday" [December 19, 1911?], Hand Papers. See also *The Promise*, 115.

57. H.C., *The Promise*, 369. See also 357.

58. Ibid., 359.

59. Ibid., 191.

60. Ibid., 360–61.

61. Ibid., 361–62.

62. Ibid., 364–65.

63. Ibid., 366.

64. Ibid., 370. Lustig (*Corporate Liberalism*, 210) argues that this proposal was taken directly from Henry George.

65. Ibid., 370–71.

66. Ibid., 372.

67. Ibid.

68. Ibid., 372–73.

69. Ibid., 373–78; quotation at 378.

70. Ibid., 379.

71. See Kloppenberg, *Uncertain Victory*, 256. Municipal ownership of utilities was quite common. See McCormick, *From Realignment to Reform*, 156–57.

72. H.C., *The Promise*, 127.

73. Ibid., 126–31.

74. Ibid., 385–88; quotation at 387.

75. Ibid., 205.

76. Ibid., 367.

77. Ibid., 381–84.

78. Ibid., 384. Roosevelt had called for an inheritance tax and discussed an income tax in his December 1906 message to Congress. See Gould, *The Presidency of Theodore Roosevelt*, 162, 245.

79. For an overview of progressivism and urban reform, see Wiebe, *The*

Search for Order, 166–74. See also Michael H. Ebner and Eugene Tobin, eds., *The Age of Urban Reform: New Perspectives on the Progressive Era* (Port Washington, N.Y.: Kennikat Press, 1977).

80. Thompson, *Reformers and War,* 120.

81. William E. Leuchtenburg, "Progressivism and Imperialism: The Progressive Movement and American Foreign Policy, 1898–1916," *Mississippi Valley Historical Review* 39 (December 1952): 483.

82. Ibid., 498. On Roosevelt and progressive foreign policy, see also Wiebe, *The Search for Order,* chapter 9.

83. Ibid., 501.

84. H.C., *The Promise,* 289.

85. Ibid., 310. Compare Croly's brief argument to the writings of such contemporaries as Brooks Adams. See Adams, *The Law of Civilization and Decay* (New York: Macmillan, 1896), *America's Economic Supremacy* (New York: Macmillan 1900), and other works.

86. Ibid., 308.

87. Ibid., 308–9.

88. Ibid., 293.

89. Ibid., 293–94, 300–303.

90. Ibid., 297–98.

91. Ibid., 309.

92. Mowry, *Era of Theodore Roosevelt,* 280–81.

93. H.C., *The Promise,* 154–67.

94. Ibid., 167.

95. Crunden, *Ministers of Reform,* 276–77. McCormick, *The Party Period and Public Policy,* 271, agrees that most progressives were evangelical.

96. Ibid., 276.

97. Hand to Roosevelt, April 8, 1910, Hand Papers, Harvard Law School. Hand praised the book highly in letters to Croly. Lodge also recommended the book to Roosevelt, who ordered another copy. See Roosevelt to Lodge, April 27, 1910, in Elting E. Morison, ed., *The Letters of Theodore Roosevelt* (Cambridge, Mass.: Harvard University Press, 1954), 7: 76–77.

98. Roosevelt to Hand, April 22, 1910, Hand Papers.

99. Roosevelt to Croly, quoted in Croly to Hand, August 1, 1910, Hand Papers. Levy cites Ray Stannard Baker as visiting Oyster Bay in this period and seeing *The Promise* with Roosevelt's comments in the margins. Levy, *Herbert Croly,* 139.

CHAPTER FIVE. PROGRESSIVISM
AND "PROGRESSIVE DEMOCRACY"

1. Levy, *Herbert Croly,* 132–36, discusses the reception of the book and summarizes a number of reviews.

2. Alvin Johnson, *Pioneer's Progress* (New York: Viking Press, 1952), 232.

3. Theodore Roosevelt, *Social Justice and Popular Rule,* vol. 19 of *Works of Theodore Roosevelt,* Memorial Edition, ed. H. Hagedorn (New York: Charles Scribner's Sons, 1925), 86; see also 138 for a reference to Croly's work.

4. Hand to H.C., February 6, 1911, Hand Papers, Harvard Law School.

5. H.C. to Hand, March 5, 1911, Hand Papers.

6. H.C. to Hand, February 3, 1911. Croly used the "disfigurement" point

specifically about a series of articles he wrote for the *Cleveland Leader*, but it seems applicable to other writings as well.

7. H.C. to Hand, "Monday, 1913" [Summer 1913], Hand Papers. The Straights invited Croly to form the *New Republic* in the summer of 1913 (see below). See the Croly-Hand correspondence for a more general discussion of Croly's finances.

8. H.C., "Democratic Factions and Insurgent Republicans," *North American Review* 191 (May 1910): 626–35.

9. H.C., *The Promise*, 163.

10. Ibid., 171.

11. H.C., "Democratic Factions and Insurgent Republicans," 626.

12. Ibid., 628, 629.

13. Ibid., 631.

14. Ibid., 631–32.

15. Ibid., 633–35.

16. Ibid., 634.

17. Ibid., 634–35.

18. On the conservation commission, see Loomis Havemeyer, *Conservation of Our National Resources* (New York: Macmillan, 1931), 8–12. On the Ballinger-Pinchot affair, see Alpheus T. Mason, *Bureaucracy Convicts Itself: The Ballinger-Pinchot Controversy of 1910* (New York: Viking Press, 1941); James L. Penick, Jr., *Progressive Politics and Conservation: The Ballinger-Pinchot Affair* (Chicago: University of Chicago Press, 1968).

19. Frederick Jackson Turner, "Social Forces in American History," [December 28, 1910, presidential address to the AHA], in Frederick Jackson Turner, *The Frontier in American History* (New York: Henry Holt and Company, 1920), 312, 317–18.

20. Ibid., 319–20. On the connection of monopolies to conservation, see also the writings of Charles Van Hise, especially his *Conservation of Natural Resources in the United States* (New York: Macmillan, 1910). Van Hise was soon to agree with Croly on the regulation of corporations, as opposed to the Brandeis argument for antitrust prosecution.

21. John M. Cooper, Jr., *The Warrior and the Priest: Woodrow Wilson and Theodore Roosevelt* (Cambridge, Mass.: Harvard University Press, 1983), 147.

22. The title was given to the collection of speeches published by the *Outlook* in 1910. See Theodore Roosevelt, *The New Nationalism*, ed. William E. Leuchtenburg (Englewood Cliffs, N.J.: Prentice-Hall, 1961) for a slightly abbreviated edition.

23. Ibid., 36.

24. See William E. Leuchtenburg, "Introduction" to ibid., for an argument that Roosevelt was more influential on Croly than Croly on Roosevelt; yet, Leuchtenburg argues that "in Croly's work, we can find a more systematic statement of Roosevelt's New Nationalism than Roosevelt himself ever found time to set down." (13). Mowry, *Era of Theodore Roosevelt*, 222, argues that most of the ideas in the speeches could be found in T.R.'s earlier presidential messages. Cooper, *The Warrior and the Priest*, argues that "aside from a somewhat greater specificity about regulatory legislation, nothing in *The New Nationalism* was new to Roosevelt except the phrase" (145). Cooper argues for a coincidence of opinions. Levy, *Herbert Croly*, argues for an "unspectacular, quiet, confirming influence" of Croly on Roosevelt (140).

25. Roosevelt, *The New Nationalism*, 165. Roosevelt noted that his chief "development" was to adapt a quotation from Lincoln.

26. Levy relies on a Walter Lippmann recollection. See Levy, *Herbert Croly,* 140. However, Elting E. Morison's chronology of Roosevelt's appointments in this period shows no meeting with Croly between August 1 and the Osawatomie speech on August 31, 1910. Croly did have lunch with T.R. on October 6, 1910. See Morison, ed., *Letters of Theodore Roosevelt*, 8:1470–71.

27. Roosevelt, *The New Nationalism*, 170.

28. H.C. to Hand, "Thursday, 1910," Hand Papers. (The text of this letter seems to indicate that it was written just after the election, despite a customary dating of October 20, 1910.) See also Croly to Hand, October 29, 1910.

29. H.C. to Hand, November 4, 1910, Hand Papers. Emphasis in the original. Croly's sarcasm clearly indicates an awareness of the very limited influence he was likely to have on T.R.

30. Hand to H.C., November 7, 1910, Hand Papers.

31. Mowry, *Era of Theodore Roosevelt*, 272–73; Cooper, *The Warrior and the Priest*, 152–53.

32. H.C. to Hand, "Thursday, 1910," Hand Papers. See note 28.

33. John D. Buenker, *Urban Liberalism and Progressive Reform* (New York: Charles Scribner's Sons, 1973), 222. See chapter 7 for Buenker's full statement of the argument that there are many progressivisms, and that urban, Democratic liberalism grew gradually from 1904 up to the 1928 election and the New Deal.

34. Barnett, *The Operation of the Initiative, Referendum and Recall in Oregon*, 191. On judges, see 289. U'Ren wrote widely on Oregon developments, including a summary article in *LaFollette's Magazine* in 1910. See Barnett, 226, for his writings. On U'Ren, see also Mowry, *Era of Theodore Roosevelt*, 77.

35. William S. U'Ren to H.C., December 18, 1911, Houghton Library, Harvard University.

36. H.C., "State Political Reorganization," in *Proceedings of the American Political Science Association* (Concord, N.H.: Rumford Press, 1912), 8: 122–25.

37. Ibid., 125, 128.

38. Ibid., 131.

39. Ibid., 132.

40. William S. U'Ren, "Remarks on Mr. Herbert Croly's Paper on 'State Political Reorganization,' " in ibid., 136–39; quotation at 139. See also U'Ren's progressive program on 137.

41. Chester H. Rowell, "Remarks on Mr. Herbert Croly's Paper on 'State Political Reorganization,' " ibid., 140–51; quotation at 143. The paper is a nice summary of progressive political achievements.

42. See H.C., *Marcus Alonzo Hanna*, 311–14.

43. H.C. to Hand, February 24, 1911, Hand Papers.

44. H.C., *Marcus Alonzo Hanna*, 306.

45. Ibid., 326.

46. Ibid.

47. Levy, *Herbert Croly,* 146–50, argues that Croly seriously compromised his intellectual convictions in this biography. I think this judgment is harsh.

48. H.C. to Hand, January 12, 1912. See also Hand to H.C., November 24, 1911; H.C. to Hand, December 10, 1911, on meeting with Roosevelt, Hand Papers.

49. Levy, *Herbert Croly,* 154.

50. See Roosevelt to H.C., February 29, 1912, commenting on these issues, in Morison, ed., *Letters of Theodore Roosevelt,* 7: 512.

51. H.C. to Hand, July 13, 1912, Hand Papers.

52. Ibid. recounts a meeting that was scheduled but not held. See also H.C. to Roosevelt, July 26, 1912, Roosevelt Papers, Library of Congress, in which Croly responds to their "conversation" by assuming that Roosevelt had suggested that Croly might someday write his biography: "I shall keep the possible assignment constantly in mind." Roosevelt replied by gently evading any commitment. See Roosevelt to H.C., July 30, 1912, in Morison, *Letters of Theodore Roosevelt* 7: 582.

53. H.C., "A Test of Faith in Democracy," *American Magazine* 75 (November 1912): 21–23.

54. Ibid., 22.

55. Ibid.

56. Ibid., 23. The phrasing "social democratic ideal" is new and points toward Croly's argument in *Progressive Democracy.*

57. Ibid.

58. John A. Gable, *The Bull Moose Years,* 100. The Gable book is an excellent source on the Progressive campaign. The Croly draft apparently no longer exists, but it is referred to in platform committee minutes.

59. Ibid., 100–102.

60. Ibid., 117–18, 190.

61. Theodore Roosevelt, "Address to the Progressive Party National Convention," August 6, 1912, in Harbaugh, ed., *The Writings of Theodore Roosevelt,* 109.

62. Ibid., 112. Roosevelt cited the work of Charles Van Hise to support his economic analysis. See Charles Van Hise, *Concentration and Control* (New York: Macmillan, 1912). Roosevelt attempted to reconcile his emphases by saying that any corporation that did not accept regulation would be subject to the Sherman Act.

63. Quoted in John Wells Davidson, ed., *A Crossroads of Freedom: The 1912 Campaign Speeches of Woodrow Wilson* (New Haven, Conn.: Yale University Press, 1956), 161–62. On the Wilson campaign, see Arthur Link, *Wilson: The Road to the White House* (Princeton, N.J.: Princeton University Press, 1947), 482–528; Cooper, *The Warrior and the Priest,* 187–205.

64. Link, *Road to the White House,* 493; Gable, *Bull Moose Years,* 121; Norman Hapgood, *The Changing Years: Reminiscences of Norman Hapgood* (New York: Farrar and Rinehart, 1930), 225. Hapgood was fired in mid-October by Robert Collier, who supported Roosevelt. Levy, *Herbert Croly,* 188.

65. Hand to Frankfurter, September 12, 1912, quoted in Levy, *Herbert Croly,* 156.

66. Quoted in Gable, *Bull Moose Years,* 123.

67. See Harbaugh, *Writings of Theodore Roosevelt,* 333–44.

68. Roosevelt and Wilson quoted in Cooper, *The Warrior and the Priest,* 196–97.

69. Roosevelt did best in the Midwest. Alfred Chandler, "The Origins of Progressive Leadership," in Morison, ed., *The Letters of Theodore Roosevelt,* 8: 1462–65, emphasizes that the Progressive party leaders were overwhelmingly professional, upper-middle-class, native-born Protestants. Most had previously

been Republicans. Wilson perhaps drew support from a newer and broader progressivism.

70. Thomas McGraw, *Prophets of Regulation*, 116.

71. Roosevelt to H.C., January 7, 1913, quoted in Levy, *Herbert Croly,* 159.

72. Herbert Croly, *Progressive Democracy* (New York: Macmillan, 1914), 1–2.

73. Ibid., 3–15. Note the comment that Mark Hanna had run on a "frankly and crassly conservative platform" (3).

74. Ibid., 208.

75. Ibid., 11.

76. Ibid., 335.

77. Ibid., 334–35.

78. Ibid., 335.

79. Ibid., 16.

80. Ibid., 337.

81. Ibid., 344.

82. Ibid., 338.

83. Ibid., 339.

84. On the 1913 elections, see Gable, *Bull Moose Years*, 179–80.

85. H.C., *Progressive Democracy,* 25.

86. Ibid., 100, for example.

87. Ibid., 176, 184, 278 as examples.

88. Ibid., 184. The analogy runs from 184 to 194.

89. Ibid., 190.

90. Ibid., 191.

91. Ibid., 192.

92. Ibid., 196. On Croly's pragmatism, see below.

93. Ibid., 197. Croly does not cite specific social psychologists in *Progressive Democracy.* David Noble has suggested that James Mark Baldwin and Charles H. Cooley are two social psychologists who could have influenced Croly. See Noble, *Paradox of Progressive Thought*, chapters 5 and 6. However, in a letter to Willard Straight at the time, Croly did mention reading Foster F. Wood, *Applied Sociology;* E. A. Ross, *Social Control* (New York: Macmillan, 1901); and Charles Ellwood, *Sociology in Its Psychological Aspects* (New York: D. Appleton, 1912). See H.C. to Willard Straight, August 6, 1913, Willard Straight Papers. It is also likely that Croly would have read Arthur Bentley's *The Process of Government* (Chicago: University of Chicago Press, 1908), a seminal work in pluralist theory.

94. Ibid., 317; see also 320.

95. Ibid., 197. Oliver Wendell Holmes, Jr., wrote to Croly praising *Progressive Democracy* but noting that he thought Croly had overestimated the importance of the nation. Holmes to H.C., November 22, 1914, Houghton Library, Harvard University. The bulk of the letter is a commentary on a brief discussion of Croly's on the economic theory of rent.

96. Ibid., 32.

97. Ibid., 32–35, 58–59.

98. Ibid., 147.

99. Holmes to Croly, November 22, 1914, Houghton Library, Harvard University.

100. H.C., *Progressive Democracy,* 151.

101. Ibid., 308.

102. See Ibid., 276–78 for a veiled discussion of an elite, which is then rejected for a "progressive democratic society."

103. James Kloppenberg has made this suggestion in a letter to the author. See Kloppenberg's discussion of Dewey's democracy in *Uncertain Victory,* 140–42, 383–84, 402–3.

104. See Walter Weyl, *The New Democracy* (New York: Macmillan, 1912; reprint, New York: Harper Torchbooks, 1964). See Weyl's diary for accounts of dinners with the Crolys and meeting Croly at a Progressive party conference in December 1912. Weyl Papers, Rutgers University. Croly met with Weyl regularly from the fall of 1913 while planning the *New Republic.*

105. H.C., "The Breach in Civilization" (unpublished book manuscript), Houghton Library, Harvard University, 24, 28, 44, and passim. This manuscript is discussed in chapter 8.

106. H.C., *Progressive Democracy,* 35.

107. Ibid.

108. Ibid., 37–38.

109. Ibid., 225. See also 271–72, 226–27, 217–18, and 120–21 for passages on the concept of rights.

110. Ibid., 78–79, 346.

111. Ibid., 112. We will consider Croly's views on private property further in dealing with his economic policy recommendations.

112. See Ibid., 125, 404–5. See also 412–13 for an argument against the "morality of repression and restraint" that is close to an endorsement of negative freedom.

113. Ibid., 384.

114. Ibid., 418–19. See also 119, 380–81.

115. Ibid., 25, 171–72, 198. See also 192, 429.

116. Ibid., 199.

117. Ibid., 404–5. See 421 and 423 for very definite references to Dewey's educational theory. A passage on 426–27 is a possible exception to the balance; Croly is very close to an organic theory here.

118. Ibid., 177–78.

119. Ibid., 217. See also 121, 183, 219, 240, 246, and 371 for passages showing Croly's pragmatism.

120. Ibid., 427.

121. Ibid., 425.

122. Ibid., 429–30. Compare Marx's hope that communism would bring a society that "makes it possible for me to do one thing today and another tomorrow, to hunt in the morning, fish in the afternoon, rear cattle in the evening, criticise after dinner, just as I have a mind." Karl Marx and Friedrich Engels, *The German Ideology,* in Robert Tucker, ed., *The Marx-Engels Reader,* 2d ed. (New York: W. W. Norton and Company, 1978), 160. Croly's utopia is appropriately more specialized.

123. Ibid., 217.

124. Ibid., 240. On 243 Croly suggests adopting a federal grants-in-aid program for the states.

125. Ibid., 271.

126. Ibid., 351.

127. Ibid., 369.

128. Ibid., 370. See also 360, 363–64, and 371 for additional descriptions of

the bureaucracy.
129. Ibid., 352.
130. Ibid., 353.
131. On the Progressive Service, see Gable, *Bull Moose Years*, 162–72, 184–88; Donald R. Richberg, *Tents of the Mighty* (New York: Willett, Clark and Colby, 1930), 40–48. On Croly's attendance at the Progressive meeting, see Walter Weyl diaries, December 15, 1912, Weyl Papers, Rutgers University.
132. H.C., *Progressive Democracy,* 236.
133. Ibid., 349. See also 99, 342.
134. Ibid., 304.
135. Ibid., 254, 306.
136. Ibid., 268.
137. Ibid., 272, 325.
138. Ibid., 264.
139. Ibid., 265.
140. Theodore Roosevelt, "Two Noteworthy Books on Democracy," *Outlook* 108 (November 1914): 648–51. The review is reprinted in Harbaugh, ed., *Writings of Theodore Roosevelt*, 344–52.
141. H.C., *Progressive Democracy,* 284–302.
142. Ibid., 295.
143. Ibid., 300.
144. Ibid., 301.
145. Ibid., 308.
146. Ibid., 292–93.
147. Ibid., 135, 142.
148. Ibid., 149; see also 234–35.
149. Ibid., 231; see also 245.
150. Ibid., 400.
151. Franklin D. Roosevelt, "Campaign Address on Progressive Government" at the Commonwealth Club, San Francisco, September 23, 1932, in Samuel I. Rosenman, ed., *The Public Papers and Addresses of Franklin D. Roosevelt* (New York: Random House, 1938) 1: 752.
152. H.C., *Progressive Democracy,* 402.
153. Ibid., 402–3.
154. Ibid., 403.
155. Ibid., 391–93.
156. Ibid., 407.
157. Ibid., 113.
158. Ibid., 116. Croly adds another point: that his proposed policy would "seek to create a system of special discipline, coextensive with the system of special privilege, the object of which will be the assurance, as a result of its operation, of socially desirable fruits" (116). I take this to be an argument for regulation of business practices.
159. Ibid., 11.
160. In explaining why *Progressive Democracy* didn't sell very well, Croly wrote to Willard Straight that "people are not seriously concerned with domestic social and political problems now. They are still so much preoccupied by the war . . . that they cannot concentrate upon a book which is confined entirely to the discussion of domestic policy." H.C. to Willard Straight, December 17, 1914, Willard Straight Papers.

CHAPTER SIX. DOMESTIC LIBERALISM
IN A "NEW REPUBLIC"

1. Diary of Dorothy Straight, courtesy of Karolyn Gould.
2. The best source on Straight is Herbert Croly, *Willard Straight* (New York: Macmillan, 1924). On Straight's work from November 1915 to April 1917 as vice president of the American International Corporation, a business consortium seeking concessions in underdeveloped countries during World War I, see Harry N. Scheiber, "World War I as Entrepreneurial Opportunity: Willard Straight and the American International Corporation," *Political Science Quarterly* 84 (September 1969): 486–511.
3. Willard Straight to H.C., December 29, 1914, Willard Straight Papers, Cornell University.
4. On Dorothy Straight, see W. A. Swanberg, *Whitney Father, Whitney Heiress* (New York: Charles Scribner's Sons, 1980).
5. Gilbert Harrison memorandum of interview with Dorothy Straight Elmhirst, March 3, 1964, Dorothy Straight Elmhirst Papers, Cornell University.
6. Ibid. See also Croly's account in *Willard Straight*, 472–73.
7. The finances of the *New Republic* are detailed in the Dorothy Straight Elmhirst Papers, Cornell University.
8. H.C., *Willard Straight*, 473–74.
9. As an illustration of the journal's independence, note that Willard Straight published his own endorsement of Charles Evans Hughes in 1916, after the editors had individually endorsed Wilson. But see also Herbert Croly to Walter Lippmann, "Saturday morning" [1916]: "I promised Willard before he went away that whatever else we did we would not nag Roosevelt. We have not done that but in his state of mind he will think we have," Series I, Box 7, Folder 303, Walter Lippmann Papers, Yale University. This comment is a very rare instance in which Straight's views may have affected editorial policy. There are many letters in which it is clear that Croly did not follow Straight's suggestions or use material Straight had submitted. See especially Willard Straight to H.C., March 1, 1915, Willard Straight Papers. On the relationship to the Straights, see also David Levy, *Herbert Croly*, 205–9. David Seideman, *The New Republic: A Voice of Modern Liberalism* (New York: Praeger, 1986), 10–45, is less sanguine about the paper's editorial purity.
10. Walter Weyl Diary, Weyl Papers, Rutgers University. The entry is dated September 28, 1912, but from chronological location it must be September 28, 1913. On Weyl, see Forcey, *Crossroads of Liberalism*, 52–87.
11. H.C. to Learned Hand, December 21, 1913, Hand Papers.
12. H.C. to Learned Hand, January 5, 1914, Hand Papers.
13. See H.C. to Learned Hand, July 29, 1914, regarding Hand's participation. Croly apparently also asked George Rublee, his and Hand's Cornish, N.H., neighbor. See H.C. to Hand, December 21, 1913, Hand Papers.
14. See David Levy, *Herbert Croly*, 203–4, on the editorial arrangements. There are many comments in Croly's letters attesting to his reluctance to be identified as chief; see, for example, H.C. to Eduard Lindeman, July 23, 1924, Lindeman Papers. See also H.C., *Willard Straight*, 473, regarding the editorial board.
15. Walter Lippmann to John Lothrop, November 23, 1914, Series I, Box 17, Folder 690, Lippmann Papers.

16. Ibid.

17. Untitled four-page typescript, noted "Croly" and "1914" in Series I, Box 22, Folder 875, Lippmann Papers. The similarity of the phrasing to the concluding pages of *Progressive Democracy* is clear. Croly goes on to say that the paper would afford a contributor the opportunity "of laboring in cooperation with right-minded associates for the benefit of an ultimate human ideal."

18. H.C., *Willard Straight*, 473.

19. H.C. to Willard Straight, November 29, 1914, Willard Straight Papers. Of his new associates, Croly noted: "I am depending on my own influence over them gradually to make them see the problem and the work as I see it."

20. H.C. to Randolph Bourne, June 3, 1914, Bourne Papers, Columbia University.

21. H.C. to Learned Hand, August 17, 1914, Hand Papers.

22. H.C. "The Obligation of the Vote," *NR* 4 (October 9, 1915): part 2, 5–6.

23. H.C., "The Future of the State," *NR* 12 (September 15, 1917): 182–83. See also "The Expert and American Society," *NR* 15 (May 4, 1918): 5–8, especially 7–8, for a discussion of subordinate social units. (This article is unsigned, as were all editorial "leaders" and most lead articles in the *NR*. Editorials had no titles and are therefore cited only by issue and page; articles were titled.)

24. H.C., "The Obligation of the Vote," *NR* 4 (October 9, 1915): 6.

25. See, for example, "Who Owns the Universities," *NR* 3 (July 31, 1915): 269–70; editorial leader on Columbia University, *NR* 10 (March 10, 1917): 149–50; and the statement by Charles A. Beard, *NR* 13 (December 29, 1917): 249–50.

26. "Liberalism in the National Army," *NR* 12 (September 8, 1917): 147–48; John Dewey, "Conscience and Compulsion," *NR* 11 (July 14, 1917): 297–98.

27. "Amnesty for Conscientious Objectors," *NR* 17 (January 11, 1919): 299–300.

28. See the following chapter.

29. O. W. Holmes to H.C., May 12, 1919; reprinted in Mark DeWolfe Howe, ed., The *Holmes-Laski Letters*, 1916–1935 (Cambridge, Mass.: Harvard University Press, 1953), 1: 203.

30. H.C., "Counsel of Humility," *NR* 13 (December 15, 1917): 176.

31. Harold J. Laski, "The Apotheosis of the State," *NR* 7 (July 22, 1916) 302–4.

32. H.C., "The Meaning of It," *NR* 4 (August 7, 1915): 10–11.

33. *NR* 7 (June 24, 1916): 181.

34. George Santayana, "Classic Liberty," *NR* 4 (August 21, 1915): 65–66; "German Freedom," *NR* 4 (August 28, 1915): 94–96; "Liberalism and Culture," *NR* 4 (September 4, 1915): 123–25.

35. See, for example, *NR* 15 (July 27, 1918): 356: "Liberal fighting spirit . . . made of England a combination of the freest and the best governed country in the world."

36. *NR* 1 (November 7, 1914): 5.

37. "The Burden of Presidential Office," *NR* 3 (June 19, 1915): 162. This article is almost certainly by Croly. See also "Majority Rule," *NR* 4 (August 21, 1915): 58–60.

38. "Executive Leadership," *NR* 4 (August 14, 1915): 31–32.

39. "Preparedness—A Trojan Horse," *NR* 5 (November 6, 1915): 6–7.

40. "Disintegrated America," *NR* 6 (March 11, 1916): 141–43.

41. "The Failure of the States," *NR* 9 (December 16, 1916): 170–72.

42. *NR* 1 (January 30, 1915): 5. See also "Majority Rule," *NR* 4 (August 21, 1915): 58–60.

43. *NR* 1 (January 23, 1915): 3–4.

44. *NR* 2 (March 6, 1915): part 2.

45. Charles A. Beard, "Reconstructing State Government," *NR* 4 (August 21, 1915): part 2, 1–16.

46. "The Future of the Two-Party System," *NR* 1 (November 14, 1914): 11.

47. See "Control of Births," *NR* 2 (April 17, 1915): 273–75; "Age of Birth Control," *NR* 4 (September 25, 1915): 195–97.

48. See especially (on the Leo Frank case) "Georgia and the Nation," *NR* 4 (September 4, 1915): 112–14.

49. There were several articles praising Booker T. Washington at his death. See especially "A Leader of Humanity," *NR* 5 (November 20, 1915): 60–61.

50. See, among many comments, "Brandeis," *NR* 6 (February 5, 1916): 4–6; "The Close of the Brandeis Case," *NR* 7 (June 10, 1916): 134–35.

51. Thomas K. McGraw, *Prophets of Regulation,* 114–28, provides an excellent brief account of this legislation. I have followed McGraw. See also Arthur S. Link, *Wilson: The New Freedom* (Princeton, N.J.: Princeton University Press, 1956), 417–44.

52. Ibid., 122–24. McGraw points out that Rublee's drafting was inexact and the FTC didn't live up to its potential in the early years partly because of legal challenges. Ibid., 124–28.

53. Link, *Wilson: The New Freedom,* 443, 432.

54. Ibid., 199–240; quotation at 238.

55. "A Narrow Escape for the Democrats," *NR* 1 (November 7, 1914): 8. The article is almost certainly by Croly.

56. Ibid., 9.

57. See Link, *Wilson: The New Freedom,* 469–70.

58. "Presidential Complacency," *NR* 1 (November 21, 1914): 7. Arthur Link writes: "It was Croly, not Wilson, who read correctly the further course of American political history. It was only the New Freedom phase of progressivism that had ended in the autumn of 1914.... Indeed, in the months to come it was Wilson himself who would lead the American people forward in their progress toward a more democratic economic and social order." Ibid., 471.

59. "An Unseen Reversal," *NR* 1 (January 9, 1915): 7–8. This article was probably written by Learned Hand. See H.C. to Hand, January 15, Hand Papers, mentioning a check for "Unseen Reversal."

60. "The Tolerated Unions," *NR* 1 (November 7, 1914): 11–12; "Unionism Vs. Anti-Unionism," *NR* 8 (September 23, 1916): 178–80. See also "Recognition for Labor," *NR* 13 (November 24, 1917): 84–86.

61. "Salvaging the Unemployed," *NR* 4 (October 2, 1915): 221–23.

62. "The Railroads and the Nation," *NR* 1 (November 21, 1914): 11–12; quotation at 12. See also "Railroad Regulation on Trial," *NR* 1 (December 19, 1914): 8–9; "The Logic of the Railroad Inquiry," *NR* 9 (December 2, 1916): 108–10.

63. *NR* 2 (February 13, 1915): 30.

64. See Arthur S. Link, *Wilson: Campaigns for Progressivism and Peace* (Princeton, N.J.: Princeton University Press, 1965), 56–60.

65. Arthur S. Link, *Woodrow Wilson and the Progressive Era* (New York: Harper and Row, 1954), 226–27, 235–37.

66. "The Other-Worldliness of Wilson," *NR* 2 (March 27, 1915): 194–95.

67. *NR* 3 (September 18, 1915): 163; H.C., "Unregenerate Democracy," *NR* 6 (February 5, 1916): 17–19. But see *NR* 5 (December 11, 1915): 130 for an early favorable comment on administration.

68. "Timid Neutrality," *NR* 1 (November 14, 1914): 7–8.

69. "The Leader Roosevelt Is," *NR* 3 (May 8, 1915): 5.

70. See Morison, ed., *Letters of Theodore Roosevelt*, 8: 826 and 1486, respectively.

71. *NR* 1 (December 12, 1914): 5.

72. H.C. to Willard Straight, December 10, 1914, Willard Straight Papers.

73. H.C. to Willard Straight, December 13, 1914, Willard Straight Papers.

74. David Levy, *Herbert Croly*, 239.

75. H.C. to Theodore Roosevelt, January 11, 1915, Theodore Roosevelt Papers.

76. Theodore Roosevelt to H.C., January 15, 1915, Theodore Roosevelt Papers.

77. See Walter Lippmann to Graham Wallas, December 18, 1915, Graham Wallas Papers, London School of Economics.

78. "The Newer Nationalism," *NR* 5 (January 29, 1916): 319–21. Roosevelt wrote a bitter letter to Willard Straight in reply, terming the editors "nice, well-meaning geese—early Victorian geese. . . . They are simply talking like nice, kindly old ladies over their knitting." Theodore Roosevelt to Willard Straight, February 8, 1916, in Morison, ed., *Letters of Theodore Roosevelt*, 8: 1019–21. See also Walter Lippmann to Willard Straight, April 6, 1916, replying to a Straight cable on Roosevelt: "If my conscience troubled me about our attitude towards him it would be that we have not been as candid about Roosevelt as we have been about Wilson," Willard Straight Papers.

79. "A Luncheon and a Moral," *NR* 6 (April 8, 1916): 251.

80. On the 1916 Progressive convention and T.R.'s rejection of the nomination, see John A. Gable, *The Bull Moose Years*, 246–49.

81. "The Progressive Party—An Obituary," *NR* 7 (June 17, 1916): 159–61. See also *NR* 7 (July 1, 1916): 209, for a criticism of the Progressive National Committee for eventually endorsing Hughes.

82. "Homeless Radicals," *NR* 7 (July 1, 1916): 211–13.

83. "Woodrow Wilson," *NR* 7 (June 24, 1916): 185–87, quotation at 186. The article is unsigned but almost certainly by Croly.

84. See especially "The Two Mr. Wilsons," *NR* 8 (September 9, 1916): 128–29.

85. H.C., "The Two Parties in 1916," *NR* 8 (October 21, 1916): 286–91, quotation at 286. Walter Lippmann's biographer cites Lippmann as claiming that he brought Croly to the endorsement. I do not find this persuasive given Croly's comments as early as June. See Ronald Steel, *Walter Lippmann and the American Century* (Boston: Little, Brown, 1980), 104–6.

86. Ibid., 290.

87. "Wilson and Roosevelt," *NR* 9 (November 4, 1916): 3–5. See *NR* 1 (January 16, 1915): 3, for an earlier linkage of the two leaders.

88. H.C., "The Effect on American Institutions of a Powerful Military and Naval Establishment," *Annals of the American Academy of Political and Social Science*, 66:164.

CHAPTER SEVEN. LIBERALISM AND WAR

1. Walter Lippmann, "Notes for a Biography," *NR* 63 (July 16, 1930): part 2, 250.

2. H.C. to Learned Hand, August 17, 1914, Hand Papers.

3. Ronald Steel, *Walter Lippmann and the American Century*, 88.

4. "The End of American Isolation," *NR* 1 (November 7, 1914): 9–10. The article is unsigned but is identified as Croly's by Lippmann, "Notes for a Biography," *NR* 63 (July 16, 1930): part 2, 251.

5. "Pacifism vs. Passivism," *NR* 1 (December 12, 1914): 6–7. The article is probably by Croly.

6. *NR* 2 (February 27, 1915): 84.

7. "A League of Peace," *NR* 2 (March 20, 1915): 167–68. This editorial is probably by Lippmann.

8. H.C. to Walter Lippmann, June 18, 1915, Series I, Box 7, Folder 303, Lippmann Papers.

9. "The Other Cheek," *NR* 2 (March 6, 1915): 113–14.

10. Ibid., 113.

11. *NR* 3 (May 15, 1915): 24.

12. "Germany's Real Offense," *NR* 3 (May 22, 1915): 55.

13. See Forcey, *Crossroads of Liberalism*, 228–31, on the *NR*'s generally anglo-phile staff.

14. Walter Lippmann to Graham Wallas, April 21, 1916, Wallas Papers.

15. "Not Our War," *NR* 3 (June 5, 1915): 108–10. Quotations at 109 and 110, respectively. Robert M. Lovett, an associate on the *NR*, attributed this article to Croly. See Box 11, Folder 20, Lovett Papers, University of Chicago Library. This material was brought to my attention by Fred Ragan. See also "The Next Step," *NR* 3 (July 31, 1915): 322–23.

16. H.C., "The Meaning of It," *NR* 4 (August 7, 1915): 10–11. Theodore Roosevelt later criticized American war policy as a "limited liability" policy, which he termed a "sharp practice." See John M. Cooper, *The Warrior and the Priest*, 326–27.

17. *NR* 4 (October 23, 1915): 293.

18. "Evasions by Mr. Wilson," *NR* 5 (November 13, 1915): 29–30.

19. "War at Any Price," *NR* 5 (November 27, 1915): 84–85.

20. "Pro-German," *NR* 5 (December 4, 1915): 107–8; see also [Lippmann], "Are We Pro-German?" *NR* 5 (December 18, 1915): 161–62.

21. *NR* 5 (January 15, 1916): 260. See also Walter Lippmann to Joseph Lee, January 8, 1916, Series I, Box 17, Folder 701, Lippmann Papers.

22. "The Ultimate Controversy," *NR* 7 (May 27, 1916): 77–78. The phrasing of this article almost certainly identifies it as Croly's.

23. "Aggressive Pacifism," *NR* 5 (January 15, 1916): 263–65; quotation at 264.

24. "An Appeal to the President," *NR* 6 (April 22, 1916): 303–5. The article is by Lippmann and is reprinted in Arthur Schlesinger, Jr., ed., *Walter Lippmann: Early Writings* (New York: Liveright, 1970), 31–36.

25. Woodrow Wilson, "An Address in Washington to the League to Enforce Peace," in Arthur S. Link, ed., *The Papers of Woodrow Wilson* (Princeton, N.J.: Princeton University Press, 1981), 37: 113–16. Quotation at 115–16. (hereafter *PWW*.) Forcey, *Crossroads of Liberalism*, claims that Wilson was influenced by *NR* editorials (254).

26. "Mr. Wilson's Great Utterance," *NR* 7 (June 3, 1916): 102. Reprinted in Schlesinger, ed., *Walter Lippmann: Early Writings*, 37–41.

27. Ibid., 103.

28. The New Republicans were not unanimous in hoping for peace in the summer of 1916. Learned Hand wrote to Graham Wallas: "I cannot share with Croly and Lippmann the belief that peace would be best now," May 23, 1916, Wallas Papers.

29. H.C. to Willard Straight, March 18, 1916, Willard Straight Papers.

30. See H.C. to Willard Straight, March 24, 1916, Willard Straight Papers.

31. Walter Lippmann to Graham Wallas, August 29, 1916, Wallas Papers; reprinted in John M. Blum, ed., *Public Philosopher: Selected Letters of Walter Lippmann* (New York: Ticknor and Fields, 1985), 58–60.

32. Steel, *Walter Lippmann*, 107.

33. H.C., "The Structure of Peace," *NR* 9 (January 13, 1917): 287–91.

34. Ibid., 287, 290. It is interesting to note that Kant makes a similar argument in his *Perpetual Peace*.

35. Ibid., 289.

36. Ibid., 290.

37. "A Report of a News Conference by Charles Merz," quoted in Link, ed., *PWW*, 40: 423. Emphasis in the original.

38. Woodrow Wilson, "An Address to the Senate," January 22, 1917, ibid., 533–39.

39. Ibid., 538. See also page 535 for a conditional endorsement of the league.

40. Ibid.

41. See "Peace without Victory," *NR* 9 (December 23, 1916): 201–2. This article was by Lippmann. See Steel, *Walter Lippmann*, 109.

42. On House's influence on Wilson and his reliability as a source for historians, see Cooper, *The Warrior and the Priest*, 244–45, 293–95, and especially 398 n. 26. See also Robert Crunden, *Ministers of Reform*, 225, 229–31.

43. Edward M. House to Woodrow Wilson, January 22, 1917, in Link, ed., *PWW*, 40: 539.

44. H.C. to Woodrow Wilson, January 23, 1917, Wilson Papers; reprinted in ibid., 559.

45. Ibid.

46. Woodrow Wilson to H.C., January 25, 1917, in ibid., 41: 13. Wilson also thanks Croly for his suggestion about the speeches. Arthur Link naturally believes that the editorial referred to is "Peace without Victory." However, the content of that editorial is quite different from Wilson's speech; a number of other *NR* editorials in the period were much more similar.

47. See "A Review of the Growth and Prospects of The New Republic," pamphlet of August 1916, Willard Straight Papers.

48. Levy, *Herbert Croly*, 255.

49. Walter Lippmann, "Notes for a Biography," *NR* 63 (July 16, 1930), part 2: 251. Compare Charles Forcey's analysis in *Crossroads of Liberalism*, in which he compares the *NR* intellectuals to moths around the flame of political power. While admitting that they were more consistent in changing their allegiance to Wilson than if they had continued to support the more militaristic T.R., Forcey still comments that "the moths had charred more than a wing or two in their new flight toward power" (262). I think Croly was fairly consistent in his views; "singe" might be a better verb.

50. "Postscript" [dated February 1, 1917], *NR* 10 (February 3, 1917): n.p.

51. "Justification," *NR* 10 (February 10, 1917): 36–38; "Armed Neutrality," *NR* 10 (March 3, 1917): 120–21.

52. "The Defense of the Atlantic World," *NR* 10 (February 17, 1917): 59–61; quotation at 61.

53. *NR* 10 (March 17, 1917): 177; *NR* 10 (March 24, 1917): 210. See also the supplement to the issue of March 10, 1917, summarizing their stands on the war from 1914 on.

54. "The Effect of America in the War," *NR* 10 (March 17, 1917): 181. See also "A War Program for Liberals," *NR* 10 (March 31, 1917): 249–50.

55. "The Great Decision," *NR* 10 (April 7, 1917): 280. The article was by Lippmann. See Lippmann to Woodrow Wilson, April 3, 1917, in Link, ed., *PWW*, 41: 537–38, which quotes passages.

56. See Willard Straight to Walter Lippmann, April 19, 1917: "glad and proud Dorothy and I feel . . . to place you and Herbert in a position where you have made your influence and your genius talk . . . through affecting the action of the President . . . upon the future of the world," Series I, Box 31, Folder 1166, Lippmann Papers. The letter indicates that Straight sent a similar letter to Croly.

57. H.C. to Willard Straight, "Wednesday," April [11?] 1917, Willard Straight Papers.

58. Steel, *Walter Lippmann*, 116–54. Croly was perhaps marginally involved in the Inquiry. See Walter Lippmann to Herbert Croly, November 22, 1917, Series I, Box 7, Folder 303, Lippmann Papers.

59. See *NR* 11 (June 2, 1917): 118; *NR* 11 (July 28, 1917): 342.

60. "What Democracy Demands of the Allies," *NR* 11 (June 9, 1917): 146.

61. See Thompson, *Reformers and War*, 204–6, for other progressive publicists' views of the Allies.

62. "Liberalism in the National Army," *NR* 12 (September 8, 1917): 148.

63. "Darkening Counsel," *NR* 12 (October 27, 1917): 341. Robert M. Lovett identifies this article as Croly's; see note 15 above. See also *NR* 13 (December 15, 1917): 159; "Never Again," *NR* 12 (August 18, 1917): 60–62.

64. H.C., "Counsel of Humility," *NR* 13 (December 15, 1917): 174. Croly's pluralism is evident in the conclusion.

65. Walter Lippmann Diary, October 5, 1917, quoted in Steel, *Walter Lippmann*, 126.

66. "A Victory of Justice vs. a Victory of Power," *NR* 16 (October 5, 1918): 271–72.

67. Ibid. See also "The Defeatists," *NR* 16 (October 19, 1918): 327–29.

68. H.C. to Learned Hand, October 30, 1918, Hand Papers.

69. See Thompson, *Reformers and War*, 210–20 for an excellent discussion of progressive views of "the war at home."

70. "Economic Dictatorship in War," *NR* 11 (May 12, 1917): 38.

71. "Government Ownership or Railway Reaction," *NR* 11 (July 7, 1917): 262–63.

72. "Recognition for Labor," *NR* 13 (November 24, 1917): 84.

73. "Financing the War," *NR* 10 (April 7, 1917): 282–83.

74. "After the War—Reaction or Reconstruction," *NR* 13 (January 19, 1918): 331.

75. Ibid.

76. "A War Program for Liberals," *NR* 10 (March 31, 1917): 250, point 2. For a comparison of Croly's views to those of other progressives on this issue, see Thompson, *Reformers and War*, 220–33, 258–63.

77. "War Propaganda," *NR* 12 (October 6, 1917): 255–57.

78. John Dewey, "In Explanation of Our Lapse," *NR* 13 (November 3, 1917): 18.

79. H.C. to Woodrow Wilson, October 19, 1917, Woodrow Wilson Papers; reprinted in Link, ed., *PWW,* 44: 408–10.

80. Ibid. On Croly's contacts with the government, see also a letter to Colonel House, April 17, 1917, in Link, ed., *PWW,* 42: 89–90, and a petition that he and Dorothy Straight signed with Lillian Wald, Jane Addams, and others on free speech and "constitutional rights and liberties." See Link, ed., *PWW,* 42: 118–19.

81. Woodrow Wilson to H.C., October 22, 1917, Wilson Papers; reprinted in Link, ed., *PWW,* 44: 420.

82. On Wilson's position on censorship, see Cooper, *The Warrior and the Priest,* 320.

83. "America Tested by War," *NR* 15 (June 22, 1918): 221. See also "Mob Violence and War Psychology," *NR* 16 (August 3, 1918): 5–7, and John Dewey, "The Cult of Irrationality," *NR* 17 (November 9, 1918): 34–35.

84. H.C. to Dorothy Straight, June 25, 1918, Dorothy Straight Elmhirst Papers. See also her stout defense of the *NR* to a friend who accused Croly of "disloyalty," Dorothy Straight to J. Scheifflein, August 30, 1918, Dorothy Straight Elmhirst Papers. On the *Nation,* see *NR* 16 (September 21, 1918): 210.

85. H.C. to H. L. Mencken, August 1, 1919, Mencken Papers, New York Public Library.

86. See Zechariah Chafee, Jr., "Freedom of Speech," *NR* 17 (November 16, 1918): 66–69; Chafee, "Legislation Against Anarchy," *NR* 19 (July 23, 1919): 379–85; Chafee, *Freedom of Speech* (New York: Harcourt Brace and Howe, 1920).

87. "The Mob in High Places," *NR* 17 (December 7, 1918): 150.

88. *NR* 18 (February 15, 1919): 67; "Freedom of Speech: Whose Concern?" *NR* 18 (February 22, 1919): 102–4; *NR* 18 (April 19, 1919): 362.

89. Liva Baker, *The Justice from Beacon Hill: The Life and Times of Oliver Wendell Holmes* (New York: HarperCollins, 1991), 539. See 513–41 for a survey of this range of cases and for a discussion of the influences on Holmes.

90. Quoted in ibid., 539–40.

91. "The Call to Toleration," *NR* 20 (November 26, 1919): 360–62. The article is identified as Croly's by Harold J. Laski (who often wrote for the *NR*) in a letter to Holmes, November 27, 1919, in Howe, ed., *Holmes-Laski Letters,* 1: 222. Laski says: "I did read with pride Croly's admirable piece on your dissent." See also Holmes to Croly, May 12, 1919, praising an earlier *NR* article on Burleson, in ibid., 202–4.

92. H.C. to Leonard Elmhirst, June 23, 1927, Dorothy Straight Elmhirst Papers. Croly sought the Elmhirsts' support to catalogue the abuses "so that when the next war comes, there will be no excuse for repeating" these mistakes.

93. Walter Lippmann, "Notes for a Biography," 252.

94. "War and Revolution," *NR* 10 (March 24, 1917): 212–14. Wilson's initial reaction was also favorable. See Link, ed., *PWW,* 41: 524.

95. "Justice to Russia," *NR* 12 (August 4, 1917): 5–7.

96. "The Salvation of Russia," *NR* 12 (September 22, 1917): 202–3.

97. "What Is at Stake in Russia," *NR* 14 (February 2, 1918): 6–8.

98. *NR* 14 (March 16, 1918): 185; "Europe, America and the Russian Revolution," *NR* 14 (March 16, 1918): 188–90.

99. "For and against the Bolsheviki," *NR* 14 (April 6, 1918): 280; "Our Case against the Soviet Republic," *NR* 19 (July 2, 1919): 265.

100. See "Intervention in Russia," *NR* 15 (June 1, 1918): 130–32; *NR* 16 (August 31, 1918): 120; "The Rescue of Russia," *NR* 16 (October 12, 1918): 301–2; "Revolution vs. Reaction in Russia," *NR* 17 (January 4, 1919): 267–70.

101. "Our Case against the Soviet Republic," *NR* 19 (July 2, 1919): 265.

102. George F. Kennan, "Walter Lippmann, the *New Republic*, and the Russian Revolution," in Marquis Childs and James Reston, eds., *Walter Lippmann and His Times* (New York: Harcourt, Brace and Company, 1959), 38, 59.

103. They were worried about Allied revenge even early in the war. See "A Negligible Germany," *NR* 5 (December 25, 1915): 184–86.

104. *NR* 17 (November 30, 1918): 113.

105. H.C., "Victory without Peace," *NR* 17 (January 11, 1919): 301–3; quotations at 302, 303.

106. See especially "The Republican Defeatists," *NR* 18 (March 8, 1919): 160–61; "Insisting on American Sovereignty," *NR* 18 (March 22, 1919): 232–34; "The Test of Events," *NR* 18 (April 5, 1919): 290–94.

107. *NR* 18 (April 12, 1919): 321.

108. H.C., "The Obstacle to Peace," *NR* 18 (April 26, 1919): 403–7.

109. Walter Lippmann, "Notes for a Biography," 252.

110. "Peace at any Price," *NR* 19 (May 24, 1919): 100. The article is unsigned but is clearly by Croly.

111. Ibid., 101–2.

112. See particularly "Mr. Wilson Forgets," *NR* 19 (July 23, 1919): 370–72; "Shantung," *NR* 19 (July 30, 1919): 405–7; "Mr. Wilson Alone," *NR* 20 (October 8, 1919): 277–79.

113. "The Treaty," *NR* 20 (November 26, 1919): 363.

CHAPTER EIGHT. LIBERALISM
IN AN "AGE OF NORMALCY"

1. See *NR* 22 (March 3, 1920): "In March will appear a new book by Herbert Croly... entitled The Breach in Civilization" (35).

2. H.C. to Learned Hand, January 27, 1930. Felix Frankfurter also apparently advised Croly against publication. Years later, Frankfurter wrote: "I can only give you the central difficulty that I had with his manuscript, namely, that he used technical religious terms, not in the sense in which an avowed Christian would use them, but with a private content of his own, and I told him I thought that was not a permissible thing to do. . . . I believe there are very few men who would have been so honest with himself"; Felix Frankfurter to Richard Rothstein, March 12, 1963, Frankfurter Papers. No doubt this was a factor in Croly's decision, but as he published a part of *The Breach in Civilization* (New York: Macmillan, 1920) in the *NR* (chapter 7 was published as "Regeneration," *NR* 23 [June 9, 1920]: 40–47), I wonder if it was the major reason. See also H.C. to Walter Lippmann, "Thursday" [1919]: "I have felt like a man who was rolling a heavy stone up a steep hill. . . . Certainly this little book has cost me far more tugging and pulling than it should"; Series I, Box 7, Folder 303, Lippmann Papers.

3. Croly, *The Breach.* Page proofs of 1–137 and 144–52 are in Houghton Library, Harvard University. Corrected page proofs are available in the Frankfurter Papers (microfilm reel 135, frames 570–672), including 138–143. The Frankfurter Papers also contain other Croly manuscripts from the 1920s. They probably were sent to Frankfurter by Louise Croly because he agreed in the late 1930s to write

the introduction to a collection of Croly's articles. He apparently never did. See letters of Louise Croly to Dorothy Straight Elmhirst in the late 1930s, Dorothy Straight Elmhirst Papers.

4. H.C., *The Breach*, 64.

5. Ibid.

6. H.C., autobiographical fragment, titled "Introduction" and noted "HC" in Frankfurter Papers, 1 (microfilm reel 136, frames 60–84 at frame 60).

7. H.C., *The Breach*, 65.

8. H.C., "The Eclipse of Progressivism," *NR* 24 (October 27, 1920): 210. The parallel article on international affairs is H.C.,"Liberalism vs. War," *NR* 25 (December 8, 1920): 35–39.

9. Ibid., 211, 212.

10. Ibid., 212.

11. Ibid., 213.

12. Ibid., 214.

13. Ibid., 215.

14. Editorial note, *Nation* 111 (November 3, 1920): 489.

15. Randolph Bourne, "Conscience and Intelligence in War," [September, 1917], in Lillian Schlissel, ed., *The World of Randolph Bourne* (New York: E. P. Dutton, 1965), 129–33, quotation at 130. On Bourne, see Edward Abrahams, *The Lyrical Left: Randolph Bourne, Alfred Stieglitz and the Origins of Cultural Radicalism in America* (Charlottesville: University of Virginia Press, 1986).

16. See Randolph S. Bourne, *War and the Intellectuals: Essays by Randolph S. Bourne*, ed. Carl Resek (New York: Harper Torchbooks, 1964). The quotation comes from an unfinished manuscript, "The State," ibid., 65–104, at 71.

17. H.C., "Liberalism vs. War," 37.

18. Ibid.

19. Ibid., 35.

20. Ibid., 38.

21. Croly's judgment in *The Breach* is most severe: "It was utterly tragic, because never before in human history was so much goodwill and loyalty, so much disinterested self-dedication, so much potential enthusiasm for human welfare, such a huge volume of technical skill, applied science and co-operative organization,—so many of those impulses and attainments which are particularly capable of contributing to the enhancement of human life—lavished upon its frustration" (5).

22. H.C., *The Breach*, 11.

23. Ibid., 35. See also 32, 38, 39, 59.

24. Ibid., 62.

25. Ibid., 62–63. The phrase "reformist liberalism" as a conscious description of his own theory is used repeatedly in a manuscript, "Why Liberalism Fails," which was either a draft of a chapter of *The Breach* or, more likely, a later manuscript from the 1925–1927 period. See Frankfurter Papers (microfilm reel 136, frames 2–18).

26. H.C., *The Breach*, 53.

27. Ibid., 54.

28. Ibid., 53–54.

29. H.C., "The Better Prospect," *NR* 27 (August 24, 1921): 349.

30. "America as the Promised Land," *NR* 32 (October 4, 1922): 136. The article is unsigned but is almost certainly Croly's.

31. "Obstreperous Liberalism," *NR* 45 (December 23, 1925): 124. See also

H.C., "The Human Potential in the Politics of the Pacific," *NR* 52 (October 5, 1927): 164–72, especially 171.

32. "Sick of Politics," *NR* 31 (June 7, 1922): 34. The article is unsigned but clearly by Croly.

33. See particularly H.C., "The Outlook for Progressivism in Politics," *NR* 41 (December 10, 1924): 60–64. This article is one of the very few in which Croly seems to question the "middle way" of liberalism. See also "The Progressive Direction," *NR* 43 (July 15, 1925): 192–94.

34. "Obstreperous Liberalism," *NR* 45 (December 23, 1925): 123.

35. George Soule, "Herbert Croly's Liberalism," *NR* 63 (July 16, 1930): 255.

36. These articles were unsigned. However, Bruce Bliven, his associate and successor as editor in chief, has identified them as "very likely" Croly's. Bruce Bliven to the author, June 18, 1965.

37. "Dictating to the Future," *NR* 52 (October 26, 1927): 247–49, quotation at 249. Compare to Louis Hartz, *The Liberal Tradition in America* (New York: Harcourt, Brace and World, 1955).

38. "Constructive Class Consciousness," *NR* 52 (November 9, 1927): 300–302, quotation at 302.

39. "Realistic Liberalism," *NR* 53 (November 23, 1927): 5, 6.

40. Ibid., 6–7. See also "Socratic Liberalism," *NR* 53 (December 28, 1927): 155–57.

41. See the many letters to Dorothy Straight Elmhirst in the 1920s, Dorothy Straight Elmhirst Papers, especially December 4, 1926, where Croly notes he is writing sections of such a work. Some of the manuscripts in the Frankfurter Papers were probably drafts of sections of this book.

42. Croly to Dorothy Straight, September 11, 1920, Dorothy Straight Elmhirst Papers. Croly notes, of *The Breach*: "The last chapter of my unfortunate book is the first crude expression of a renewed faith." See also Louise Croly to Dorothy Straight: "Herbert has had a conversion in these last two years. He has literally become religious. . . . I think it's the war." Louise Croly to Dorothy Straight, "Sunday," n.d. [August, 1923?], Dorothy Straight Elmhirst Papers.

43. Leonard Elmhirst to Daniel Mebane [treasurer of the *NR*], May 6, 1955, Leonard Elmhirst Papers, Library of Dartington Hall, Totnes, Devon.

44. Learned Hand to Graham Wallas, August 24, 1921, Wallas Papers.

45. Harold Laski to O. W. Holmes, January 4, 1920, in Howe, ed., *Holmes-Laski Letters*, 1:231.

46. Ibid., 2:836, 1050 (letters of 1926 and 1928, respectively).

47. H.C., "Christianity as a Way of Life," *NR* 39 (July 23, 1924): 230.

48. See Croly to Dr. Carter, chairman of the commission, January 10, 1924, Dorothy Straight Elmirst Papers. See also H.C. to Eduard Lindeman, April 20, 1923, for a draft questionnaire for the group, Eduard Lindeman Papers.

49. H.C., "Religion in Life," unpublished manuscript, n.d., Houghton Library, Harvard University. Quotation from 15–16. A copy of this manuscript is also available in the Frankfurter Papers (microfilm reel 135, frames 690–713).

50. Ibid., 30, 35.

51. On Gurdjieff, see James Webb, *The Harmonious Circle: The Lives and Works of G. I. Gurdjieff, P. D. Ouspensky, and Their Followers* (New York: G. P. Putnam's Sons, 1980). Orage may also have been associated with the "Christian Way of Life" group.

52. T. S. Matthews, *Name and Address: An Autobiography* (New York: Simon and Schuster, 1960): 204–7.

53. See H.C. to Learned Hand, February 3, 1926, Hand Papers. See also a humorous description of a session with Orage in Louise Croly to Dorothy Straight Elmhirst, "Sunday," January 24, [1926?], Dorothy Straight Elmhirst Papers.

54. See A. R. Orage, "Religion in America," *NR* 41 (December 31, 1924): 141–42; A. R. Orage, "On Religion," *NR* 45 (February 10, 1926): 317–19.

55. H.C. to Felix Frankfurter, October 18, 1927, Frankfurter Papers.

56. H.C., unpublished 25-page manuscript, noted "1925," in the Dorothy Straight Elmhirst Papers, at page 18.

57. Eduard C. Lindeman, *Social Discovery* (New York: Republic Publishing Co., 1924). Croly's introduction was published separately also as "Social Discovery," *NR* 39 (May 28, 1924): 18–20.

58. See Dorothy Straight to Walter Lippmann, November 21, 1922, asking him to join. Series I, Box 31, Folder 1166, Lippmann Papers.

59. Bruce Bliven to the author, June 18, 1965. See also Bruce Bliven, *Five Million Words Later* (New York: John Day Company, 1970), especially 165–66, noting Croly's process of writing his lead editorial.

60. See "Americanism in the Present Crisis," *NR* 20 (November 12, 1919): 305; "Why a Labor Party?" *NR* 18 (April 26, 1919): 397–400; "The Policeman and the Police Power," *NR* 20 (October 1, 1919): 246–48.

61. "The Political Function of the Supreme Court," *NR* 29 (January 25, 1922): 236.

62. "The Uses of Politics," *NR* 38 (March 5, 1924): 31.

63. See Frankfurter to Walter Lippmann, June 11, 1926, Series I, Box 10, Folder 427, Lippmann Papers. Frankfurter also supplied Lippmann with extensive materials for Lippmann's editorials in the *New York World*.

64. H.C. to Walter Lippmann, September 21, 1927, Series I, Box 7, Folder 303, Lippmann Papers. See also H.C. to Leonard Elmhirst, October 6, 1927, reporting on the dinner, commenting on the case at length, and also asking if Dorothy would support collecting an archive; Dorothy Straight Elmhirst Papers. Edmund Wilson wrote that Croly had wanted him to write a history of the case, Edmund Wilson to Sylvester Gates, December 26, 1927, in Edmund Wilson, *Letters on Literature and Politics, 1912–1972*, ed. Elena Wilson (New York: Farrar, Straus and Giroux, 1977), 137.

65. Walter F. White, " 'Work or Fight' in the South," *NR* 18 (March 1, 1919): 144–46.

66. Bliven, *Five Million Words Later*, 173.

67. H.C. to Leonard K. Elmhirst, June 23, 1927, Dorothy Straight Elmhirst Papers; also in Leonard Elmhirst Papers, Dartington Hall.

68. H.C., *The Breach*, 104. See chapter 6, "Bolshevism," for Croly's most extended discussion of communism in these years.

69. See John P. Diggins, *Mussolini and Fascism: The View from America* (Princeton, N.J.: Princeton University Press, 1972), especially 227–36. The "pro-Fascism" quotation is on 232. See also Diggins's earlier version of the argument, "Flirtation with Fascism: American Pragmatic Liberals and Mussolini's Italy," *American Historical Review* 71 (January 1966): 487–506, especially 495–98.

70. *NR* 49 (January 12, 1927): 212–13.

71. "An Apology for Fascism," *NR* 49 (January 12, 1927): 207–9, quotations at 207.

72. Ibid.

73. *NR* 50 (March 2, 1927): 47.

74. "Liberalism vs. Fascism," *NR* 50 (March 2, 1927): 34–35.

75. Ibid., 35.

76. Croly wrote: "In Italy the fascist dictatorship treats the liberal opposition almost as roughly and contemptuously as do the Communist dictators in Russia." H.C., unpublished manuscript, "Christianity and Modern Life," Frankfurter Papers (microfilm reel 135, frames 715–53, at frame 726).

77. On the Hoover boomlet, see "A New National Party," *NR* 22 (March 24, 1920): 108–10. Croly endorses Christensen in H.C., "The Eclipse of Progressivism," *NR* 24 (October 27, 1920): 210–16.

78. "Progressivism Reborn," *NR* 33 (December 13, 1922): 56–57.

79. H.C. to Dorothy Straight, "Saturday" [July 1924], Dorothy Straight Elmhirst Papers.

80. H.C., "Why I Shall Vote for LaFollette," *NR* 40 (October 29, 1924): 222–23.

81. "The Progressive Direction," *NR* 53 (July 15, 1925): 192–94. On H.C.'s private reservations about supporting a "candidate in whom we did not more than half believe," see H.C. to Dorothy Straight Elmhirst, December 1, 1927, Dorothy Straight Elmhirst Papers.

82. See "Governor Smith and the Progressives," *NR* 53 (February 1, 1928): 284–86.

83. H.C., "Smith of New York," *NR* 54 (February 22, 1928): 9–14.

84. H.C. to Leonard Elmhirst, July 27, 1928, Dorothy Straight Elmhirst Papers; also in Leonard Elmhirst Papers, Dartington Hall.

85. Ibid.

86. H.C., "How Is Hoover," *NR* 55 (June 27, 1928): 138–40, quotation at 140.

87. H.C., "The Progressive Voter: He Wants to Know!" *NR* 55 (July 25, 1928): 242–47, quotations from 243.

88. H.C. to Dorothy Elmhirst, August 23, 1928, Dorothy Straight Elmhirst Papers.

89. "Why Progressives Should Vote for Smith," *NR* 56 (September 5, 1928): 58–60, quotation at 59.

90. "Agitation through Action," *NR* 56 (September 12, 1928): 84–86, quotation at 84.

91. On the New School, see Peter M. Rutkoff and William B. Scott, *New School: A History of the New School for Social Research* (New York: Free Press, 1986). See also Alvin Johnson, *Pioneer's Progress* (New York: Viking Press, 1952; reprint, Lincoln: University of Nebraska Press, 1960).

92. Ibid., 10.

93. H.C., "A Great School of Political Science," *World's Work* 20 (May 1910): 12887–88.

94. Rutkoff and Scott, *New School,* 11.

95. H.C., "A School of Social Research," *NR* 15 (June 8, 1918): 167–71, quotation at 167.

96. Alvin Johnson, *Pioneer's Progress,* 276

97. Rutkoff and Scott, *New School,* 27–34. Croly was not entirely opposed to adult education. See H.C., "Education for Grown-ups," *NR* 37 (December 12, 1923): 59–61.

98. H.C., *Willard Straight.*

99. H.C. to Dorothy Straight, September 27, 1922, Dorothy Straight Elmhirst Papers.

100. See H.C. to Dorothy Elmhirst, December 4, 1926, and another letter, n.d. [1926?] to Dorothy Elmhirst, Dorothy Straight Elmhirst Papers.

101. Walter Lippmann to Felix Frankfurter, June 24, 1921, Frankfurter Papers. Lippmann goes on to say that the paper is no longer "the paper I would want to make it." See also a four-page memo in Lippmann's papers in which he suggests changes in the *NR*, Series I, Box 22, Lippmann Papers.

102. H.C. to Dorothy Straight, November 18, 1924, Dorothy Straight Elmhirst Papers.

103. See David Levy, *Herbert Croly,* 271–74, 278–81 for a full discussion of the staffing of the *NR* in the 1920s.

104. The Croly-Dorothy Straight Elmhirst correspondence is full of detailed commentary from Croly on the workings of the paper—on the finances, staffing, space requirement, and many other details involved in its production. See the Dorothy Straight Elmhirst Papers.

CHAPTER NINE. CONCLUSIONS

1. The classic account is Edmund Wilson, " 'H.C.,' " *NR* 63 (July 16, 1930): 266–68. See also Felix Frankfurter's comments, quoted in Harlan B. Phillips, ed., *Felix Frankfurter Reminisces* (Garden City, N.Y.: Anchor Books, 1962), especially page 117.

2. Harold Laski to Walter Lippmann, January 29, 1919, Series I, Box 17, Folder 688, Lippmann Papers.

3. Quoted in Phillips, ed., *Felix Frankfurter Reminisces,* 112, 115.

4. Edmund Wilson to Arthur Schlesinger, Jr., 1964, in Wilson, *Letters on Literature and Politics,* 198. Wilson noted that Croly dominated discussions on politics while they were colleagues on *New Republic* and complained that "everything had had to be kept within the frame of the philosophy of *The Promise"* (198).

5. One attempt by a commentator to summarize "liberal ideology" is Morton White, *Social Thought in America: The Revolt against Formalism* (Boston: Beacon Press, 1957). White writes that liberal theory "was anti-formalistic, evolutionary, historically-oriented; it was deeply concerned with the economic aspects of society" (107). Croly's theory fits many of these criteria, though his religious convictions (treated below) might set him apart in some respects.

6. See his comment that "although liberals have no reason to relinquish their traditional suspicion of the state and they have every reason to cherish their deep concern for human liberty, they cannot afford to fall back on unreconstructed liberalism." H.C., "Why Liberalism Fails," Frankfurter Papers (microfilm reel 136, frame 14).

7. Alvin Johnson, interview with the author, May 19, 1965.

8. See particularly Theodore Lowi, *The End of Liberalism: Ideology, Policy, and the Crisis of Public Authority* (New York: W. W. Norton and Company, 1969), especially chapters 2, 3, and 8.

9. Otis L. Graham, Jr., *An Encore for Reform: The Old Progressives and the New Deal* (New York: Oxford University Press, 1967), 4. Graham mentions the "obvious debt of NRA to the ideas of the 'Concentration School' going back to Van Hise and Croly" (8), but his research also establishes that many progressives who lived into the 1930s in fact opposed the New Deal. Bruce Bliven later claimed of the *NR* that "almost all the ideas of the New Deal had been threshed out in our

pages . . . years before Roosevelt became President." Bruce Bliven, *Five Million Words Later*, 168.

10. Edmund Wilson, " 'H.C.,' " *NR* 63 (July 16, 1930): 267.

11. Among Niebuhr's many works, see particularly his "Intellectual Autobiography" in Charles W. Kegley and Robert Bretall, eds., *Reinhold Niebuhr: His Religious, Social and Political Thought* (New York: Macmillan, 1956).

12. John Rawls, *A Theory of Justice*, 22.

13. See, for example, Michael Walzer, "Liberalism and the Art of Separation," *Political Theory* 12 (August 1984): 315–30.

14. See especially Gabriel Kolko, *The Triumph of Conservatism*, 215–16; R. Jeffrey Lustig, *Corporate Liberalism*, 127, 132, 212, 222–23.

15. N. H. Brailsford to Louise Croly, June 25, 1930, Dorothy Straight Elmhirst Papers.

Selected Bibliography

MANUSCRIPT COLLECTIONS

Randolph Bourne Papers, Columbia University Library
Herbert Croly Letters and Manuscripts, Houghton Library,
     Harvard University
Dorothy Straight Elmhirst Papers, Cornell University Library
Leonard Elmhirst Papers, Dartington Hall, Totnes, England
Felix Frankfurter Papers, Library of Congress
Learned Hand Papers, Harvard Law School Library
Eduard C. Lindeman Papers, in the possession of Prof. Charles Forcey
Walter Lippmann Papers, Yale University Library
Theodore Roosevelt Papers, Library of Congress
Sorosis Papers, Sophia Smith Collection, Smith College Library
Willard Straight Papers, Cornell University Library
Graham Wallas Papers, Library of the London School of Economics
     and Political Science
Walter Weyl Papers, Rutgers University Library
Woodrow Wilson Papers, Library of Congress

WORKS BY HERBERT CROLY

Books

[William Herbert, pseud.]. *Houses for Town and Country.* New York: Duffield and
     Co., 1907.
Marcus Alonzo Hanna: His Life and Work. New York: Macmillan, 1912. Reprint.
     Hamden, Conn.: Archon Books, 1965.
Progressive Democracy. New York: Macmillan, 1914.

The Promise of American Life. New York: Macmillan, 1909. Reprint. Hamden, Conn.: Archon Books, 1963.
Willard Straight. New York: Macmillan, 1924.
Desmond, Harry W., and Herbert Croly. *Stately Homes in America.* New York: D. Appleton and Company, 1903.

Articles (Signed) in The New Republic

"The Meaning of It." 4 (August 7, 1915): 10–11.
"The Obligation of the Vote." 4 (October 9, 1915) Pt. 2: 5–10.
Review of *The Reconciliation of Government with Liberty,* by John W. Burgess. 5 (November 20, 1915) Pt. 2: 2–3.
"Unregenerate Democracy." 6 (February 5, 1916): 17–19.
"Commonwealth of Greater Britain." 7 (July 22, 1916): 309–12.
"The Two Parties in 1916." 8 (October 21, 1916): 286–91.
"The Structure of Peace." 9 (January 13, 1917): 287–91.
"The Future of the State." 12 (September 15, 1917): 179–83.
"Counsel of Humility." 13 (December 15, 1917): 173–76.
"A School of Social Research." 15 (June 8, 1918): 167–71.
"Victory without Peace." 17 (January 11, 1919): 301–3.
"The Obstacle to Peace." 18 (April 26, 1919): 403–7.
"Disordered Christianity." 21 (December 31, 1919): 136–39.
"The Paradox of Lincoln." 21 (February 18, 1920): 350–53.
"Regeneration." 23 (June 9, 1920): 40–47.
"The Eclipse of Progressivism." 24 (October 27, 1920): 210–16.
"Liberalism vs. War." 25 (December 8, 1920): 35–39.
"The Better Prospect." 27 (August 24, 1921): 344–49.
"The Meaning of the Conference." 28 (November 16, 1921) Pt. 2: 1–14.
"Hope, History, and H. G. Wells." 29 (November 30, 1921): 10–12.
"In Memoriam, Willard Straight." 29 (December 21, 1921): 94–96.
"Behaviorism in Religion." 29 (February 22, 1922): 367–70.
"Reconstruction of Religion." 31 (June 21, 1922): 100–102.
"Surely Good Americanism." 32 (November 15, 1922): 294–96.
"The *New Republic* Idea." 33 (December 6, 1922) Pt. 2: 3–16.
"Naturalism and Christianity." 34 (February 28, 1923): 9–11.
"American Withdrawal from Europe." 36 (September 12, 1923): 65–68.
"Education for Grown-ups." 37 (December 12, 1923): 59–61.
"Economics and Statesmanship." 38 (February 27, 1924): 17–19.
"Social Discovery." 39 (May 28 1924): 18–20.
"Christianity as a Way of Life." 39 (July 23, 1924): 230–37.
"Why I Shall Vote for LaFollette." 40 (October 29, 1924): 221–24.
"The Outlook for Progressivism in Politics." 41 (December 10, 1924): 60–64.
"What Ails American Youth?" 41 (February 11, 1925): 301–3.
"Christians Beware!" 45 (November 25, 1925): 12–14.
"Consciousness and the Religious Life." 45 (January 27, 1926): 262–65.
"Religion as Method." 47 (June 30, 1926): 174–77.
"Mexico and the United States." 50 (March 30, 1927): 159–64.
"The Human Potential in the Politics of the Pacific." 52 (October 5, 1927): 164–72.
"Smith of New York." 54 (February 22, 1928): 9–14.

"How Is Hoover?" 55 (June 27, 1928): 138–40.
"The Progressive Voter: He Wants to Know!" 55 (July 25, 1928): 242–47.

Other Articles

"American Artists and Their Public." *Architectural Record* 10 (January 1901): 256–62.
"The Architect in Recent Fiction." *Architectural Record* 17 (February 1905): 137–39.
"Art and Life." *Architectural Record* 1 (October-December 1891): 219–27.
"Democratic Factions and Insurgent Republicans." *North American Review* 191 (May 1910): 626–35.
"The Effect on American Institutions of a Powerful Military and Naval Establishment." *Annals of the American Academy of Political and Social Science* 66 (July 1916): 157–72.
"A Great School of Political Science." *World's Work* 20 (May 1910): 12887–88.
"Henry James and His Countrymen." *Lamp* 28 (February 1905): 47–53.
"The New World and the New Art." *Architectural Record* 12 (June 1902): 135–53.
"New York as the American Metropolis." *Architectural Record* 13 (March 1903): 193–206.
"State Political Reorganization." *Proceedings of the American Political Science Association.* Concord, N.H.: Rumford Press, 1912. 8: 122–35.
"A Test of Faith in Democracy." *American Magazine.* 75 (November 1912): 21–23.
"Why I Wrote My Latest Book: My Aim in `The Promise of American Life.' " *World's Work* 20 (June 1910): 13086.

OTHER PRIMARY SOURCES

Barnett, James. *The Operation of the Initiative, Referendum, and Recall in Oregon.* New York: Macmillan, 1915.
Beard, Charles A. "Reconstructing State Government." *New Republic* 4 (August 21, 1915), Pt. 2: 1–16.
Bliven, Bruce. *Five Million Words Later.* New York: John Day Company, 1970.
———. "Herbert Croly and Journalism." *New Republic* 63 (July 16, 1930): 258–60.
Blum, John M., ed. *Public Philosopher: Selected Letters of Walter Lippmann.* New York: Ticknor and Fields, 1985.
Bourne, Randolph S. *War and the Intellectuals.* Edited by Carl Resek. New York: Harper Torchbooks, 1964.
Conklin, Groff, ed. *New Republic Anthology: 1915–1935.* New York: Dodge Publishing Co., 1936.
Croly, David Goodman. *Glimpses of the Future.* New York: G. Putnam's Sons, 1888.
———. *Miscegenation.* New York: H. Dexter, Hamilton and Co., 1864.
———. *A Positivist Primer: Being a Series of Familiar Conversations on the Religion of Humanity.* New York: David Wesley and Co., 1871.
———. *The Truth about Love.* New York: David Wesley and Co., 1872.
Croly, Jane Cunningham [Jennie June, pseud.] Articles in *Demorest's Monthly Magazine*, 1860–1889.
———. *For Better or Worse.* Boston: Lee and Shepard, 1875.

———. *The History of the Woman's Club Movement in America*. New York: Henry G. Allen, 1898.

———. *Jennie Juneiana: Talks on Women's Topics*. Boston: Lee and Shepard, 1864.

———. *Thrown on Her Own Resources; Or, What Girls Can Do*. New York: Crowell and Company, 1891.

Davidson, John W., ed.. *A Crossroads of Freedom: The 1912 Campaign Speeches of Woodrow Wilson*. New Haven, Conn.: Yale University Press, 1956.

Dewey, John. "Conscience and Compulsion." *New Republic* 11 (July 14, 1917): 297–98.

———. "The Cult of Irrationality." *New Republic* 17 (November 9, 1918): 34–35.

———. "In Explanation of Our Lapse." *New Republic* 13 (November 3, 1917): 17–18.

———. *The Public and Its Problems*. New York: Henry Holt and Co., 1927. Reprint. Denver: Allen Swallow, n.d.

———. *Reconstruction in Philosophy*. New York: Henry Holt, 1920. Reprint. Boston: Beacon Press, 1957.

DeWitt, Benjamin. *The Progressive Movement*. New York: Macmillan, 1915. Reprint. Seattle: University of Washington Press, 1968.

Elmhirst, Dorothy. "Herbert Croly." *New Republic* 63 (July 16, 1930): 243.

Frank, Waldo. "The Promise of Herbert Croly." *New Republic* 63 (July 16, 1930): 260–63.

Frankfurter, Felix. "Herbert Croly and American Political Opinion." *New Republic* 63 (July 16, 1930): 247–50.

Green, Thomas Hill. "Liberal Legislation and Freedom of Contract." In R. L. Nettleship, ed., *Works of Thomas Hill Green*. London: Longmans, Green and Co., 1888. 3: 365–86.

Grant, Robert. *Unleavened Bread*. New York: Charles Scribner's Sons, 1900.

Hackett, Francis. *I Chose Denmark*. New York: Doubleday, Doran and Co. 1940.

Hapgood, Norman. *The Changing Years: Reminiscences of Norman Hapgood*. New York: Farrar and Rinehart, 1930.

Harbaugh, William, ed. *The Writings of Theodore Roosevelt*. Indianapolis: Bobbs-Merrill Company, 1967.

Hobhouse, Leonard. *Liberalism*. 1911. Reprint. New York: Oxford University Press, 1964.

Howe, Frederic C. *The Confessions of a Reformer*. New York: Charles Scribner's Sons, 1925.

Howe, Mark DeWolfe, ed. *The Holmes-Laski Letters, 1916–1935*. 1 and 2. Cambridge, Mass.: Harvard University Press, 1953.

Johnson, Alvin S. *Pioneer's Progress: An Autobiography*. New York: Viking Press, 1952. Reprint. Lincoln: University of Nebraska Press, 1960.

Laski, Harold J. "The Apotheosis of the State." *New Republic* 7 (July 22, 1916): 302–4.

Lindeman, Eduard C. "A Man of Wisdom." *New Republic* 63 (July 16, 1930): 263–65.

———. *Social Discovery*. New York: Republic Publishing Co., 1924.

Link, Arthur S., ed., *The Papers of Woodrow Wilson*. vols. 40–44. Princeton, N.J.: Princeton University Press, 1982, 1983.

Lippmann, Walter. *Drift and Mastery*. New York: 1914. Reprint. Englewood Cliffs, N.J.: Prentice-Hall, 1961.

———. "Liberalism in America." *New Republic* 21 (December 31, 1919): 150–51.
———. "Notes for a Biography." *New Republic*. 63 (July 16, 1930): 250–52.
———. *A Preface to Politics.* New York: 1913; Reprint. Ann Arbor: University of Michigan Press, 1962.
Littell, Philip. "As A Friend." *New Republic* 63 (July 16, 1930): 243–45.
Lovett, Robert Morss. *All Our Years.* New York: Viking Press, 1948.
———. "Herbert Croly." *Harvard College Class of 1890, Fiftieth Anniversary Report, 1890–1940.* Norwood, Mass.: privately printed, 1940, 113–14.
———. "Herbert Croly's Contribution to American Life." *New Republic* 63 (July 16, 1930): 245–46.
Matthews, T. S. *Name and Address: An Autobiography.* New York: Simon and Schuster, 1960.
———. "One Generation to Another." *New Republic* 63 (July 16, 1930): 270–71.
Mill, John Stuart. *Auguste Comte and Positivism.* 1873. Reprint. Ann Arbor: University of Michigan Press, 1961.
Morgan, Ruth. "One Who Stood Firm." *New Republic* 63 (July 16, 1930): 271.
Morison, Elting E., ed. *The Letters of Theodore Roosevelt.* Vols. 7 and 8. Cambridge, Mass.: Harvard University Press, 1954.
Morse, Caroline, ed. *Memories of Jane Cunningham Croly, "Jennie June."* New York: G. P. Putnam's Sons, 1904.
Munsterberg, Hugo. *The Americans.* Translated by Edwin B. Holt. New York: McClure, Phillips and Co., 1904.
"The New Books." *Outlook* 93 (December 4, 1909): 788–89.
Orage, A. R. "On Religion." *New Republic* 45 (February 10, 1926): 317–19.
———. "Religion in America." *New Republic* 41 (December 31, 1924): 141–42.
Phillips, Harlan B., ed. *Felix Frankfurter Reminisces.* Garden City, N.Y.: Anchor Books, 1962.
Pinchot, Amos. *History of the Progressive Party, 1912–1916.* Edited by Helene M. Hooker. New York: New York University Press, 1958.
Platt, Charles A. "Herbert Croly and Architecture." *New Republic* 63 (July 16, 1930): 257.
Richberg, Donald R. *Tents of the Mighty.* New York: Willett, Clark and Colby, 1930.
Roosevelt, Theodore. *Social Justice and Popular Rule.* Vol. 19 of *Works of Theodore Roosevelt.* Edited by H. Hagedorn. New York: Charles Scribner's Sons, 1925.
———. *The New Nationalism.* Edited by William E. Leuchtenburg. Englewood Cliffs, N.J.: Prentice-Hall, 1961.
———. "Two Noteworthy Books on Democracy." *Outlook* 108 (November 1914): 648–51.
Rowell, Chester H. "Remarks on Mr. Herbert Croly's Paper on 'State Political Reorganization.' " *Proceedings of the American Political Science Association.* Concord, N.H.: Rumford Press, 1912. 8: 140–51.
Royce, Josiah. *The Philosophy of Loyalty.* New York: Macmillan, 1908.
———. *The World and the Individual.* Vols. 1 and 2. New York: Macmillan, 1900, 1901.
Santayana, George. "Classic Liberty." *New Republic* 4 (August 21, 1915): 65–66.
———. "German Freedom." *New Republic* 4 (August 28, 1915): 94–96.
———. "Liberalism and Culture." *New Republic* 4 (September 4, 1915): 123–25.
Schlesinger, Arthur, Jr., ed. *Walter Lippmann: Early Writings.* New York: Liveright, 1970.
Soule, George. "Hard-boiled Radicalism." *New Republic* 65 (January 21, 1931): 261–65.

————. "Herbert Croly's Liberalism: 1920–1928." *New Republic* 63 (July 16, 1930): 253–57.

Stearns, Harold. *Liberalism in America*. New York: Boni and Liveright, 1919.

Turner, Frederick Jackson. *The Frontier in American History.* New York: Henry Holt and Co., 1920.

U'Ren, William S. "Remarks on Mr. Herbert Croly's Paper on `State Political Reorganization.' " *Proceedings of the American Political Science Association*. Concord, N.H.: Rumford Press, 1912. 8: 136–39.

Van Hise, Charles. *Concentration and Control*. New York: Macmillan, 1912.

Villard, Oswald Garrison. *Fighting Years: Memoirs of a Liberal Editor*. New York: Harcourt, Brace and Co., 1939.

Wells, H. G. *The Future in America: A Search after Realities*. New York: Harper and Brothers, 1904.

Walter Weyl: An Appreciation. Philadelphia: privately printed, 1922.

Weyl, Walter. *The New Democracy.* New York: Macmillan, 1912. Reprint. New York: Harper Torchbooks, 1964.

White, William Allen. *The Old Order Changeth*. New York: Macmillan, 1910.

Wilson, Edmund. "An Appeal to Progressives." *New Republic* 65 (January 14, 1931): 234–38.

————. " 'H.C.' " *New Republic* 63 (July 16, 1930): 266–68.

————. *Letters on Literature and Politics, 1912–1972*. Edited by Elena Wilson. New York: Farrar, Straus and Giroux, 1977.

Wilson, Woodrow. *The New Freedom*. Edited by William E. Leuchtenburg. Englewood Cliffs, N.J.: Prentice-Hall, 1961.

Young, Stark. "With H.C." *New Republic* 63 (July 16, 1930): 268–70.

SECONDARY SOURCES

Aaron, Daniel. *Men of Good Hope: A Story of American Progressives*. New York: Oxford University Press, 1951.

Abrams, Richard M. *Conservatism in a Progressive Era: Massachusetts Politics, 1900–1912*. Cambridge, Mass.: Harvard University Press, 1964.

Baker, Liva. *The Justice from Beacon Hill: The Life and Times of Oliver Wendell Holmes*. New York: HarperCollins, 1991.

Bensel, Richard Franklin. *Yankee Leviathan: The Origins of Central State Authority in America, 1859–1877*. Cambridge: Cambridge University Press, 1990.

Berlin, Isaiah. *Four Essays on Liberty.* New York: Oxford University Press, 1969.

Blair, Karen J. *The Clubwoman as Feminist: True Womanhood Redefined, 1868–1914*. New York: Holmes and Meier, 1980.

Blum, John M. *The Republican Roosevelt*. New York: Atheneum, 1962.

Buenker, John. *Urban Liberalism and Progressive Reform*. New York: Charles Scribner's Sons, 1973.

Chamberlain, John. "Croly and the American Future." *New Republic* 51 (November 8, 1939): 33–35.

————. *Farewell to Reform*. 2d ed. New York: John Day Company, 1933.

Chapman, William. "Herbert Croly's `The Promise of American Life.' " *South Atlantic Quarterly* 59 (Autumn 1960): 543–55.

Cooper, John M., Jr. "Progressivism and American Foreign Policy: A Reconsideration." *Mid-America; An Historical Review* 51 (October 1969): 260–77.

————. *The Warrior and the Priest: Woodrow Wilson and Theodore Roosevelt.* Cambridge, Mass.: Harvard University Press, 1983.

Crunden, Robert. *Ministers of Reform: The Progressives' Achievements in American Civilization, 1889–1920.* New York: Basic Books, 1982.

Danbom, David B. *"The World of Hope": Progressives and the Struggle for an Ethical Public Life.* Philadelphia: Temple University Press, 1987.

Dexter, Byron. "Herbert Croly and the Promise of American Life." *Political Science Quarterly* 70 (June 1955): 197–218.

Diggins, John P. *Mussolini and Fascism: The View from America.* Princeton, N.J.: Princeton University Press, 1972.

Ebner, Michael H., and Eugene Tobin, eds. *The Age of Urban Reform: New Perspectives on the Progressive Era.* Port Washington, N.Y.: Kennikat Press 1977.

Effross, Harris I. "The Political Philosophy of Herbert Croly." Ph.D. diss., Department of Political Science, Rutgers University, 1959.

Faulkner, Harold U. *Politics, Reform and Expansion.* New York, 1959. Reprint. New York: Harper Torchbooks, 1963.

Forcey, Charles. *The Crossroads of Liberalism: Croly, Weyl, Lippmann, and the Progressive Era, 1900–1925.* New York: Oxford University Press, 1961.

Gable, John A. *The Bull Moose Years: Theodore Roosevelt and the Progressive Party.* Port Washington, N.Y.: Kennikat Press, 1978.

Goldman, Eric F. *Rendezvous with Destiny: A History of Modern American Reform.* New York: Alfred A. Knopf, 1952.

Gould, Lewis L., *The Presidency of Theodore Roosevelt.* Lawrence: University Press of Kansas, 1991.

Graham, Otis L., Jr. *An Encore for Reform: The Old Progressives and the New Deal.* New York: Oxford University Press, 1967.

Haber, Samuel. *Efficiency and Uplift: Scientific Management in the Progressive Era, 1890–1920.* Chicago: University of Chicago Press, 1964.

Hays, Samuel P. *The Response to Industrialism, 1885–1914.* Chicago: University of Chicago Press, 1957.

Hofstadter, Richard. *The Age of Reform: From Bryan to F.D.R.* New York, 1955. Reprint. New York: Vintage Books, 1960.

Holmes, Stephen. "The Liberal Idea." *American Prospect* Number 7 (Fall 1991): 81–96.

Kaplan, Sidney. "The Miscegenation Issue in the Election of 1864." *Journal of Negro History* 34 (July 1949): 274–343.

————. "Social Engineers as Saviors: Effects of World War I on Some American Liberals." *Journal of the History of Ideas* 17 (June 1956): 346–369.

Kennan, George F. "Walter Lippmann, the `New Republic,' and the Russian Revolution." In Marquis Childs and James Reston, eds. *Walter Lippmann and His Times.* New York: Harcourt, Brace and Company, 1959.

Kloppenberg, James T. *Uncertain Victory: Social Democracy and Progressivism in European and American Thought, 1870–1920.* New York: Oxford University Press, 1986.

Kohn, Hans. *American Nationalism: An Interpretive Essay.* New York: Collier Books, 1961.

Kolko, Gabriel. *The Triumph of Conservatism.* New York: Free Press, 1963. Reprint. Chicago: Quadrangle Books, 1967.

Kuklick, Bruce. *The Rise of American Philosophy: Cambridge, Massachusetts, 1860–1930.* New Haven, Conn.: Yale University Press, 1977.

La Porte, Robert Sherman. *Leaders of Reform: Progressive Republicans in Kansas, 1900–1916.* Lawrence: University Press of Kansas, 1974.

Leuchtenburg, William E. "Progressivism and Imperialism: The Progressive Movement and American Foreign Policy, 1898–1916." *Mississippi Valley Historical Review* 39 (December 1952): 483–504.

Levy, David W. *Herbert Croly of the New Republic: The Life and Thought of an American Progressive.* Princeton, N.J.: Princeton University Press, 1985.

Link, Arthur S. *Wilson: Campaigns for Progressivism and Peace.* Princeton: Princeton University Press, 1965.

———. *Wilson: The New Freedom.* Princeton, N.J.: Princeton University Press, 1956.

———: *Wilson: The Road to the White House.* Princeton, N.J.: Princeton University Press, 1947.

———. *Woodrow Wilson and the Progressive Era.* New York: Harper and Row, 1954. Reprint. New York: Harper Torchbooks, 1963.

Lustig, R. Jeffrey. *Corporate Liberalism: The Origins of Modern American Political Theory, 1890–1920.* Berkeley: University of California Press, 1982.

Mason, Alpheus T. *Brandeis: A Free Man's Life.* New York: Viking Press, 1946.

May, Henry S. *The End of American Innocence.* Chicago: Quadrangle Books, 1964.

McCormick, Richard L. *From Realignment to Reform: Political Change in New York State, 1893–1910.* Ithaca, N.Y.: Cornell University Press, 1981.

———. *The Party Period and Public Policy: American Politics from the Age of Jackson to the Progressive Era.* New York: Oxford University Press, 1986.

McGraw, Thomas K. *Prophets of Regulation.* Cambridge, Mass.: Harvard University Press, 1984.

———. ed. *Regulation in Perspective.* Cambridge, Mass.: Harvard University Press, 1981.

Mowry, George. *The Era of Theodore Roosevelt and the Birth of Modern America.* 1958. Reprint. New York: Harper Torchbooks, 1962.

———. *Theodore Roosevelt and the Progressive Movement.* 1946. Reprint. New York: Hill and Wang, 1960.

Muncy, Robyn. *Creating a Female Dominion in American Reform, 1890–1935.* New York: Oxford University Press, 1991.

Noble, David. *The Paradox of Progressive Thought.* Minneapolis: University of Minnesota Press, 1958.

Pringle, Henry. *Theodore Roosevelt.* 1931. Reprint. New York: Harvest Books, 1956.

Rawls, John. *A Theory of Justice.* Cambridge, Mass.: Harvard University Press, 1971.

Rothstein, Richard J. "Herbert Croly and the Philosophy of Fulfillment." B.A. honors thesis, Department of Government, Harvard University, 1963.

Rozwenc, Edwin C., ed. *Roosevelt, Wilson and the Trusts.* Boston: Heath and Co., 1950.

Rutkoff, Peter M., and William B. Scott. *New School: A History of the New School for Social Research.* New York: Free Press, 1986.

Schlesinger, Arthur, Jr. "Croly and the Promise of American Life." *New Republic* 152 (May 8, 1965): 17–22.

Schlesinger, Elizabeth. "The Nineteenth Century Woman's Dilemma and Jennie June." *New York History* 42 (October 1961): 365–79.

Scheiber, Harry N. "World War I as Entrepreneurial Opportunity: Willard Straight and the American International Corporation." *Political Science Quarterly* 84 (September 1969): 486–511.

Schlissel, Lillian, ed. *The World of Randolph Bourne.* New York: E. P. Dutton, 1965.

Seideman, David. *New Republic: A Voice of Modern Liberalism.* New York: Praeger, 1986.

Sen, Amartya. "Individual Freedom as a Social Commitment." *New York Review of Books* 37 (June 14, 1990): 49–54.

Shaver, Muriel. "David Goodman Croly." *Dictionary of American Biography.* New York: Charles Scribner's Sons, 1929. 2: 560.

———. "Jane Cunningham Croly." *Dictionary of American Biography.* New York: Charles Scribner's Sons, 1929. 2: 560–61.

Steel, Ronald. *Walter Lippmann and the American Century.* Boston: Little, Brown, 1980.

Swanberg, W. A. *Whitney Father, Whitney Heiress.* New York: Charles Scribner's Sons, 1980.

Thelen, David. *The New Citizenship: Origins of Progressivism in Wisconsin, 1885–1900.* Columbia: University of Missouri Press, 1972.

Thompson, John A. *Reformers and War: American Progressive Publicists and the First World War.* New York: Cambridge University Press, 1987.

Villard, Oswald Garrison. "Herbert David Croly." *Dictionary of American Biography.* Edited by Harris E. Starr. New York: Charles Scribner's Sons, 1944. Vol. 21 (supplement I): 209–210.

Ward, John William. Introduction to Herbert Croly. *The Promise of American Life.* Indianapolis: Bobbs-Merrill Co., 1965.

Weinstein, James. *The Corporate Ideal in the Liberal State: 1900–1918.* Boston: Beacon Press, 1968.

White, Morton. *Social Thought in America: The Revolt Against Formalism.* Boston: Beacon Press, 1957.

Wiebe, Robert H. *Businessmen and Reform: A Study of the Progressive Movement.* Cambridge, Mass.: Harvard University Press, 1962. Reprint. Chicago: Quadrangle Books, 1968.

———. *The Search for Order, 1877–1920.* New York: Hill and Wang, 1967.

Yellowitz, Irwin. *Labor and the Progressive Movement in New York State 1897–1916.* Ithaca, N.Y.: Cornell University Press, 1965.

Young, Michael. *The Elmhirsts of Dartington.* London: Routledge and Kegan Paul, 1982.

Index